AUSTERLITZ

The Eagle's sun

F.-G. HOURTOULLE

Uniform plates by d'André Jouineau
Maps by Jean-Marie Mongin
Translated from the French by Alan McKay

HISTOIRE & COLLECTIONS - PARIS

(© E. Micheletti)

To the Memory of the thousands of Saint-Cyr Cadets who, on 2 December each year, on the occasion of their traditional 2S re-enact the Battle of Austerlitz under the command of their *"Père système"* dressed up as Napoleon, before going off to serve France and die in great numbers for the values learnt in that school.

"A genoux les hommes, debout les officiers"

* The 2S refers to the internal code at Saint-Cyr. It designates each of the ten months spent at the school with one letter of the word Austerlitz. The first month, October, is represented by A, November by U and December by S, thus 2S means 2nd December

(RR)

Histoire & Collections
© 2003

AUSTERLITZ
The Empire at its Zenith

CONTENTS

INTRODUCTION

I should like to thank my friend Jacques Garnier, like myself, a fanatical admirer of this battle. We have been talking about it for more than fifteen years, particularly the action of the right wing under Davout with Friant's division and the 48th of the Line as the stars. Jacques Garnier is well-known for his work with Jean Tulard and for his official reports on Austerlitz. Moreover he has the great advantage of having been to the site, bringing back photographs and unpublished documents. His documentation on the subject is most complete and if this book is a success then it is thanks to him.

I should like to thank Pierre Bréteigner and his inexhaustible information about Russian artillery and Austrian uniforms

THE THIRD COALITION

The peace treaty signed at Amiens on 25 March 1802 was broken in 1803 by England which decided to put an embargo on French and Dutch ships. The Emperor responded by occupying Hanover where he put Mortier in charge, later replaced by Bernadotte.

The English were very worried when the camp at Boulogne opposite them on the other side of the Channel was set up, and did everything to get this army to move off back into Europe.

● They started by winning over **Tsar Alexander**, giving him large subsidies in order to levy large numbers of troops. They decided to pay these Russian mercenaries a lot, about 300 francs a man. A force of 200 000 men was planned.

It was made up of three armies:

— **Kutusov** led the first with 55 000 men, of which 8 000 cavalry and 200 cannon.

— **Buxhoeven** led the second with 40 battalions and 85 squadrons.

— **Benningsen** formed a third army with 33 battalions and 35 squadrons. He would join the Prussians if they decided to join the Coalition.

— **Essen** was to lead the vanguard of 10 000 men which arrived at Olmutz too late.

—**Lieutenant general Tolstoy** moreover joined the Russian troops in their action with the English and Swedes against Holland.

● Austria only joined the Coalition on 7 July 1805. Thanks to English subsidies to reinforce its army, which consisted of:

— **An Army of Germany** whose nominal commander was Archduke Ferdinand; he was accompanied by General Mack – who had the Emperor's favour

— **A general headquarters** for this force of 60 000 men which entered Bavaria to recover troops. Unfortunately for the Coalition, the Elector of

From left to right.
The leaders of the Third Coalition: Tsar Alexander I, Franz II of Austria, the King of Sweden and William Pitt, the "soul of the plot", and Queen Marie-Caroline of Naples.
(RR)

Bavaria remained loyal to France and fell back in front of the Austrians. Mack responded by tightening his grip on the area.

— **Archduke Charles** led an army of 100 000 men in Italy.

— **Archduke John** commanded an army of 22 000 men in the Tyrol.

● **Sweden,** supported by the English threatened Northern Germany and Holland with, if needs be, the support of Tolstoy.

● **Marie-Caroline of Naples** opened its borders to the Russians and the English, thus creating a second front.

● There remained **Prussia**, courted by the Russians and especially the English who were prepared to increase the allowance given to each mercenary recruited in that country. The Prussians were happy just to be mediators. They allowed the Russians, however, to cross their territory to join up with the Austrians.

The Army in the camp of Boulogne

Faced with this other threat, Napoleon got his army in the Camp at Boulogne ready to move down towards the Danube. Daru received precise directives about organising the force into army corps led by the marshals. These large three-arm units were autonomous and powerful and made up the "seven torrents" which swept down onto Austria with unbelievable speed for the period; this was in stark contrast to the enemy's slow movements which were planned by a triumvirate made up of Winzigrode, Schwarzenberg and Mack.

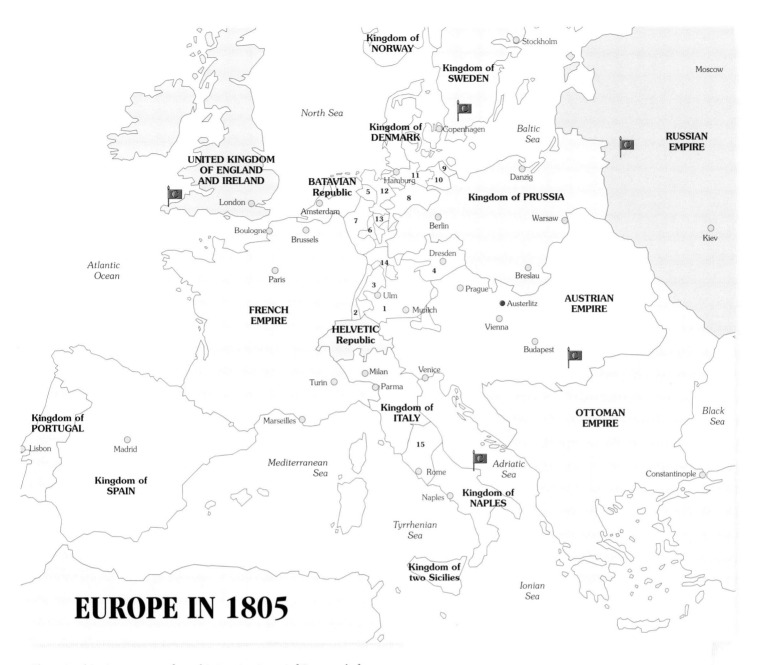

EUROPE IN 1805

The main objective was to confront this Austrian Army *of Germany before the Russians could come to its help.

Where the secondary theatres of operations were concerned, the Army of Italy was entrusted to Masséna who had 60 000 men. A force was organised in Holland and Gouvion-Saint-Cyr had 20 000 men in Calabria with which he could attack Naples or later if necessary, join up with Masséna.

THE MARCH TOWARDS AUSTERLITZ

Speed was the hallmark of this campaign. The 150 000 men from Boulogne swept down to the Danube and cut Mack's army (in Ulm waiting for the first Russian army to arrive) off from its line of retreat towards Munich.

The Emperor did not have enough transport, so he requisitioned 3 500 four-horse carriages each driven by two carters. A lot of them deserted when they learnt they were off to Germany. Others brought their best horses.

These carriages were to be left in relays at each halt. The seven streams of the Grande Armée – now at its height, with soldiers trained at the camp at Boulogne by excellent cadres and veterans of the Revolutionary Wars - swept along the wide roads of the time. The pattern for these marches was laid down in great detail.

The infantry battalions marched in two files one on either side of the road, leaving the centre of the road for the carriages and the artillery. One third of the drummers were placed in the van, one in the centre and one at the rear; they took turns beating the step. There was a five-minute pause every hour and at the three-quarter journey stage, there was a half-hour break.

The whole band had to play during the halts

THE GERMAN STATES

1. **Bavaria.**	9. **Swedish Pomerania**
2. **Baden.**	10. **Mecklenburg**
3. **Württemberg**	11. **Hanover**
4. **Saxony**	12. **Oldenburg**
5. **Berg**	13. **Hesse**
6. **Hesse-Kassel**	14. **Württemberg**
7. **Nassau**	15. **Papal States**
8. **Hanover**	

Generals had the right to a carriage; colonels rode their horses at the head of their regiment. A hundred paces separated the battalions. Each stage was covered at an average of a league per hour.

The most famous forced march of the campaign was that carried out by Friant's division with Davout. Leaving the Vienna area, they covered the distance to the battlefield 70 miles in forty hours, i.e. in effect thirty-six hours marching.

For cavalry, it was the same: they marched in two files with the same rules. The troops were billeted by division at each halt.

The infantry were issued with a greatcoat and two pairs of shoes. Food was found on the way in the villages through which the army passed.

When he saw them pass, a former Austrian officer of dragoons said: "Some of them are veritable walking larders." The ordnance officers helped by other officers organised the billets at each halt before the troops arrived.

5

DÉCRET IMPÉRIAL

Concernant les Militaires ou Employés à la suite de l'Armée, convaincus d'avoir excité leurs Camarades à la désertion.

Au Palais des Tuileries, le 23 Ventôse an 13.

NAPOLÉON, EMPEREUR DES FRANÇAIS;

Sur le rapport du Ministre de la guerre;

Vu l'article LXVII de l'arrêté du 19 vendémiaire an 12, ainsi conçu:

« Sera puni de mort,
» 1.º Le déserteur à l'ennemi;
» 2.º Tout chef de complot de désertion,
» 3.º Tout déserteur étant en faction, &c. »

L'article LXVIII du même arrêté, portant:

« Seront réputés déserteurs à l'ennemi, ceux qui ont été qualifiés
» comme tels par la loi du 21 brumaire an 5.

» Seront réputés chefs de complot, ceux qui ont été qualifiés comme
» tels par la loi précitée. »

Les articles V et VI du titre I.er de la loi du 21 brumaire an 5; ainsi conçus:

» Art. V. Tout militaire ou autre individu employé à l'armée et
» à sa suite, qui sera convaincu d'avoir excité ses camarades à passer
» chez l'ennemi, sera réputé chef de complot, et puni de mort,
» quand même la désertion n'aurait point eu lieu.

» Art. VI. Lorsque des militaires auront formé le complot de passer

» à l'ennemi, et que le chef du complot ne sera pas connu, le plus
» élevé en grade des militaires complices, ou, à grade égal, le plus
» ancien de service, sera réputé chef du complot, et puni comme tel.

» Si le complot a été formé seulement par des employés à la
» suite de l'armée, le plus élevé en grade, et, à grade égal, le plus
» ancien de service, sera réputé chef du complot, et puni comme tel. »

Considérant que la loi du 21 brumaire an 5, à laquelle renvoie l'arrêté du 19 vendémiaire an 12, pour la définition du chef de complot de désertion, ne contient aucune disposition qu'on puisse appliquer textuellement aux chefs de complot de désertion à l'étranger ou à l'intérieur; qu'il est urgent de s'expliquer à ce sujet;

Le Conseil d'état entendu,

DÉCRÈTE:

ART. I.er A l'avenir, tout militaire ou autre individu employé à la suite de l'armée, qui sera convaincu d'avoir excité ses camarades à déserter, soit à l'ennemi, soit à l'étranger, soit à l'intérieur, sera réputé chef de complot, et, comme tel, puni de mort.

II. Le Ministre de la guerre est chargé de l'exécution du présent décret.

Signé NAPOLÉON,

Par l'Empereur:

Le Secrétaire d'état, signé HUGUES B. MARET.

Le Ministre de la guerre,

Signé M.al BERTHIER.

Above.
This imperial decree specified what the charges and penalties were for the soldiers of the Grande Armée convicted of desertion or intelligence with the enemy.
(Recto-verso reconstituted, Private Collection)

Opposite, right.
**This page comes from the campaign diary of an officer of Engineers.
It shows the cabins built in the camp at Boulogne.**
(Private Collection)

Below.
Napoleon leaving Augsburg and haranguing men from Marmont's II Corps before going to Weissenhorn. He is reassuring and 'motivating' them.
(RR)

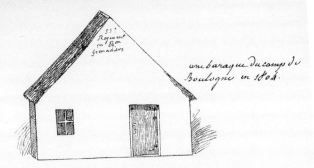

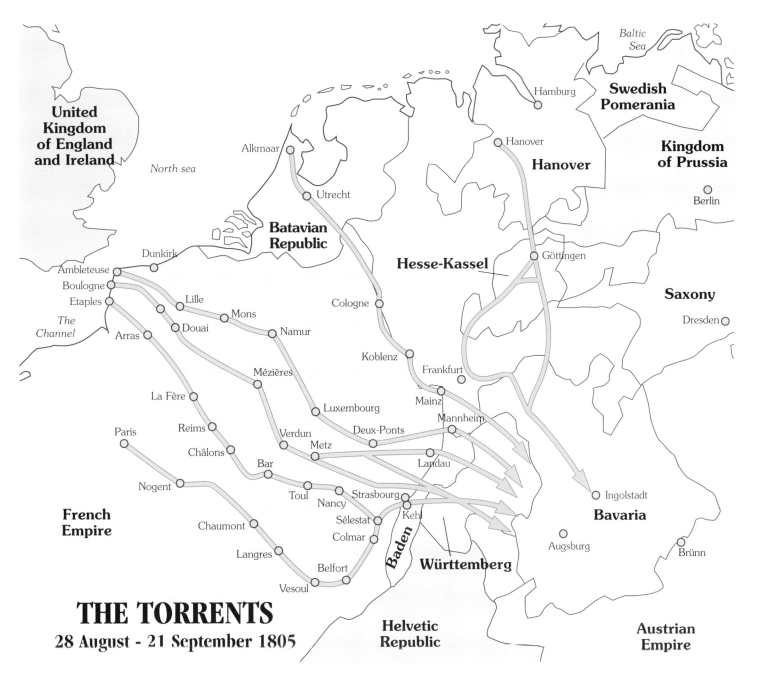

THE TORRENTS

28 August - 21 September 1805

THE TORRENTS

BATTLE PRELIMINARIES

Bernadotte's corps left from Hanover for Wurzburg. It had to cross the territory of Anspach which belonged to the Prussians.

Marmont's corps came from Holland in the direction of Wurzburg. From there onwards, the two corps protected the left of the army consisting of 60 000 men and headed for Munich to join the Bavarians.

The other corps gradually surrounded Ulm. Mack was waiting for the French when they came out of the Black Forest. He had gathered together his magnificent army of 60 000 men and was completely oblivious of things to come. Nevertheless he started to prepare an attack along the left bank of the Danube where Dupont was rather isolated at Albeck. Murat made up for his mistake of having neglected the left bank by recapturing the bridge at Elchingen in order to relieve Dupont. Dupont had won at Haslach but he was still threatened by Werneck's two divisions who were on their way to occupy Elchingen. The battle for which Ney received his duke's title shut the rest of the Austrians up in Ulm. Only Werneck was able to get away on the left bank and Archduke Ferdinand decided to try his luck with his available cavalry and join up with him.

Murat was sent to pursue these escaping forces. But 25 000 men remained trapped in Ulm and Mack gave in on 17 October. His 25 000 men surrendered on 20 October, filing past in front of their victors. They abandoned 60 hitched-up cannon and laid down 40 flags.

This was a disgrace for the Austrians. Mack was court-martialled, reduced to the ranks and sentenced to 10 years' prison. He was eventually pardoned; he retired and died in St Polten in 1828.

Murat reached Werneck and obtained the surrender of 8 000 men, 50 cannon and 18 flags.

Archduke John was caught at Furth, near Nuremberg; the artillery, wagons and a thousand men were taken on 20 October.

But on the 21st there was Trafalgar, and France lost its navy. Napoleon learnt of this on 1 November.

The King of Prussia had been increasingly hesitant about joining the Coalition was stopped in his tracks by the surrender at Ulm.

Napoleon launched **Ney and his 6th Corps** towards the Tyrol helped by **Augereau (7th Corps)**; **Bernadotte's** and **Marmont's** 1st and 2nd Corps covered the right with the Bavarians. In the centre Murat with Davout, Soult and the Guard were on the road to Vienna.

Lannes' 5th Corps was reinforced by Klein, Dupont and the Dutch

7

under Dumonceau. He covered the left. The Austrians abandoned Braunau with all its resources; it was used as a depot and entrusted to Lauriston.

Kienmayer and Merveldt and their Austrian troops were gradually pushed back; Archduke Charles was called back from Italy where he was facing Masséna. He set off and Masséna, seeing him leave, followed him.

Their objective was Kutusov who, no longer wanting to go to Vienna, headed towards Moravia in order to find Buxhoewden and his corps.

The Austrians were beginning to distrust the Russians, their excesses and their scornful haughtiness.

Napoleon had Mortier together with Gazan's division supported by Dupont and Dumonceau cross over to the left bank of the Danube at Passau, in order to try and cut Kutusov off on the northern road. The Emperor had reached Linz. Merveldt split up from Kutusov and the road to Vienna seemed to be open. There was no longer any point in counting on the Russians to save the capital.

Davout stopped Merveldt at Maria-Zell and took 4 000 prisoners, one flag, 16 cannon and 80 carriages.

Kutusov was now at Krems with the 40 000 men of Bagration, Dokhturov, Maltitz, Miloradovitch, Essen II and the very competent Austrian quarter-master Schmidt. Bagration knew that Mortier only had Gazan's division and decided to attack him at Dürrenstein.

The battle took place on 11 November. After heroic fighting, the men of Gazan's division were saved by the arrival of Dupont's Division. Fabvier in particular distinguished himself as did Bazancourt with his 4th Light whose Major Guyardet was wounded. Generals Graindorge and Campana, Colonel Ritay and Major Henriod of the 100th of the Line also distinguished themselves. The Austrian General Schmidt, Weyrother's superior, was killed.

The General Mack Commanding Suabe's Army
(RR)

Above and opposite page
These three pictures illustrate the main stages of the campaign which finished at Austerlitz.

The cavalry of the 18th Dragoon Regiment passing before Ney at Elchingen.
(J. Girbal, Author's Collection)

Murat's glorious ride of 16 – 20 October, close on the heels of Werneck and Archduke Charles.
(H. G. Chartier, c. Roger Viollet)

The surrender of Ulm: seventeen Austrian generals came to surrender to the Emperor of the French.
(Thévenin, ©. RMN)

Kutusov was saved and returned towards Brünn and Moravia, and the Russian Second Army.

Murat reached the gates of Vienna and Kienmayer gave up. It was most important to capture the bridges intact. Murat, Lannes, Bertrand and Dode feigned a truce in order to trick Prince Auersperg and captured the bridge over the Tabor without hindrance.

Napoleon set himself up in Schönbrunn Palace with the Guard. Murat was sent off to chase Kutusov, Marmot cut the road to Italy up in the mountains. The resources discovered in the Vienna arsenals were huge.

Murat, who had been tricked for a moment before Hollabrünn, got the order to attack and used Oudinot's grenadiers and Legrand's infantry. Oudinot was wounded quite seriously. Bagration lost 1 200 men, 12 cannon and a hundred or so wagons, but with this sacrifice he enabled Kutusov to get away once and for all.

Napoleon chose Brünn, the Allies preferred Olmutz; the scene was thus set for the coming battle at Austerlitz where the big issue was to be settled.

9

LES FORCES ALLIÉES

FOR THE RUSSIANS
● **The Tsar** was nominally in command. With him was his advisor Czartorinsky with his young aide de camps Dolgorukov, Gagarin, Volkonsky, Wintzingerode and Lieven.

● **Kutusov was Commander-in-Chief.**

The Quartermasters were Weyrother for the Austrians and **Sukhtelen** and **Gerhard** for the Russians. General Intzov and Colonel Toll.

— **Count Araktcheyev** was Inspector-General of the Artillery with General Meller Zakomelski and General Bogdanov for the Mounted artillery. General Glikov was the Russian Chief-Engineer.

FOR THE AUSTRIANS
● **Emperor Franz II, prince Schwarzenberg** and the **Prince of Liechtenstein**. General Lamberti was the Emperor's aide de camp. There were also some English emissaries, present as advisors and observers. They were lord Granville, Charles Stuart and General John Ramsay.

— **Two squadrons of the Kaiser's Guard** (cuirassiers) made up the headquarters escort. The plans of attack were drawn up by Weyrother.

THE VANGUARD UNDER BAGRATION.
(11 750 men of which 3 000 cavalry and 30 guns + 12 at the end.)

— **General Dolgorukov's 1st Brigade:** 5th and 6th Chasseurs.

— **Kamensky II's 2nd Brigade:** the Arkhangelgorod Regiment.

— **Major-general Engelhardt's 3rd Brigade:** the Old-Ingria and Pskov Regiments.

— **Wittgenstein's 4th Brigade:** Pavlograd and Marioupol Hussars.

— **Voropaitzky's 5th Brigade:** the Empress' Leib-Cuirassiers and the Tver and St-Petersburg Dragoons.

● **Chaplitz Cossacks:** 15 squadrons from Khanjenkov, Kiselev and Malakhov.

● **Battalion Artillery:** 18 guns for 9 battalions, 6-pounders or 10-pounder unicorns.

● **Field Artillery: Russian Mounted Artillery:** six 6-pounders and six 10-pounder unicorns.

● **Two Austrian Mounted Artillery Batteries** with four 6-pounder guns each and two howitzers. They came from Olmutz as reinforcements during the afternoon.

THE RUSSIAN GUARD UNDER GRAND-DUKE KONSTANTIN
(8 500 men of which 2 600 cavalry, and 40 cannon).

● **The Infantry under Major-General Maliutin**

— **Major-General Deperadovitch's First brigade I:** Preobrajensky, Semenovsky, Ismaïlovsky and the Chasseurs of the Guard.

— **Major-General Libanov's Second Brigade.** Grenadiers of the Guard, or grenadiers from the corps, 3 battalions.

— **Pioneers,** 100 men.

● **Lieutenant-General Kologrivov's Cavalry.**

— **Jankovitch's First Brigade:** Hussars of the Guard (5 squadrons), Cossacks of the Guard (2 squadrons).

— **Dereradovitch's Second Brigade II:** Life Guards Regiment, Horse guards.

— **Battalion Artillery:** 20 pieces either 6-pounders or 10-pounder unicorns.

— **Field Artillery:** 5 Mounted Artillery 6-pounders and ten 10-pounder unicorns. Plus a heavy battery: six 12-pounders and four 18-pounder unicorns.

The Guard's strength was 8 500 combatants with 40 guns.

PRINCE LIECHTENSTEIN'S CAVALRY
(4 600 cavalrymen with 24 cannon)

● **Prince of Hohenlohe** (Austrians)

— **Carramelli's First Brigade:** 5th Nassau-Usingen Cuirassiers (6 squadrons), 300 cavalrymen; 7th Lothringen Cuirassiers (6 squadrons),

300 cavalrymen.

— **Weber's Brigade:** 1st Kaiser Regiment (6 squadrons), 425 men. Two squadrons protected headquarters (140 cavalrymen); one battery of mounted artillery with four 6-pounders and two howitzers.

● **Lieutenant-General Essen II and Skepelov (Russians).**

— **First Brigade:** Uhlans of Grand-Duke Konstantin (10 squadrons), 950 men.

— **Uvarov's Brigade:** Elisabethgrad Hussars (10 squadrons), 950 men; 2nd Kharkov Dragoons (5 squadrons), 500 men; Tchernigov's 3rd Dragoons (5 squadrons), 366 men.

— **Cossacks:** Denisov Cossacks, 50 men; Gordeyev Cossacks (5 squadrons), 300 men; Isayev Cossacks (4 squadrons), 240 men.

— **Artillery.** The Russian Mounted Artillery was made up of six 6-pounders and six 10-pounder unicorns and half a mounted battery with six 6-pounders.

Total for the column: 4 622 cavalry and 24 cannon.

THE ATTACKING FORCE OF FIVE COLUMNS
THE VANGUARD UNDER KIENMAYER.
(about 5 000 men of which 1 000 cavalry, 500 Cossacks and 12 cannon.)

— **General Carneville:** 7th Frontier (Grenz) Regiment, 350 survivors of two battalions; 1st and 2nd Szekler, 2 100 men; 3 companies of pioneers (250 men).

— **Stutterheim's Brigade:** O'Reilly's Chevau-Léger (8 squadrons), 700 men; 25 Merveldt Uhlans; two mounted batteries with four 6-pounders and two howitzers each.

— **Nostitz-Rieneck's Brigade:** Hesse-Homburg Hussars (6 squadrons), 360 men; 50 Schwarzenberg Uhlans.

— **Moritz Liechtenstein's Brigade:** Szekler (Frontier Hussars) Regiment, 600 men; Melentev Cossacks, 300 men; Sysoyev Cossacks, 200 men.

The vanguard's total strength was 4 935 combatants with 12 cannon.

The first three columns were under the command of General Buxhoewden.

THE FIRST COLUMN UNDER DOKHTUROV
(7 752 men and 64 cannon).

Russian regiments had two or three battalions; those with three had one grenadier battalion and two musketeer battalions except for special cases.

— **Levis (?) Brigade:** 1st Battalion of 7th Chasseurs, 470 men. New-Ingria Regiment, 1 173 men.

— **Urusov's Brigade:** Yaroslav Regiment (reduced to two battalions after heavy initial losses), 754 men; Vladimir Regiment (3 battalions), 1 649 men; Bryansk Regiment (3 battalions), 829 men.

— **Major-General Lüders Third Brigade:** Vyatka Regiment (3 battalions), 379 men; Kiev Grenadier Regiment (3 battalions), 716 men; Moscow Regiment (3 battalions), 882 men.

— **Cavalry and other arms:** Denisov Cossacks (5 squadrons), 210 men; 90 pioneers; 40 cannon, of which eight 12-pounders and four 18-pounder unicorns, the other cannon being 6-pounders.

Total column strength: 7 752 men and 64 cannon.

THE SECOND COLUMN UNDER LANGERON.
(10 283 men of whom 360 cavalry and 30 cannon)

— **Olsufiev's Brigade:** 8th Chasseurs (2nd and 3rd Battalions), 333 men; Viborg Regiment (3 battalions), 1 881 men; Kursk Regiment (3 battalions), 1 908 men: Perm Regiment (3 battalions), 1 911 men.

— **Kamenski's Brigade I:** Fanagoria Regiment (3 battalions), 2 017 men; Ryazan Regiment (3 battalions), 1783 men.

— **Cavalry and other Arms:** Colonel Black's St-Petersburg Dragoons (20 men) and 40 Isayev Cossacks; 90 pioneers. The artillery was made up of 30 guns, 2 per battalion; there were 6-pounders and 10-pounder unicorns.

Total: 10 283 men and 30 cannon.

THE THIRD COLUMN UNDER PRZYBYSZEWKSI
(about 7 500 men with 30 cannon)

— **Miller's Brigade III:** 7th Chasseurs (2nd and 3rd battalions), 1 020 men; Galicia Regiment, 1 564 men.

— **Strick's Brigade:** Butyrsk Regiment (3 battalions), 864 men; Narva Regiment (3 battalions), 7 321 men.

— **Wimpfen's Brigade:** 8th Chasseur Regiment (1st Battalion), 79 men; Podolia Regiment (3 battalions), 509 men; Azov Regiment (3 battalions), 591 men.

— **Artillery and Engineers:** 90 pioneers; thirty 6-pounders or 10-pounder unicorns.

Total in the column: 5 448 men and 30 cannon.

THE FOURTH COLUMN UNDER KOLLOWRATH AND MILORADOVITCH
(Slightly more than 12 000 men with 40 cannon)

— **Lieutenant-Colonel Monakhtin's Vanguard:** Apsheron Musketeers (1 battalion), 137 men; Novgorod Regiment (2 battalions of which one of grenadiers), 513 men; Arch-Duke John's Dragoons, 100 cavalrymen.

— **Berg's Brigade:** Novgorod Regiment (1 battalion), 256 men; Little Russia Regiment (3 battalions), 1 011 men.

— **Repinsky's Brigade:** Apsheron Regiment (2 battalions of which one of grenadiers), 273 men; Smolensk Regiment (3 battalions), 685 men.

— **Rottermund's Brigade (Austrian):** Salzburg regiment N°23 (6 battalions), 3 044 men; Wenzel-Kaunitz Regiment N°20 (1 battalion coming from the depot), 500 men.

— **Jurczik's Brigade (Austrian):** Kaiser Franz N°1 (1 depot battalion), 600 men; Czartorisky-Saggusko Regiment N°9 (1 depot battalion), 600 men; Lindenau regiment N°29 (4th Battalion), 500 men; Wurtemberg Regiment N° 38 (3rd Battalion), 600 men; Carl Anesperg Regiment N°24 (1 depot battalion), 600 men; Kerpen Regiment N°49 (1 depot battalion), 700 men; Reuss-Greitz Regiment N°55 (1 depot battalion), 600 men; Beaulieu Regiment N° 58 (1 depot battalion), 600 men; Vienna Volunteers (2 companies), 200 men.

— **Artillery and Engineers:** Pioneers, 2 companies of 180 men. The artillery was made up of twenty-four 6-pounders (battalion guns) for the Russians, 10-pounder unicorns and twenty-eight 3- and 6-pounders for the Austrians. A heavy Russian battery consisting of four medium 12-pounders, four short 12-pounders, and four 18-pounder unicorns.

Two Austrian batteries consisting of four 12-pounders and two howitzers.

Total for the Column: 12 099 men and 76 guns.

Total of the Allied Forces:
72 789 infantry, 14 139 cavalrymen and 318 cannon; just under 100 000 men with which they definitely out-numbered the French

Above, from left to right and top to bottom.
The prince of Liechtenstein commanding the Coalition army's cavalry.
Miloradovitch commanding the fourth column.
Field-Marshal Kollowrath commanded the Austrians of the fourth column.
General Kamensky was at he head of Bagration's vanguard.
General Volkonsky.
Grand-Duke Constantin commanding the Russian Imperial Guard.
Schwarzenberg was present with the Austrian Emperor.
Langeron was at the head of the second column. *(RR)*

Below, left
Fusiliers, Grenadiers and a German Infantry regiment officer
in the Austrian Army. The German-speaking troops were distinguishable
from the so-called "Hungarian" units by their all-white uniform
and the fact that they wore a helmet instead of the shako.
(Author's Collection)

Below, right
Hussars (foreground) and Ublans (background) of the Austrian Cavalry,
in marching dress. *(Author's Collection)*

THE RUSSIAN VANGUARD
under lieutenant-general, Prince Bagration

Infantryman from
the 5th Chasseurs.

Officer from the
6th Chasseurs wea-
ring a greatcoat.

Infantryman from
the 6th Chasseurs.

There were a lot of differences between the Russian infantry of 1805 and that of 1812 as can be seen from these plates.
The grenadier regiments consisted of 3 battalions; one was of grenadiers with four companies and two of fusiliers in which one company was grenadiers and three companies of fusiliers. The musketeer regiments consisted of one four-company battalion of grenadiers and two battalions of musketeers consisting of one company of grenadiers and three of musketeers. The regiments of chasseurs consisted of three battalions with three chasseur companies and one of grenadiers each.

Officer from the 5th Chasseurs in campaign dress.

Colonel's flag
of the Old-Ingria
(Vieille-Ingrie)
Regiment.

Old-Ingria Regiment.

Fusilier from the Old-Ingria
Regiment.

André Jouineau © Histoire et collections 2003

THE RUSSIAN VANGUARD
under lieutenant-general, Prince Bagration

Colonel Flag,
Arkhangelgorod
Regiment.

Colonel Flag,
Pskov Regiment.

Arkhangelgorod Regiment.

Pskov Regiment.

Fusilier, Arkhangelgorod
Regiment.

Fusilier,
Pskov Regiment.

Tver regiment of Dragoons.

Left.
Cavalryman in campaign dress.

Right.
Trumpeter in marching dress,
horse trousers worn
over cavalry boots.

André Jouineau © Histoire et collections 2003

THE RUSSIAN VANGUARD
under lieutenant-general, Prince Bagration

Pavlograd Hussar,
marching dress.

Marioupol Hussar.

Trumpeter,
Mounted Artillery.

Cossack in marching dress.
These cavalrymen were not
all dressed so uniformly.

Trumpeter
in the Marioupol Hussars.
The Russian Hussar trumpeters
wore swallows nests.

THE AUSTRIAN VANGUARD
under lieutenant-general Kienmayer

Brooder Frontier Infantry regiment.

Szekler Infantry Regiment N°2.

Szekler Infantry Regiment N°1.

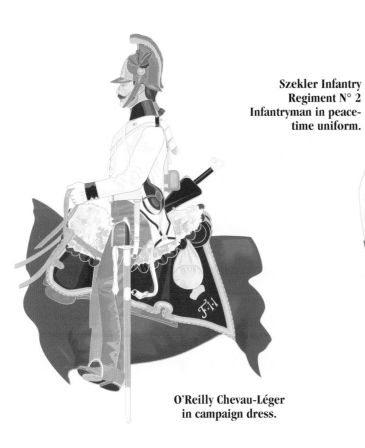

O'Reilly Chevau-Léger in campaign dress.

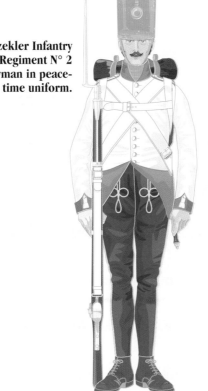

Szekler Infantry Regiment N° 2 Infantryman in peace-time uniform.

Szekler Infantry Regiment N° 1, Officer.

André Jouineau © Histoire et collections 2003

THE AUSTRIAN VANGUARD
under lieutenant-general Kienmayer

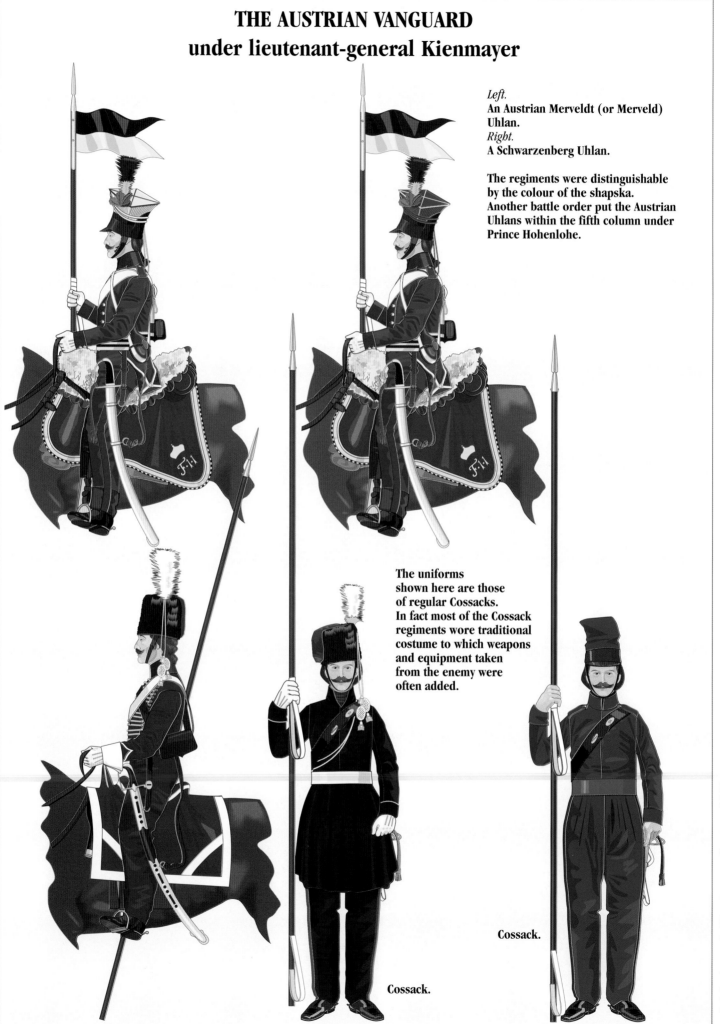

Left.
An Austrian Merveldt (or Merveld) Uhlan.
Right.
A Schwarzenberg Uhlan.

The regiments were distinguishable by the colour of the shapska. Another battle order put the Austrian Uhlans within the fifth column under Prince Hohenlohe.

The uniforms shown here are those of regular Cossacks. In fact most of the Cossack regiments wore traditional costume to which weapons and equipment taken from the enemy were often added.

Cossack.

Cossack.

André Jouineau © Histoire et collections 2003

THE AUSTRIAN VANGUARD
under lieutenant-general Kienmayer

Hesse-Homburg Hussar in full dress
with ' à la Hongroise' trousers.

Szekler Hussar. It was the only
regiment of this type
(Frontier Regiment)
within the Austrian cavalry.

Pioneer from an
Austrian Engineer
company.

Austrian Wagon
train driver.

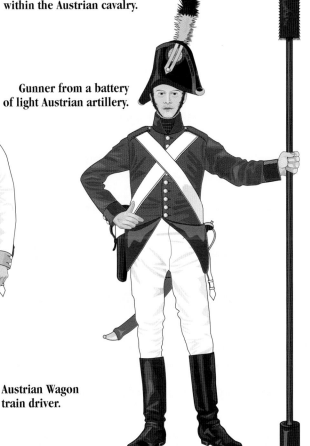

Gunner from a battery
of light Austrian artillery.

André Jouineau © Histoire et collections 2003

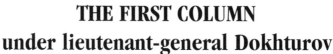

THE FIRST COLUMN
under lieutenant-general Dokhturov

Unlike the Russian infantry of the Line,
the Chasseurs wore a light green
uniform with black strappings,
but the markings of the NCOs
and the officers were the same
as the rest of the infantry.

Infantryman in the 7th Chasseur Regiment.

Infantryman in the
5th Chasseur Regiment.

Infantry Sabre-knots
(by company).

1st   3rd
2nd   4th

Flag of the Ukraine 1803
inspection type.

Kiev Regiment
Grenadier
in marching dress.
In combat,
the cloak was worn
rolled up
saltire-wise.

Kiev Regiment,
Model 1797 flag.

Kiev Regiment
Grenadier.

André Jouineau © Histoire et collections 2003

THE FIRST COLUMN
under lieutenant-general Dokhturov

Colonel Flag,
New-Ingria
Regiment,
1797 model.

Colonel Flag,
Yaroslav Regiment,
1797 model.

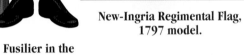

New-Ingria Regimental Flag,
1797 model.

Yaroslav Regimental Flag,
1797 model.

Fusilier in the
New-Ingria Regiment.

Musketeer in the
Yaroslav Regiment.

Colonel Flag, Bryansk
Regiment, 1797 model.

Colonel Flag, Vladimir
Regiment, 1797 model.

Bryansk Regimental Flag,
1797 model.

Vladimir Regimental Flag,
1797 model.

Fusilier in the Bryansk
Regiment.

Fusilier in the Vladimir
Regiment.

André Jouineau © Histoire et collections 2003

THE FIRST COLUMN
under lieutenant-general Dokhturov

Colonel Flag, Vyatka
Regiment,
1797 model.

Vyatka Regimental Flag,
1797 model.

Fusilier in the Vyatka Regiment.

Colonel Flag,
Moscow Regiment,
1797 model.

Moscow Regimental Flag,
1797 model.

Musketeer in the
Moscow Regiment.

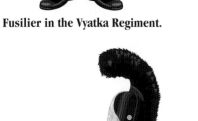

Mounted Artillery.
In the first battalion the shoulder flaps were
red, in the second they were white.

Artillery, Gunner
in the 3rd Regiment.

Pioneer
in the 2nd
Regiment
of Russian
Engineers.

He was armed with a pistol carried
in a white leather holster and with a
knife for making faggots.

André Jouineau © Histoire et collections 2003

THE SECOND COLUMN
under lieutenant-general Langeron

Infantryman in the 8th *Chasseur à pied* Regiment, 2nd and 3rd battalions. The Chasseurs were armed with the infantry rifle, except for twelve men per company who had a rifled carbine. The sabre-bayonet was worn on the left and was not fixed to the gun.

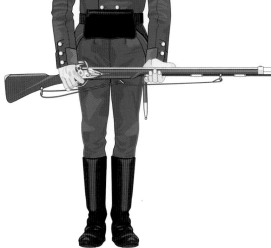

Saint-Petersburg Dragoons. The basic colour of the jacket was identical to the Chasseur regiments. The distinctive colours of the regiments were applied to the collar, the facings, the shoulder flaps and the saddle blanket.

Colonel Flag,
Viborg Regiment.

The flag of a battalion
in the Viborg Regiment.

Fusilier in the
Viborg Regiment

Fusilier wearing a greatcoat.
This coat was very ample and long, and bore
the regiment's distinctive colours on the collar
and the shoulder flaps.

André Jouineau © Histoire et collections 2003

THE SECOND COLUMN
under lieutenant-general Langeron

Soldier wearing a greatcoat. This model which could be of different shades of grey beige, was very ample. The sleeves even covered the hands. The distinctive colours of the regiment appeared on the collar and the shoulder flaps. The shako was fitted with a cover for the nape of the neck and earflaps

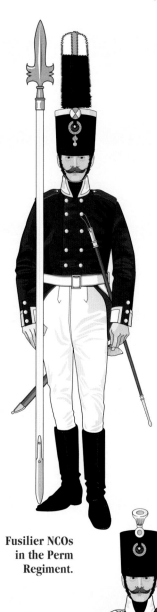

Fusilier NCOs in the Perm Regiment.

Colonel Flag, Perm Regiment.

Perm Regimental Flag.

Colonel Flag, Kursk Regiment

Subaltern in the Perm Regiment.

Musketeer, Kursk Regiment.

Battalion Flag, Kursk Regiment

André Jouineau © Histoire et collections 2003

THE SECOND COLUMN
under lieutenant-general Langeron

Grenadier in full service dress, Fanagoria Grenadier Regiment.

Colonel Flag, Fanagoria Grenadier Regiment.

The headdress was the cylindrical shako, fitted with a very voluminous black plume, for the grenadiers only. The grenadiers wore a brass grenade on the front, under the pompon and the cockade which was common to all. There were also four grenades at the four corners of the cartridge box, which also had a large round plate with the Eagle for the Line and the Star of Saint Andrew for the Guard. Only the Pavlov Regiment kept the mitre from the previous century, and it kept it until 1914. Each regiment was issued with a white colonel flag, and coloured flags for the battalions. The first battalion was given a coloured flag with the white one; the other battalions had two coloured flags.

Fanagoria Grenadiers Regimental Flag.

Colonel Flag, Ryazan Regiment.

Battalion Flag, Ryazan Regiment.

ARTILLERY

Subaltern.

NCOs.

The infantry drummers wore an identical jacket to that of the troops', but with white stripes on the sleeves and on the front of the jacket, swallows' nests at the top of the sleeves, and a red plume. The regimental distinctive colour was applied to the same parts as the soldiers' uniform.

André Jouineau © Histoire et collections 2003

THE THIRD COLUMN
under lieutenant-generals Przybyszewski and Wimpfen

Chasseur from the 2nd and
3rd Battalions of the 7th
Regiment of Chasseurs.

Chasseur from
the 1st Battalion
of the 8th Chasseur Regiment.

Fusilier from the Galitz
(Galicia) Regiment.

Colonel Flag,
Butyrsk Regiment.

Butyrsk
Regimental Flag.

Fusilier in the Butyrsk Regiment.

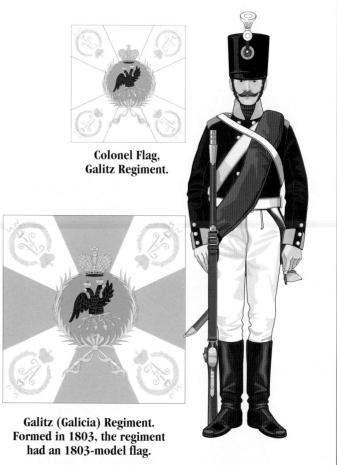

Colonel Flag,
Galitz Regiment.

Galitz (Galicia) Regiment.
Formed in 1803, the regiment
had an 1803-model flag.

André Jouineau © Histoire et collections 2003

THE THIRD COLUMN
under lieutenant-generals Przybyszewski and Wimpfen

Colonel Flag.

Colonel Flag.

Musketeer in the
Narva Regiment.

Narva Regiment.

Pdolsk Regiment.
*Formed in 1803, the regiment had an
1803-model flag.*

Colonel Flag.

Musketeer
in the Azov Regiment.

Azov Regiment.

Pioneer NCOs.

Austrian
Artillery Server.

André Jouineau © Histoire et collections 2003

THE FOURTH COLUMN
under Lieutenant-generals Kollowrath and Miloradovitch

Austrian Dragoon from Archduke John's Regiment *(Erzherzog Johann).*

Grenadier from
the Little Russia
Grenadier Regiment.

Colonel Flag, Little Russia
Grenadier Regiment.

Little Russia Regimental Flag.

Musketeer
from
the Smolensk
Regiment.

Colonel Flag,
Smolensk Regiment.

Colonel Flag,
Apsheron Regiment

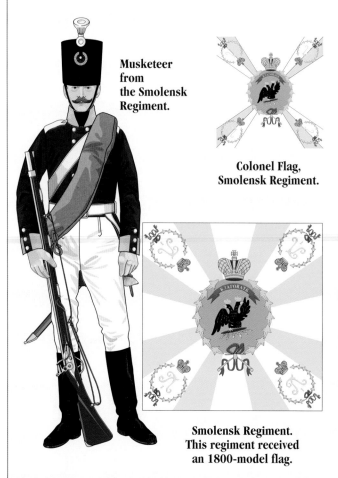

Smolensk Regiment.
This regiment received
an 1800-model flag.

Apsheron
Regimental Flag.

Musketeer from the Apsheron Regiment.

André Jouineau © Histoire et collections 2003

THE FOURTH COLUMN
under lieutenant-generals Kollowrath and Miloradovitch

Musketeer from the
Novgorod Regiment.

Colonel Flag,
Novgorod Regiment.

Novgorod Regiment.
This regiment received
an 1800-model flag.

Austrian regimental flag
of the 1792 type, common
to all infantry regiments.

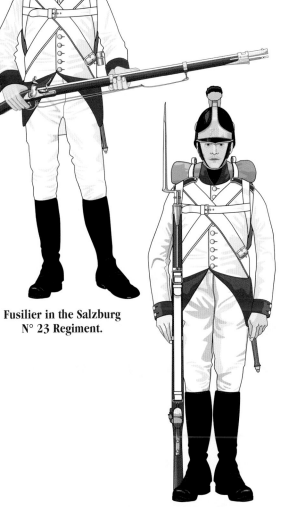

Fusilier in the Salzburg
N° 23 Regiment.

Fusilier in the Emperor's N°1 Regiment.
(Kaiser Franz)

Kaunitz Regiment N° 20
(Wenzel Kaunitz)

André Jouineau © Histoire et collections 2003

THE FOURTH COLUMN
under lieutenant-generals Kollowrath and Miloradovitch

Austrian Colonel
Flag 1792-model
(obverse) common
to all infantry
regiments.

Reverse. There
were several
variants
of this model.

Austrian
infantryman's coat.

Czartorinsky N°9 Regiment.
(Graf Czarutorisky).

Reuss-Greitz N°55 Regiment.

Fusilier, grenadier and officer in Archduke Ferdinand of Wurtemberg
N° 38 Regiment *(Erzherzog Ferdinand von Wurtemberg)*.

Beaulieu N° 58 Regiment
(Baron Beaulieu)

André Jouineau © Histoire et collections 2003

THE FOURTH COLUMN
under lieutenant-generals Kollowrath and Miloradovitch

Kerpen N° 49 Regiment
(Baron Kerpen).

**Front and rear view of a Fusilier
from Lindenau N° 29 Regiment.**

**Austrian General Officer
wearing ordinary dress.**

Drummer from the Grenadiers of Anesperg
(Carl Auersperg) **N° 24 Regiment.**

**Austrian Artilleryman
wearing a coat.**

Vienna Chasseur.

André Jouineau © Histoire et collections 2003

THE FIFTH COLUMN
under lieutenant-generals, Prince Johann of Liechtenstein and the Prince of Hohenlohe

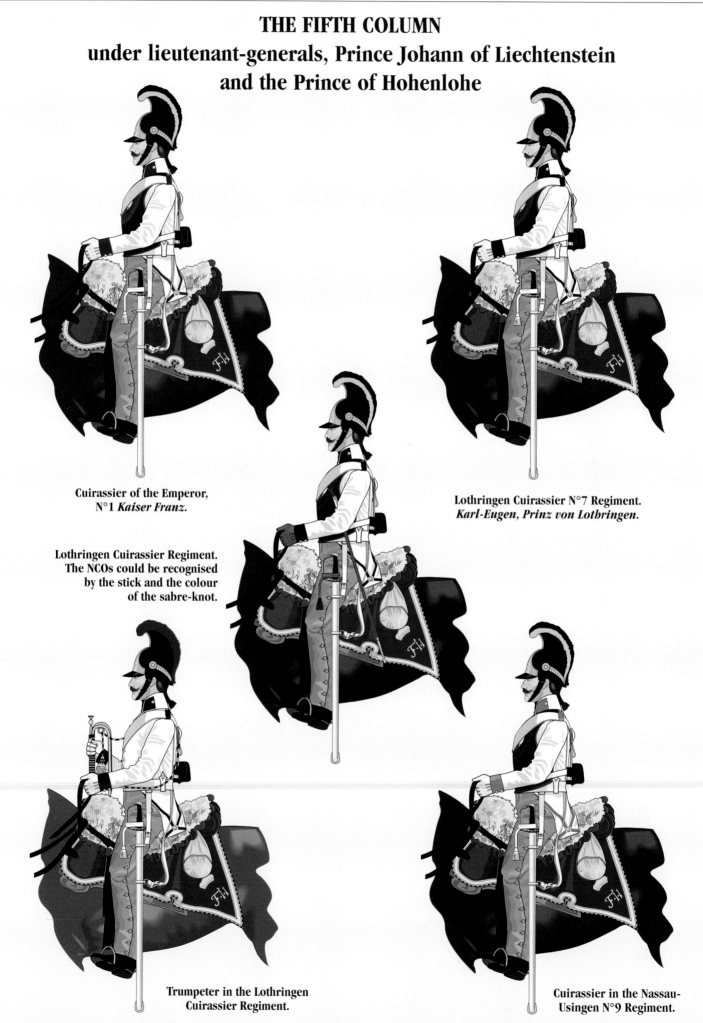

Cuirassier of the Emperor, N°1 *Kaiser Franz*.

Lothringen Cuirassier Regiment. The NCOs could be recognised by the stick and the colour of the sabre-knot.

Lothringen Cuirassier N°7 Regiment. *Karl-Eugen, Prinz von Lothringen*.

Trumpeter in the Lothringen Cuirassier Regiment.

Cuirassier in the Nassau-Usingen N°9 Regiment.

André Jouineau © Histoire et collections 2003

THE FIFTH COLUMN
under lieutenant-generals, Prince Johann of Liechtenstein and the Prince of Hohenlohe

Standard of the Empress' Cuirassiers.

An Empress' Cuirassier.

Standard of the Kharkov Dragoons.

A Kharkov Dragoon.

Standard of the Tchernigov Dragoons.

Tchernigov Dragoon Regiment.

Elisabethgrad Hussar.

André Jouineau © Histoire et collections 2003

RUSSIAN IMPERIAL GUARD
under Grand-Duke Konstantin

Corps Grenadier.

Drummer in the Chasseurs à pied
of the Russian Imperial Guard.

Colonel and regimental flags
of the Foot regiments of the Guard.
In 1800, the three regiments
Preobrajensky, Ismaïlovsky
and Semenovsky received
their flags from
Paul 1st himself.

Jäger

Cossacks
of the Guard
bivouacking.
(RR)

32

André Jouineau © Histoire et collections 2003

RUSSIAN IMPERIAL GUARD
under Grand-Duke Konstantin

Grenadier
in the Preobrajensky
Regiment.

Grenadier
in the Preobrajensky
Regiment.

Grenadier in the
Semenovsky
Regiment.

Grenadier NCOs
in the Preobrajensky
Regiment.
The NCOs carried
a half-pike and a cane.

Grenadier Drummer in the
Preobrajensky Regiment.

Grenadier in the
Ismaïlovsky Regiment.

André Jouineau © Histoire et collections 2003

RUSSIAN IMPERIAL GUARD
under Grand-Duke Konstantin

Life Guard.

Vexillum of the Life Guards (Chevalier-Garde). The regiment was given three to replace the red standards with the Maltese cross. They were taken on campaign for the Empire and were left in the village of Austerlitz before the Guard's charge.

NCOs in the Life Guards.

Cuirassier of the Guard.

Cuirassier of the Guard Standard, 1800-model. It was borne by an NCOs.

Cuirassier NCOs of the Russian Imperial Guard.

André Jouineau © Histoire et collections 2003

NCOs
of the
Hussars
of the Guard.

The Hussars of the Guard were dressed like those of the Line, but with their own distinctive colours.
The NCOs had the usual marks of rank, worn on the dolman and the brown-furred pelisse as well as an orange and white plume edged with black. The cavalrymen were issued with carbines which the NCOs did not have.

Hussar of the Guard.

The Cossacks of the Guard were created in the reign of Catherine II in 1775 and unlike those in the army were considered as regulars.
Their uniform included a winter uniform (see opposite) and summer dress comprising a red half-caftan. Arms consisted of a lance, a sabre and a pistol hooked onto a bandolier.
The NCOs did not have marks of rank but could be recognised by the black and orange-tipped plume and by the fact that they carried canes.

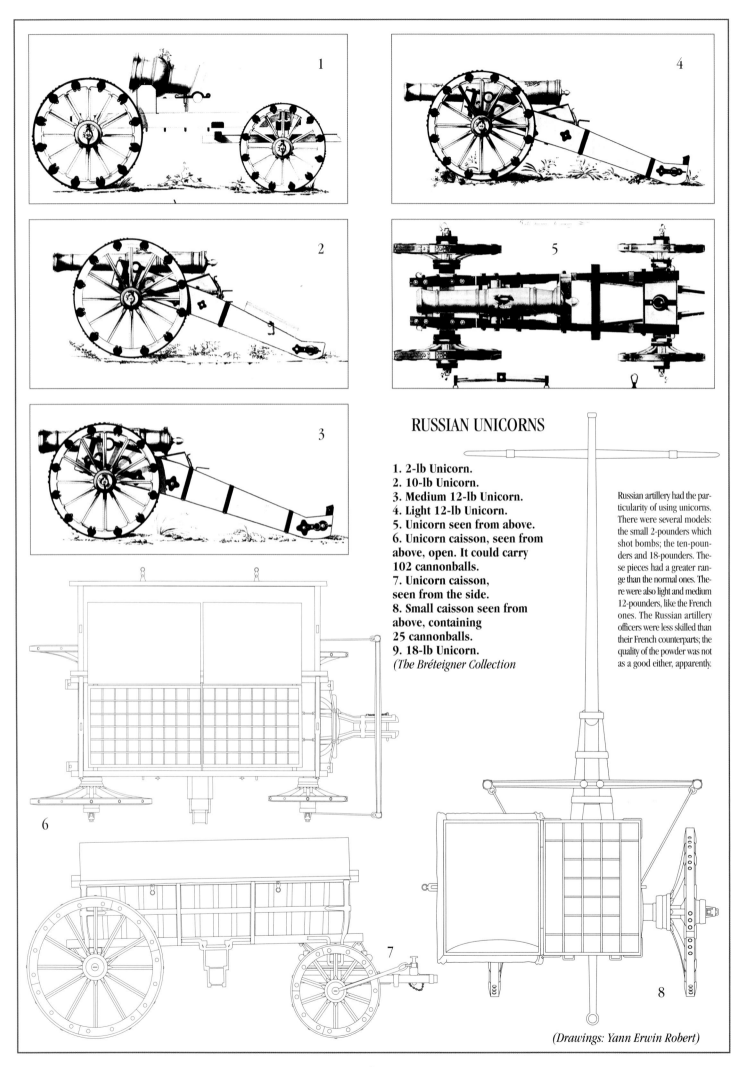

RUSSIAN UNICORNS

1. 2-lb Unicorn.
2. 10-lb Unicorn.
3. Medium 12-lb Unicorn.
4. Light 12-lb Unicorn.
5. Unicorn seen from above.
6. Unicorn caisson, seen from above, open. It could carry 102 cannonballs.
7. Unicorn caisson, seen from the side.
8. Small caisson seen from above, containing 25 cannonballs.
9. 18-lb Unicorn.
(The Bréteigner Collection

Russian artillery had the particularity of using unicorns. There were several models: the small 2-pounders which shot bombs; the ten-pounders and 18-pounders. These pieces had a greater range than the normal ones. There were also light and medium 12-pounders, like the French ones. The Russian artillery officers were less skilled than their French counterparts; the quality of the powder was not as a good either, apparently.

(Drawings: Yann Erwin Robert)

RUSSIAN IMPERIAL GUARD
under Grand-Duke Konstantin

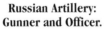

Russian Artillery:
Gunner and Officer.

Artillery train driver.

Mounted Artilleryman
wearing marching
dress.

The 'Dismounted' Artillery battalion was a creation of Paul I. Its uniform was identical with that of the Army but used the Guards' distinctives.
The Mounted Artillery wore the cavalry's heavy helmet with the Guard's star; on the right shoulder there was a yellow woollen aglet which resembled that of the Prussian cavalry.

9

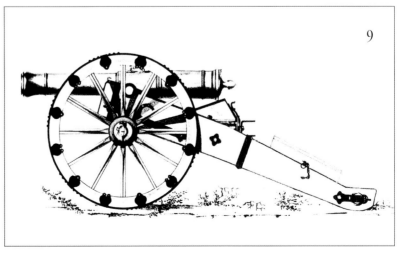

André Jouineau © Histoire et collections 2003

(Drawing by J. Girbal © DBA)

Headquarters.
— The Emperor's Household.
— Berthier's Staff.
— Daru's Administration.

THE IMPERIAL GUARD

● **The Infantry**
— **The Grenadiers:** their commanding officer Hulin was in command in Vienna and was not at the battle. 1 549 men.
— **Soulès' Chasseurs.** 1 281 men.
— **Lecchi's grenadiers of the Royal Italian Guard.** 589 men.
● **The Cavalry**
— **Ordener's Grenadiers.** 628 men.
— **Morland's Chasseurs.** 331 men.
— **The Mameluks.** 109 men.
— **Couin's Artillery.** 283 men.

BERNADOTTE'S 1st CORPS

● **Kellermann's Vanguard.**
This consisted of 4 light cavalry regiments, i.e. two brigades with a total strength of 1 856 cavalrymen.
— **Van-Marisy's Brigade:**
4th Hussars and 5th Chasseurs.
— **Picard's Brigade:** 2nd and 5th Hussars.
— **General Frère's 27th Light,** in support of the vanguard if needed. It joined Drouet's division for the battle.
● **Rivaud's Division.**
— **Dumoulin's Brigade:**
8th and 45th of the Line.
— **Pachtod's Brigade:** 54th of the Line.
● **Drouet d'Erlon's Division.**
— **Frère's Brigade** with the 27th Light.
— **Werlé's Brigade:**
94th and 95th of the Line.
The total strength of the 1st Corps was 10918 infantry and 1 856 cavalry, and 1 305 artillerymen. Generally, the infantry regiments had two battalions, but each battalion had between 600 and 1 000 men. The cavalry regiments had 3 squadrons each with 250-300 men.
Kellermann's Division was put on the left wing to reinforce Murat's cavalry which here was operating on appropriate terrain, aptly called 'the Cavalryman's Plain'. This levy irritated

Bernadotte who complained bitterly and worked to rule on the day of 2 December.

DAVOUT'S 3rd CORPS

● **Caffarelli du Falga's Division.**
This aide de camp of Napoleon's took command following General Bisson's serious wound at Lambach. It consisted of:
— **Demont's Brigade:**
only the 13th Light. 1 382 men.
— **Billy's brigade:** 17th and 30th of the Line.
— **Eppler's Brigade:**
51st and 61st of the Line.
Its strength was 6 380 men and 165 artillerymen. It was attached to the 5th Corps under Lannes to strengthen the infantry on the French left wing.
● **Friant's Division.**
Leaving the area around Vienna, it made its famous forced march of 36 leagues in 40 hours without stopping to take part in the battle. It arrived gradually at Raygern. Normally there were 5 556 men but only 3 800 men and 9 cannon were present at the beginning of the battle. It consisted of:
— **Heudelet's Brigade:** the 108th and the Voltigeurs of the 15th Light.
— **Kister's Brigade:** the remainder of the 15th Light and the 33rd.
— **Lochet's Brigade:** 48th and 111th of the Line. The 1st Dragoons of Klein's Division (329 men) joined Heudelet, the only regiment in the division which had arrived. The rest joined them at the end of the day.
— **Gudin's Brigade:** situated beyond Vienna, it began its march but did not arrive for the battle; it took part in the final pursuit.
— **Vialannes' Cavalry:** 7th Hussars, 1st, 2nd and 3rd Chasseurs. It remained with Gudin and there were only 61 cavalrymen (of whom many were mentioned in despatches) present to escort Marshal Davout.
— **Colonel Jouffroy's Artillery.** Only Friant's cannon were available.

SOULT'S 4th CORPS

● **Saint-Hilaire's Division.**
— **Morand's Brigade:** only the 10th Light.

— **Thiébault's Brigade:**
4th and 36th of the Line.
— **Waré's brigade:**
43rd and 55th of the Line.
● **Vandamme's Division.**
— **Schiner's Brigade:** only the 24th Light.
— **Ferey's Brigade:** 46th and 57th of the Line.
— **Candras' Brigade:**
4th and 28th of the Line.
● **Legrand's Division.**
— **Merle's Brigade:**
3rd of the Line, Pô Tirailleurs.
— **Levasseur's Brigade:** 18th and 75th of the Line, and the Corsican Tirailleurs.
This made 7 736 men and 213 Artillerymen.
● **Margaron's Cavalry.**
— **Franceschi's 8th Hussars.**
— **11th and 26th Chasseurs.**
In all 924 cavalrymen and 143 mounted artillerymen. The corps total strength was 24333 men and 924 cavalry and 1 135 artillerymen.

LANNES' 5th CORPS

● **Oudinot's Division.**
In fact the grenadiers and the elite Voltigeurs were regrouped into a reserve making three brigades and were kept as a first reserve in front of the Guard without taking part very much. Because of his wound at Hollbrünn where his men had distinguished themselves, Oudinot was replaced by Duroc, but because of the former's protests, Napoleon agreed to divide the command in two with 6 battalions for Duroc and four for Oudinot.
— **Laplanche-Mortière's Brigade:** the first regiment with the elite companies of the 13th and 58th of the Line. The second regiment came from the 9th and the 81st.
— **Dupas' Second Brigade:** third regiment from the 2nd and 3rd Lights. Fourth regiment coming from the 28th of the Line and 31st Light. Only these two regiments were used with Duroc at the end of the battle to seal off any escape for the Allies trapped in Sokolnitz.
— **Ruffin's Third Brigade:** fifth regiment coming from the 12th of the Line and the 15th light.
This division had 5 700 men and 10 cannon at its disposal.
● **Suchet's Division.**
— **Claparède's Brigade:**
the 17th Light alone fortified the Santon, swearing to defend it to the end.
— **Beker's Brigade:**
34th and 40th of the Line.
— **Valhubert's Brigade:**
64th and 88th of the Line. Total 6 805 men.
● **Treillard's Cavalry.**
— **Treillard's Brigade:**
9th and 10th Hussars and
— **Fauconnet's Brigade:** 13th and 21st Chasseurs. Total for the corps 15 414 men, 640 cavalry and 774 artillerymen.

THE CAVALRY RESERVE

● **Nansouty's First Heavy Cavalry Division.**
— **Piston's Brigade:** 1st and 2nd Carabiniers
— **De la Houssaye's Brigade:**
2nd and 9th Cuirassiers.
— **Saint-Germain's Brigade:**
3rd and 12th Cuirassiers.
In all 1 387 cavalry and 92 artillerymen.
● **De Hautpoul's Second Heavy Cavalry Division.**

— **St-Sulpice's Brigade:**
1st and 5th Cuirassiers.
— **Fontaine's Brigade:**
10th and 11th Cuirassiers
in all 1 043 cavalry and 85 artillerymen.
● **Klein's First Dragoon Division.**
— **Fornier** (aka Fénérols) Brigade:
1st and 2nd Dragoons.
— **Lasalle's Brigade:**
4th and 14th Dragoons (according to Six)
The 4th had been engaged at Durrenstein and had not joined up. In this division, only the 1st Dragoons was at Austerlitz. The others joined at the end of the evening at Raygern and took part in the pursuit on 3 December with Davout, who got Gudin back and led the Dragoons who were present towards Goeding.
● **Walther's Second Dragoon Division.**
— **Sébastiani's Brigade:**
3rd and 6th Dragoons.
— **Roger de Belloguet's Brigade:**
10th and 11th Dragoons.
— **Boussard's Brigade:**
13th and 22nd Dragoons.
In all 2 136 dragoons and 84 artillerymen. Roget replaced Walther who was wounded during the battle.
● **Beaumont's Third Dragoon Division.**
— **Boyé's Brigade:**
5th, 8th and 12th Dragoons.
As Beaumont was ill, Boyé was in command of this division.
— **Scalfort's Brigade:**
9th 16th and 21st Dragoons.
In all, 2 161 dragoons and 85 artillerymen.
● **Bourcier's Fourth Dragoon Division**
— **Laplanche's Brigade:**
15th and 17th Dragoons.
— **Sahuc's Brigade:** 18th and 19th Dragoons.
— **Verdière's Brigade:**
25th and 27th Dragoons.
In all 2 274 dragoons.
● **Baraguay d'Hillier's Dismounted Cuirassiers.**
They were not at Austerlitz, but Walther was allowed to make up his regiments by taking thirty men among them for each of his regiments.
● **Milhaud's Light Cavalry Reserve.**
— **Milhaud's Brigade:**
16th and 22nd Chasseurs.

The 5th Corps' cavalry was under Murat for Austerlitz.
— **Treillard's Brigade:**
9th and 10th Hussars.
— **Fauconnet's Brigade:** 13th and 21st Chasseurs. In all 729 cavalrymen.
73 100 men took part in the battle together with 139 cannon.

The changes which Napoleon made

He reinforced the left wing with cavalry because the terrain was very favourable to this arm, with the cavalry of the 1st and 5th Corps.
He reinforced his infantry with Caffarelli's Division by keeping Oudinot's Grenadiers as the first reserve before the Guard.
After his inspection on 1 December, he slipped Legrand's Division further south to block the Allies' left-wing if possible, hoping that the attack in the centre by Soult would relieve Davout and Legrand who were operating together, but who were outnumbered by the first enemy columns.

PREPARING FOR THE BATTLE

Headquarters were still at Brünn, but Soult had occupied Austerlitz and the surrounding area. Napoleon wanted to provoke the Russians into taking the offensive.

THE PRELUDE AT WISCHAU

On 25 November there was a first serious alert, so help was requested from Walther who was in Rausnitz and who sent the 3rd and 11th dragoons to Wischau to reinforce Milhaud's (16th and 22nd Chasseurs) and Treillard's (9th and 10th Hussars) brigades.

It was on 28 November that Bagration attacked the place. At one in the morning, a mass of cavalry followed a swarm of Cossacks which overran the village, followed by dragoons and hussars. Milhaud was forced to begin falling back. They went to Lutsch but bumped into Bauer's Cossacks and Hussars. Guyot (who replaced Treillard who was absent, just as Maupoint replaced Beaumont at the head of the 10th Hussars) tried to break through and finally managed to get through to Rausnitz; but seeing Milhaud in peril at Lutsch where there was heavy fighting, he turned round and went up in support with a platoon of his 9th Regiment hussars.

Milhaud was able get back. Lannes' cuirassiers and the infantry formed up to receive them. The 16th and 22nd Chasseurs had fought well, but the 22nd had lost 40 horsemen killed or taken as well as three officers; the 16th was missing 31 men and one officer. The Russians had engaged about 6 000 cavalry against 1 600.

The Allies entered Wischau and deployed. The Emperor went up to the post office at Posorzitz to see the enemy positions for himself. He gave the order to retreat back to the positions which he had carefully chosen when he inspected in detail the defiles, the villages, the high points on the Pratzen Plateau.

Passing before the 17th Light, he said to a veteran who was filling his pipe: *"Those blighters think that all they've got to do now is to gobble us up."* To which the veteran replied, *"Oh! Oh! It won't happen that way; we'll get in the way!"* The Emperor received the Prussian ambassador Haugwitz who claimed to be a mediator – which Napoleon did not believe for a moment; he nevertheless sent him to Vienna to talk with Talleyrand, who was there and who would comfort the ambassador in his favourable attitud to Prussian neutrality. From there, Napoleon galloped to the Posorsitz post office to meet his marshals.

Murat, Soult and Lannes were sitting in front of a big fire. They agreed that a retreat was

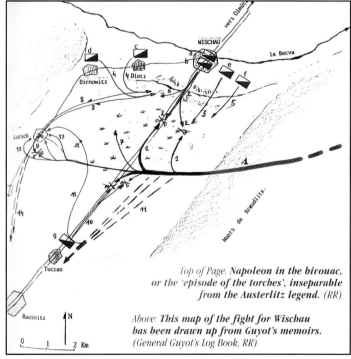

Top of Page. **Napoleon in the bivouac, or the 'episode of the torches', inseparable from the Austerlitz legend.** *(RR)*

Above: **This map of the fight for Wischau has been drawn up from Guyot's memoirs.**
(General Guyot's Log Book, RR)

Above: The present-day post office at Posorsitz on the Olmutz road, the high point of the battle of Austerlitz. (© Garnier)

39

the best solution and asked Lannes to write the appropriate recommendation, which he did. When Napoleon arrived he read the recommendation and said: *"What! Lannes's recommending a retreat? It's the first time he does that."* Turning to Soult, he asked: *"What do you think?"*

"However Your Majesty uses the Fourth Corps, be they twice our number, I will overcome them". Lannes lost his temper at this perfect courtier's hypocritical reply, going so far as to provoke Soult in front of the Emperor, who took absolutely no notice of the conflict. He too thought that it was necessary to retreat so as to draw the enemy and increase their feeling of superiority which would make them advance and try to cut the road to Vienna, by attacking the French right which he would pretend to deny them. The trap was set; all they had to do now was fall into it.

30th November

Napoleon had tightened up his dispositions in the direction of the Turas Plateau, in front of Brünn. He hoped that the enemy was going to take the bait and he observed them.

In the evening he made a proclamation. *"The positions which we now occupy are formidable and while they march on our batteries, I want their flanks to be attacked."* After the evening's reconnaissance, this text was slightly modified the following morning, saying: *"while they are marching to turn my right".* This was the text which was handed out to the different headquarters.

THE FIRST DECEMBER

The 1st Corps had arrived and Davout had also reached headquarters. Napoleon was in his bivouac which was a simple cabin at Zuran from which he had a panoramic view of the future battlefield. Vandamme was positioned in Girzikowitz, Saint-Hilaire near Kobelnitz, Legrand had stationed the Pô Tirailleurs in Sokolnitz with Margaron's Cavalry; Friant had to occupy Raygern, Treillard and Milhaud were at Bosenitz and Walther was at Bellowitz with the cuirassiers on either side of the road from Olmutz to Schlapanitz and Kritchen. The hillock called the Santon was entrusted to Claparède and the 17th light and had to be fortified; it was made steeper on the east side by digging trenches and setting up 18 Austrian cannon in a battery. This was the main linchpin for the French left.

The Emperor spent the day visiting his regiments. He saw the Allies taking over the Pratzen Plateau at about three o'clock. Bagration did not move. Reinforced by Caffarelli's Division taken from Davout's Corps, Lannes took up a position on Suchet's right which was against the fortified Santon. Reinforced by light cavalry from the 1st and 5th Corps, Murat was behind Lannes' divisions. The 1st Corps was in Lattein. Oudinot's Grenadiers who were split up between their commanding officer (only four battalions) and Duroc (the remaining six battalions) because he was wounded recently at Hollabrünn, were kept in reserve behind the Guard. During the night shooting could be heard towards the south; it continued for some time. The Emperor sent Savary to find out what was going on. He reported that Kienmayer had chased the Pô Tirailleurs out of Telnitz; but Legrand had a battalion from the 3rd of the Line retake the village.

Moreover, and especially, Savary reported that between Aujezd and Telnitz, the Allies had sent an impressive corps including all arms, which had gone down through the valley, without being seen.

That was enough for Napoleon to do his own reconnoitering. He sent for Soult, Caulaincourt, de Ségur and his usual escort. He went to Girzikowitz first. In the main street, the Dragoons of the Guard told him that they had heard the movement and the sounds of enemy troops marching, until two o'clock in the morning, heading towards the left, coming up against the French right. The Emperor risked going between the lines and unexpectedly came across a Cossack position.

The Chasseurs of the escort had to intervene so that they could get back as quickly as possible towards the Goldbach; the Surgeon Yvan got stuck in the marshy banks. Once over the stream, Napoleon carried on foot to his bivouac at Zuran. In the darkness he hit a tree stump; a grenadier tied some straw to the end of a pole and lit it to light up the way for his Emperor. From one person to the next, torches lit up; the shouting grew louder and louder: *"Long live the Emperor! Long live the anniversary of the Coronation!"*

The Allies did not understand anything of this and were alarmed by all the noise. Now that he was well-informed, Napoleon changed his plans with Soult's help. Saint-Hilaire's division went down to cross the Goldbach at Puntowitz. Levasseur's brigade positioned itself in front of Kobelnitz. The 3rd of the line was placed in Telnitz. In theory, Friant's division went back up towards Turas but had to head for Sokolnitz in order to hold up the Allies' likely attack on Telnitz and Sokolnitz.

It was Weyrother who planned the attack over this terrain which he knew well, having carried out manoeuvres recently in the area.

ALLIED PROJECT FOR THE 1st DECEMBER

Langeron explained that *"the divisions and the brigades had been all mixed up, each commanding officer having lost the regiments he had known for a very long time; and, in war, knowing your troops is very useful for a general. There was no longer any time to correct all that; but when marching towards the enemy, a commanding officer should at least be entrusted with the battalions and squadrons he was to command on the day of the battle, so that he can get used to them and they to him. We did exactly the opposite. During those five marches, a general never commanded the same regiment he had commanded the day before. Camp was reached during the night. Orders were received late, nothing could be done in the dark; although it was a full moon, the sky was too cloudy and the weather too misty for its light to be of any use to us. Each general had to look for the regiments which should have made up his column in the other four. They had to do one if not two miles just to reach him... It was always 10 or 11 o'clock before we could muster; often, columns crossed each other, a mistake which even the last and most ignorant of staff officers would not be forgiven for making.*

"We arrived late, split up to look for supplies, the village was looted; there was disorder everywhere."

It was only at 10 p.m. that the commanders of the columns, except for Bagration, got the order to go to Krenowitz, to meet with Kutusov to hear what dispositions had been taken for the morrow's battle. It was only at one a.m. that Weyrother found them gathered together. He unfolded a huge map of the area. Kutusov, sitting, was almost asleep when we arrived, and finished by falling asleep completely before we left. Buxhoewden, standing, listened but most certainly did not understand a thing. Miloradovitch was silent; only Dokhturov exami-

ned the map with attention. "The plan consisted of outflanking the French right by crossing the Goldbach between Telnitz and Kobelnitz, then converging and attacking on the front between Turas and Puntowitz.

"The first column was to take Telnitz and would then go off to the right, lining up with the second crossing the stream between Telnitz and Sokolnitz, and the third at Sokolnitz Castle." And then the heads of the three columns were to advance up to the ponds at Kobelnitz.

"Bagration's Corps, helped by Liech-tenstein's cavalry was to take the San-ton and from there attack the French left. The army was to regroup at Lat-tein and crush the French in their flight to Brünn. The columns were to leave at 7 a.m.

"Kutusov then woke up and orde-red an adjutant to be left to copy the texts which Major Toll was going to translate from the German into Russian. Langeron said he only recei-ved his copy at 8 a.m., after he had set off."

The Allies, in reality had 87 000 men according to Colin, with 278 cannon and 8 500 men of the Guard, facing 75 000 men (among whom 2 000 men in the wagon train) and the 137 cannon which Napoleon had at his disposal.

Above.
These three views of the site, taken a few years ago, give a clear picture of what was the theatre of the battle, the plateau, like the plain had changed little. Here, the photos have been taken from the Pratzen Plateau.
(© Garnier)

Above. **Napoleon during the night of 1-2 December 1805. Another element in the legend.** *(RR)*

41

THE 2 DECEMBRE: THE GREAT BATTLE

THE FRENCH DISPOSITION BEFORE THE BATTLE

Once Wischau captured, Austerlitz abandoned and the army's generalised retreat on the Goldbach line started, Napoleon pretended to be frightened and hesitant; he disposed his forces in the following manner.

ON THE LEFT WING

Murat was in overall command. The Santon was held by Claparède with the 17th Light and the 18 Austrian cannon from Brünn. The regiment had sent a small unit into Bosenitz, a position supported by Milhaud's and Treillard's light cavalry.

Lannes had Suchet's division which was in the line along the edge of the Santon. Its objective was to advance towards Bagration above the main road to Olmutz. Caffarelli's division was more to the right, above the main road and supported by Kellermann's cavalry, followed by Beaumont's (Boyé) and Walther's dragoons. Behind were Nansouty's heavy cavalry in the line and then d'Hautpoul's which were behind Suchet's division. They were on a level with Bellowitz and Kritchen.

IN THE CENTRE

There was **Soult's corps**. After crossing the Goldbach, it was placed so as to be ready to attack the Pratzen. The troops were hidden by a providentially thick fog which prevented the Allies from seeing the danger coming.

Vandamme was in front of Girzikowitz; its objective was the vine-covered Staré Vinhorady, which would be visible once the precious fog lifted.

Saint-Hilaire's departure point was Puntowitz, his objective the Pratzenberg, but by-passing if at all possible, the village of Pratzen. Levasseur's brigade was to slip along towards Kobelnitz.

Still belly-aching about losing his cavalry, **Bernadotte** was to approach Goldbach coming from Schlapanitz and follow Soult's advance and cross the Goldbach at Girzikowitz. Oudinot's grenadiers were also on a level with Schlapanitz and were ready. Napoleon was at Zuran with his Guard. It was 8 a.m.

ON THE RIGHT

Legrand had the 3rd of the Line which had recaptured Telnitz. Merle and Margaron were in Sokolnitz. **Davout** had left Raygern, moving up to Turas. He was going to have to branch out towards Telnitz and Sokolnitz to slow up the first Allied columns and prevent them from deploying beyond the Goldbach. It was a sacrificial mission and he was quite aware of this. He had Bourcier's dragoons with him, with Klein's 1st Dragoons marching with Heudelet in front.

THE ALLIES DISPOSITION BEFORE THE BATTLE

ON THEIR RIGHT

There was **Bagration** with 12 000 men, among which 3 000 were cavalry, and 40 cannon. At 8 a.m. he was in front of Kowalowitz and got under way at 9.30 a.m., occupying Holubitz and Kruh to the south. The Russian Guard came up to the heights overlooking the village of Blasowitz.

IN THE CENTRE

Everybody got into place by nightfall on the 1st, with a lot of confusion which was denounced by Langeron. This was because **Liechtenstein's cavalry** had got lost over by Pratzen. This was the origin of all the trouble with the second and third columns because until Liechtenstein had left this zone, Langeron and Przybyszewski could not move and wasted an hour. This delay was very precious for Davout's forces. The real centre was held by Miloradovitch and Kollowrath and

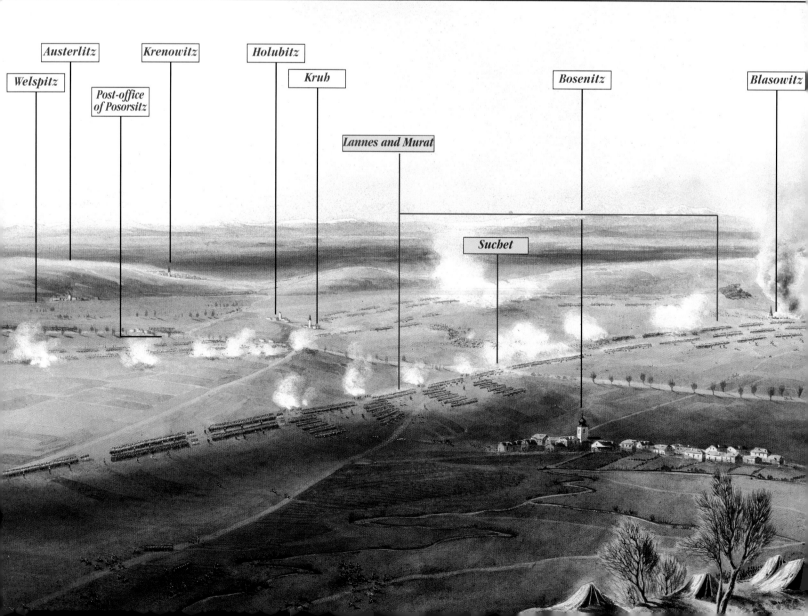

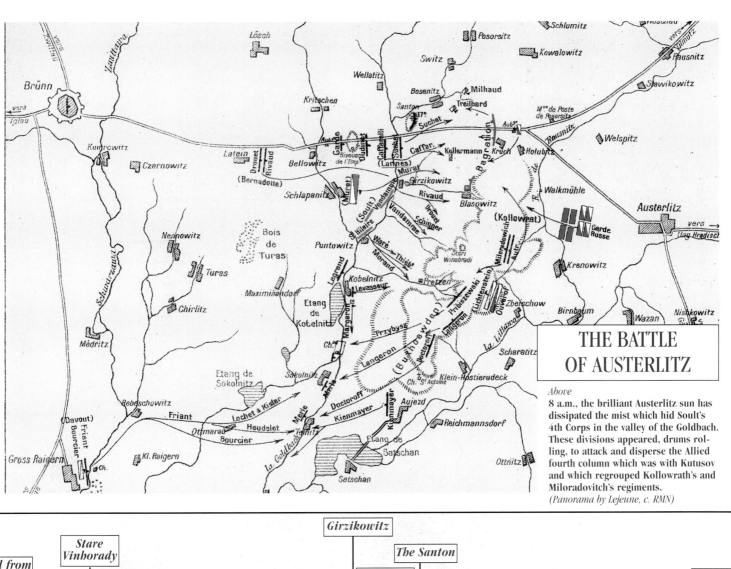

THE BATTLE OF AUSTERLITZ

Above

8 a.m., the brilliant Austerlitz sun has dissipated the mist which hid Soult's 4th Corps in the valley of the Goldbach. These divisions appeared, drums rolling, to attack and disperse the Allied fourth column which was with Kutusov and which regrouped Kollowrath's and Miloradovitch's regiments.

(Panorama by Lejeune, c. RMN)

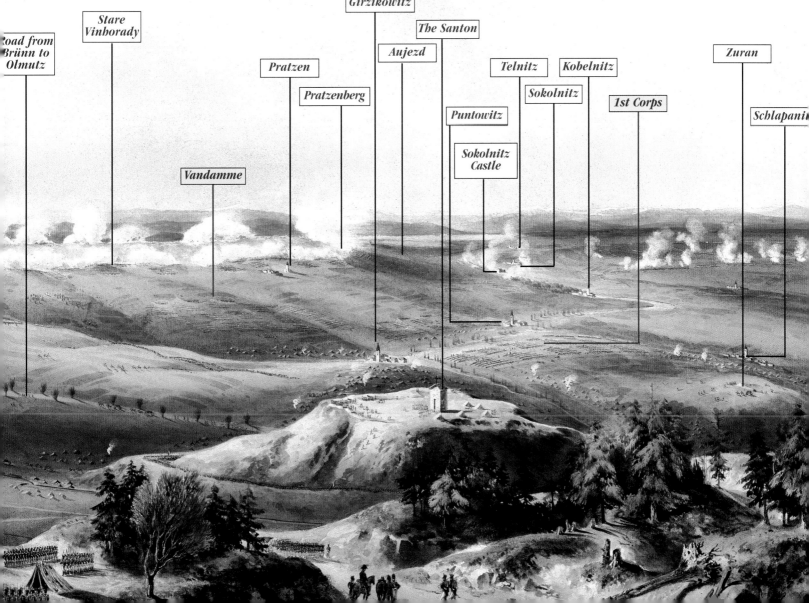

Road from Brünn to Olmutz

Stare Vinhorady

Girzikowitz

The Santon

Aujezd

Zuran

Pratzen

Telnitz

Kobelnitz

Pratzenberg

Sokolnitz

Puntowitz

1st Corps

Schlapani

Sokolnitz Castle

Vandamme

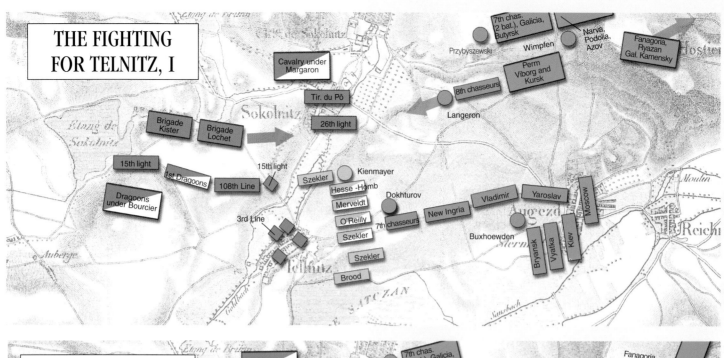

THE FIGHTING
FOR TELNITZ, I

Cavalry under
Margaron

Tir. du Pô

Brigade
Kister

Brigade
Lochet

26th light

15th light

15th light

1st Dragoons

108th Line

Dragoons
under Bourcier

3rd Line

Szekler

Kienmayer

Hesse -Homb

Merveldt

Dokhturov

O'Reilly

7th chasseurs

New Ingria

Vladimir

Yaroslav

Moscow

Szekler

Buxhoewden

Bryansk

Vyatka

Kiev

Szekler

Brood

7th chas.
(2 bat.), Galicia,
Butyrsk

Przybyszewski

Wimpfen

Narva,
Podolia,
Azov

Fanagoria,
Ryazan
Gal. Kamensky

Perm
Viborg and
Kursk

8th chasseurs

Langeron

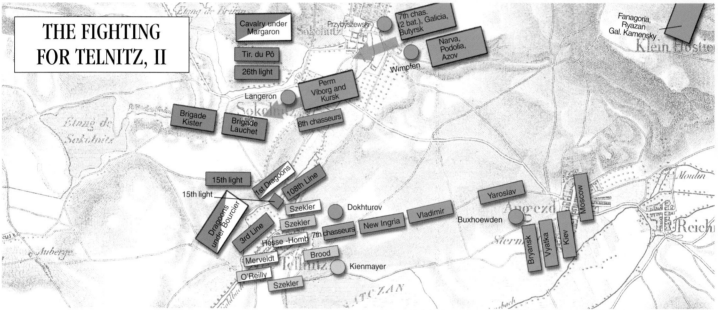

THE FIGHTING
FOR TELNITZ, II

Cavalry under
Margaron

Przybyszewski

7th chas.
(2 bat.), Galicia,
Butyrsk

Fanagoria,
Ryazan
Gal. Kamensky

Tir. du Pô

26th light

Narva,
Podolia,
Azov

Wimpfen

Langeron

Perm
Viborg and
Kursk

Brigade
Kister

Brigade
Lauchet

8th chasseurs

15th light

1st Dragoons

108th Line

15th light

Yaroslav

Moscow

Dragoons
under Bourcier

Szekler

Dokhturov

3rd Line

Szekler

Hesse -Homb

7th chasseurs

New Ingria

Vladimir

Buxhoewden

Bryansk

Vyatka

Kiev

Merveldt

Brood

O'Reilly

Kienmayer

Szekler

the fourth column commanded at that moment by Kutusov. The Tsar was following the advance.

ON THE LEFT

Towards Telnitz, Kienmayer was fighting for Telnitz with his 5 000 men among which 1 000 cavalry, and 12 cannon. Coming from Aujezd, Dokhturov's first column went to his rescue. Having disentangled himself from Liechtenstein's cavalry, Langeron moved down towards Sokolnitz with Przybyszewski and his third column; but at the beginning, the mist hindered them. The smoke from all the firing made it thicker. The Allies quite clearly out-numbered the French in this part of the field. They were able to occupy Telnitz and Sokolnitz but were not able to break out. Buxhoewden, who was in command of this wing, was in front of Aujezd with several regiments and had nothing to do.

ACTION AGAINST THE FRENCH RIGHT WING

1. THE FIGHTING FOR TELNITZ

In order to turn the French army, Weyrother's columns had to go through Telnitz and Sokolnitz. It was Davout's role, supported by Bourcier's dragoons and Legrand's division, to stop them for as long as possible in order to let Soult's attacks towards the plateau of Pratzen get under way; these would hopefully relieve him.

In theory, Kienmayer at the front of the first column, had to clear Telnitz in order

THE FIGHTING FOR TELNITZ

- **During the night of 1 December**, Kienmayer captured Telnitz by chasing out the Pô Tirailleurs which had been occupying it. The 3rd of the Line had sent a battalion to retake this village. Legrand sent two other battalions from the regiment to reinforce its defence.

- **On the 2nd, in the morning**, from 8 a.m. onwards, Kienmayer attacked the village with the 1st battalion of Szekler 1st Regiment; this was pushed back. He then sent the 2nd battalion, also without success. The Hesse-Homburg Hussars and Maurice of Liechtenstein's Szekler Hussars covered the infantry against the threat of Margaron's cavalry.

- **General Carneville** supported the assault with the Szekler 2nd Regiment and the Brood Battalion, but five consecutive attacks were driven off.

- **They had to wait for 8.30 a.m.** and Dokhturov's first column for the Russian 7th Chasseurs followed by the New-Ingria Regiment to be sent to reinforce the Austrians. The 1 200 survivors of the 3rd of the Line finally gave way and sought refuge among the vines and the ditches on the other side of the Goldbach. Buxhoewden, in command of this left wing decided to await the arrival of the second and third columns before continuing his attack. He remained in front of Aujezd with four Russian regiments.

- **Margaron** warned Davout who was moving up to Turas about the events at Telnitz. Davout then marched on Telnitz and Sokolnitz. He sent General Heudelet with the 108th of the Line, the 15th Voltigeurs of the 15th Light and the 1st Dragoons commanded by Captain Ménard.

- **In the thick fog**, Heudelet launched his men who threw the Allied troops into disorder; the New-Ingria Regiment fled, causing disorder in Dokhturov's troops who were following behind. At this moment there was a misunderstanding caused by the men of the 26th Light who had been dislodged from Sokolnitz. In the thick fog they mistook the men from the 108th for the enemy and started firing at them.

- **Davout** decided to regroup his forces further north behind the stream at Sokolnitz. Bourcier's Dragoons were there to prevent the enemy from coming out of Telnitz which was now in their hands.

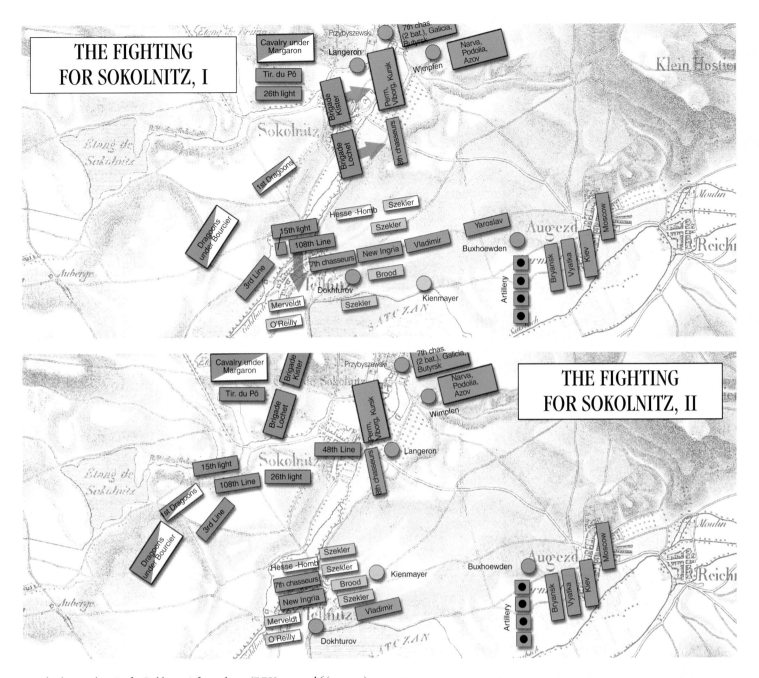

THE FIGHTING FOR SOKOLNITZ, I

THE FIGHTING FOR SOKOLNITZ, II

to make the march easier for Dokhturov's first column (7 752 men and 64 cannon). A wide road went through the village separating low houses; it was on the left bank of the Goldbach, dominated by a small rise which could be seen when coming from Aujezd and on which the Column of the Martyrs had been erected. The village was surrounded by vineyards and crops. Kienmayer had been got out of Telnitz on the previous evening by the 3rd of the Line (Legrand's Division) whose Colonel Schubert installed its four battalions in the village. Kienmayer had two Szekler Regiments (2 600 men) plus a Brood Infantry battalion (500 men), the Szekler Hussars (200 men), O'Reilly's Chevau-Légers (900 men) and 12 cannon at his disposal. They attacked the 3rd of the Line about five times without success. Buxhoewden had to wait for the arrival of the head of Dokhturov's first column in order to reinforce his attacks. Dokhturov sent his 7th Chasseurs who drew the Austrians along with them and drove the 3rd of the Line out of the village where the men then rallied. Margaron's chasseurs had not been able to check the attacks of the Austrian cavalry which committed itself whole-heartedly.

Having left Raygern at 05.30 and moving up towards Turas as planned, Davout got the order to get to Sokolnitz. He changed direction and at that moment met one of Margaron's cavalry officers who described the difficult situation in Telnitz. The marshal immediately sent the 1st Dragoons in that direction and hastened his men. Heudelet was at the head with the Voltigeurs of the 15th Light, the 108th and the 1st Dragoons in support. The thick fog made seeing anything difficult and covered the whole lake area. Bourcier's dragoons approached Telnitz.

The soldiers of the 108th met wounded from the 3rd coming back. They put their haversacks down and rested a moment before the attack. Out of the 1 637 men who had started off from Raygern, there were now only 800 fit for action. Likewise the

THE FIGHTING FOR SOKOLNITZ

- **This village was the target** for Langeron's second and Przybyszewski's third column. The disorder caused by Liechtenstein (when he came and bivouacked by mistake in the middle of the 2nd and 3rd columns the previous night) had considerably delayed their departure for Sokolnitz.

- **It was at 09.00 that Langeron** came up with the 8th Chasseurs and pioneers in the lead followed by Olsufiev's Brigade with the Viborg, Perm, and Kursk Regiments. He managed to get into the south of the village held by Merle's men: the 26th Tirailleurs and the Pô Tirailleurs. The Russian Chasseurs and the Viborg and Perm Regiments pushed the 26th out of the village, chasing them on to the hill situated to the south-west. It was there that the 26th mistook the 108th for the enemy and took shots at them while they were pulling back towards Telnitz.

- **Davout pulled the 26th** back beyond the stream at Sokolnitz. Przybyszewski tried to spill round the village towards Kobelnitz, but he was pushed back by Levasseur with the 18th, the 75th and the Corsican Tirailleurs.

- **The Allies held Sokolnitz,** but Friant's division arrived with Lochet in the lead; he cleaned out the south of the village with the 48th; the 111th was sent to support him. Eight cannon and two flags were captured even though the fighting was very fierce and the French were chased out of the village. Only the south of the village was held, by the 48th. Davout gathered his regiments together in the north and rallied them as best he could. Langeron was called back by Kamenski who was panicking having seen the disaster from the top of the Pratzen Plateau. As a result he turned around and joined the battle.

- **That left Olsufiev** alone in Sokolnitz. At 12.30, Davout was ready for the attack having rallied all his regiments.

Voltigeurs of the 15th Light accompanying them, now reduced to a hundred or so. These 900 or so elite soldiers attacked Telnitz from the north where they were

welcomed by the fire from 12 cannon placed by Kienmayer in the village's wide street. The smoke from the cannon darkened the already thick fog, but the French made a bayonet charge, pushing the Russian chasseurs of the 7th and a battalion from Carneveille's Szekler Regiment back. These men fleeing in disorder caused chaos in the ranks of battalions of the New-Ingria Regiment who had been sent to reinforce them by General Levis in the first column. Two allied flags were captured by Generals Mauzy and Pront. They were rewarded by Davout who had followed their action.

The French Tirailleurs advanced towards the east through the vineyards. Colonel Mohr who was in position with the 360 Hussars of the Hesse-Homburg led a charge against the soldiers of the 108th who were arriving on the scene. They suffered heavy casualties thanks to him and the survivors sought shelter in the vineyards which protected them from the cavalry. A tragic mistake increased the serious disorder. Soldiers from the 26th driven out of Sokolnitz towards the south, seeing the men of the 108th in the fog, mistook them for the enemy and opened fire. Captain Livadot had to brandish an Eagle and shout before the tragic mistake ceased.

In the end Telnitz remained in enemy hands, but they could not break out. Indeed, Bourcier's Dragoons had taken up a position and were shooting their few cannon at them, at the same time protecting the men of the 3rd of the Line who with other elements of the 108th were rallying and leaving the village. Buxhoewden, already almost drunk, gave the order to stay in the village and wait for the second and third columns to arrive, which were near but still in the fog. He was very satisfied with the capture of Telnitz; his first objective had been reached. He kept four Russian regiments in reserve in front of Aujezd. This reserve, which was doing absolutely nothing, could have seized Sokolnitz…

Out of the six regiments of Bourcier's fourth division, one had been kept near Raygern to keep an eye on the Vienna road. It was from this direction that the stragglers from Friant's Division and the rest of Klein's Division were coming up, encouraged by the sound of the cannon. It was Colonel Rigau's 25th which had been entrusted with this task. The 1st Dragoons of Klein's Division were still with Heudelet who was rallying the troops driven out of Telnitz. Bourcier's 15th, 17th, 18th, 19th and 27th Dragoons were in the line with their cannon to support them and prevent the Allies from going further than the Goldbach. The rest of Klein's division returned to Raygern at the end of the day, after the battle.

2. THE FIGHTING FOR SOKOLNITZ

Situated on the right bank of the Goldbach, against a little hill, the village had a wide T-shaped road; its castle had an enclosed park; further to the north there was a 600 m by 300 m wood enclosed by walls called the 'Faisanderie'. The 340 Pô Tirailleurs were in the castle with 51 Corsican Tirailleurs and Merle's Brigade with the 26th Light which had returned to hold the village under threat from the arrival of the second and third allied columns. Legrand reinforced them with the Levasseur Brigade in front of Kobel-

nitz. Margaron and his cavalry were also there. It was Langeron, an émigré in Russian service who got there first at the head of his second column. Fortunately the disorder caused by Liechtenstein's cavalry bivouacking too far south, right in Langeron's way, seriously delayed the departure of the Allies' left wing. It was Langeron who had to make up for this mistake and Liechtenstein went to take up his original position, further north near Blasowitz. Langeron waited for the third column under Przybyszewski, but nevertheless launched the attack on the village with Miller III troops which included the 8th Chasseurs and the Viborg, Perm and Kursk Regiments from Olsufiev's Brigade. Przybyszewski arrived and took part in the attack with two battalions from the 7th Chasseurs leading. The 26th Chasseurs were pushed out of the village and even off the little hill to the south. It was there that it started shooting at the 108th.

Friant was en route for a counter-attack. He arrived with Lochet's brigade (48th and 111th). It was just after 09.00. The 48th took the hill, captured six cannon and two flags and got through into Sokolnitz. The regiment was surrounded by the enemy and it took the 111th to get them out of trouble, but they took two cannon. Lochet was magnificent and regrouped the 48th in the southern part of the village where he fought like a lion and managed to hold. Davout launched the 15th Light, then the 33rd Light of the Line into this terrible battle.

The Russian reinforcements pushed the French back beyond the stream where they reformed. At the same time, Langeron realised what was going on the Pratzen and went over to Kamenski who had just warned him and who had decided to fight 'back to front' with the Fanagoria and Ryazan Regiments (made up of new conscripts) because the tail of Langeron's column (of which he was in command) was under attack by Soult's corps which was investing the Pratzen Plateau. Langeron returned to this zone. The émigré general's temporary absence gave a bit of respite to the combatants in Sokolnitz which was in total confusion. It was Olsufiev, left there by Langeron, who led the fighting in that sector. Langeron was aware of the danger of the situation and wanted to bring part of his troops who were engaged in Sokolnitz back onto the Plateau, but it was too late. Varé's 43rd came to the 36th's rescue. Vandamme and Saint-Hilaire were masters of the plateau and Kamenski's battalions were half-destroyed and forced to fall back with Kutusov on Krenowitz.

THE ATTACK ON THE PRATZEN PLATEAU

Hidden by the very thick fog, the soldiers of the 4th Corps who had crossed the Goldbach without being seen were ready to go over to the attack, drums beating and music playing. Facing them, the Allies were ready to attack. It was the fourth column which got going towards Kobelnitz. It was made up of the Russians under Miloradovitch who was in command of the Novgorod, Apsheron, Little Russia and Smolensk Regiments. At 08.30 they left Krenowitz where they were near the Emperors' headquarters. They passed through Pratzen, but Langeron criticised Miloradovitch's lack of precautions; he was

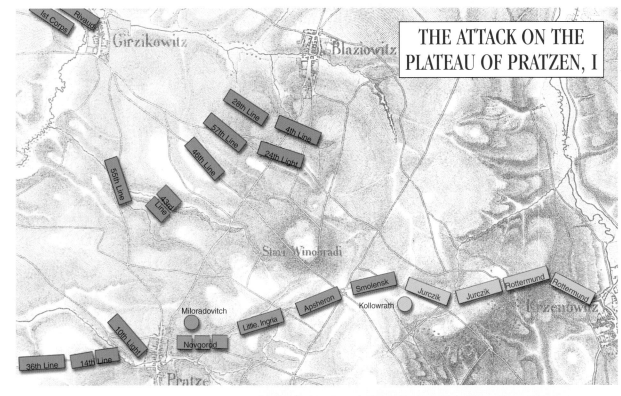

Preceding page, top.
Napoleon and his staff on a height – it could be the Staré Vinhorady depicted rather naively – following the initial deployments of his troops. In the background one can make out the Chasseurs à cheval of the escort and in the foreground, Marshal Murat, with the hat.
(*Author's Collection*)

The 1st French Corps about to cross the Goldbach. Drouet's Division divided into half battalions towards Pratzen and Rivaud's Division towards Blasowitz.

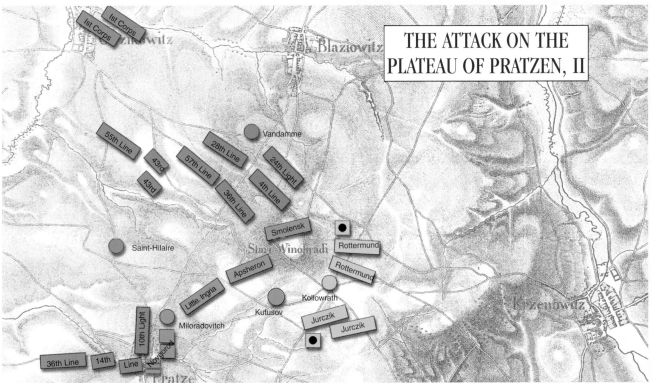

THE ATTACK ON THE PLATEAU OF PRATZEN

- **It was Miloradovitch** who, at 08.30 started to attack in the direction of Puntowitz and Kobelnitz. Lieutenant-Colonel Monakhtin led the Novgorod and Apsheron Regiments followed by the Little Russian and the Smolensk Regiments with Arch-Duke John's Dragoons. This march was carried out without scouts out in front even though fog was hiding the bottom of the hollows where Soult's men were beginning to move off. The brilliant sun rose, gradually lifting the layers of mist.

- **Morand's 10th Light** was climbing in front and met the enemy around the village of Pratzen. It was a total surprise for the Allies. A first battalion had laid in ambush on the edge of the village with men lying just behind the ridge. Thiébault was then ordered to take the village. He sent Colonel Mazas with the 1st Battalion of the 14th which fell into the trap and fled; Mazas rallied them towards Morand; he

was killed by a bullet (biscayen). Thiébault rushed and took the village. The Novgorod and Apsheron Regiment were completely routed in sight of the Tsar. General Repninski was wounded and captured as was General Berg who attempted to rally the Little-Russia Regiment.

- **Miloradovitch's men** had been dispersed in half an hour by Ferey's Brigade (46th and 57th) which was supported by Varé with the 55th and a battalion of the 43rd which later joined up with the second battalion which had been sent towards Thiébault's left in support. The Russians fell back towards Krenowitz in full flight. This first phase finished at 09.30.

- **The Austrians** went up into the line at the two places under threat: Jurczik's men (6th Battalions) towards the Pratzenberg and Rottermund's Regiments (Salzburg Regiment with six battalions with one battalion from the Auersperg and one from Kaunitz, a total strength of 4 000 men) headed for

the Staré Vinhorady where Vandamme was heading, too. The Salzburg Regiment was attacked by the 4th and the 24th with a bayonet charge; they had arrived from the west and north slopes of the hillock. The Salzburg Regiment was shoved around and forced to retreat, its artillery captured. The Austrians were routed and chased towards Aujezd. They dragged the Ismaïlovsky battalion (which had been sent by Konstantin as reinforcements at Kutusov's request) with them in their flight.

- **On the Pratzenberg,** thanks to general Kamenski's action, the Ryazan and Fanagoria Regiments, which made up the tail of Langeron's second column, turned back and climbed to the crest. Langeron had been warned by Lieutenant-Colonel Balk who commanded two squadrons of St-Petersburg Dragoons who were with this second column with Isayev's Cossacks. He left Sokolnitz, leaving Olsufiev in command in the village and he came up to help Kamenski. Volkonsky

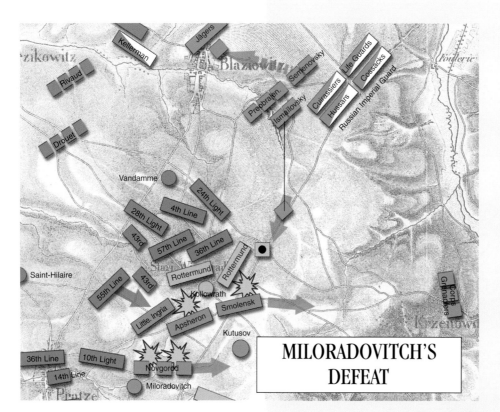

and even Weyrother went up there to direct charges.

- **It was Thiébault** who resisted Kamenski's attacks. He had the 36th which itself had the second battalion of the 14th on its left, supported in an L-shaped formation by the first battalion of the 14th, itself extending the right of Morand's 10th Light, also L-shaped, facing Jurczik's Austrians.

- **Thiébault received six 12-pounders** in reinforcement which he put with his three cannon, hiding this solid battery behind his infantry. He had to withstand several charges by the Russians with the Austrians from the 6 battalions. The unbridled firing of Thiébault's artillery and the infantry decimated the attackers who were driven off at each attempt; they fought for a long time, losing half of their strength, watched by Langeron who admired their courage.

- **Finally Kamenski** had to give and he pulled back towards Krenowitz with Kutusov. It was 11.30 and the Plateau of Pratzen had been taken. Napoleon took advantage of the fact to go to the Staré Vinohrady (298 m) from where he could better see and direct operations. He was followed by the Guard but he left behind him Oudinot's Grenadiers as a reserve in case Davout or Legrand needed them.

- **The two battalions of the 43rd** were called over towards the Pratzenberg to help Thiébault and Morand; Levasseur's Brigade moved to Thiébault's right with the 18th, the 75th and the Corsican Tirailleurs completing the line.

MILORADOVITCH'S DEFEAT

moving forward without reconnoitering the lie of the land even though he had a hundred of Arch-Duke John's Dragoons for just that.

He also pointed out that the infantry had not loaded its rifles. At the same time, Saint-Hilaire was in front of Puntowitz and was about to begin his attack. He could see his objective perfectly well; the heights of Pratzen, the Pratzenberg, 324 metres high to the south of the village of the same name. The 10th Light led on by Morand was at the front, followed by Thiébault (14th and 36th), himself followed by Varé (43rd and 55th) which made up the first reserve.

Vandamme was further to the north, in front of Girzikowitz; his objective was the little 298 metre-high summit of the Staré Vinohrady covered in vineyards. Férey's Brigade was in the lead (46th and 57th), followed by the 28th and further to the left the 4th and 24th Light covering Blasowitz. It is important to insist on Liechtenstein's mistake – when he came and set up camp the previous evening with his fifth column of cavalry too far down the valley and created chaos the following morning when he wanted to get to the start-off point higher up; this was originally situated on a level with Blasowitz to cover the linchpin of the front in Bagration's direction. He particularly got in the way of Langeron's second column which was therefore late starting off to Sokolnitz.

The Allies were even more surprised when the sun caused the mist to lift. They saw the soldiers of the 10th Light emerge and rush for their objective, the Pratzenberg. The

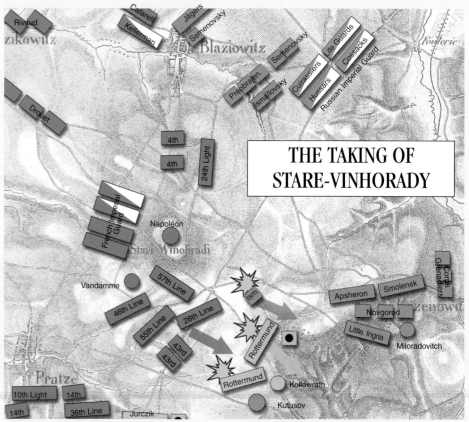

THE TAKING OF STARE-VINHORADY

General Staff and the two Emperors reached Kutusov who was supervising the fourth column and who had not yet moved. It was Miloradovitch's vanguard which took the brunt of the initial attack. The vanguard had been entrusted to Colonel Manachtine who was later killed at the Moskova. He had the Novgorod, Apsheron, Little Russia and Smolensk Regiments at his disposal. Further back the Austrians of the Salzburg Regiment and the battalions from the Austrian depots, much less war-hardened, were in the second line, forming a column on the same road. These troops were on their way to attack in the direction of Puntowitz. What a surprise they got when they saw the French emerging: the attackers were suddenly the attacked. Two battalions of the Novgorod were in Pratzen. One was lying down, in ambush behind a crest, just out of Pratzen. The second was in full flight, wreaking havoc among the Apsheron Regiment. All these fleeing soldiers passed in front of the Tsar who tried unsuccessfully to stop them. The elements of this theoretical fourth column were under the command of

Kutusov himself and General Miloradovitch. Those who took part in the fighting did not think very much of this general. He was accused of being all 'show', impressing the Tsar who took him for a hero when all he did was to get himself crushed in the onslaught. In his book, Claude Manceron related the following dialogue concerning the general.

Mounted on his superb English horse, a very fast racer, General Miloradovitch came and went very quickly among the bullets and the cannonballs. From the small hillock where, spyglass in hand, the Tsar was watching the spectacle with the same slightly strained calm with which he watched a badly rehearsed ballet at the opera, the only thing to be seen was Miloradovitch. The officers of the General Staff and even the Tsar were fascinated by him.

Constantly between the soldiers and the enemy, Miloradovitch swore, scolded, waved his sabre and fired off shots blindly with an enormous pair of pistols.

'Have you noticed that he never goes out of the Tsar's sight?' sighed Czartorins-

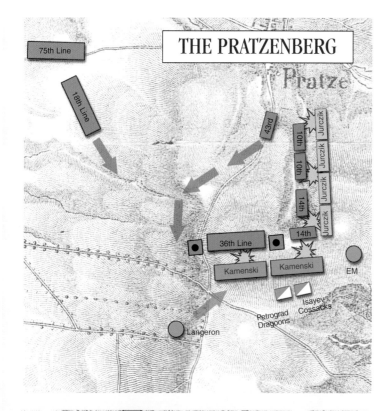

THE PRATZENBERG

75th Line · 18th Line · Pratze · 43rd · 10th Jurczik · 10th Jurczik · 14th Jurczik · Jurczik · 14th · 36th Line · Kamenski · Kamenski · EM · Isayev Cossacks · Petrograd Dragoons · Langeron

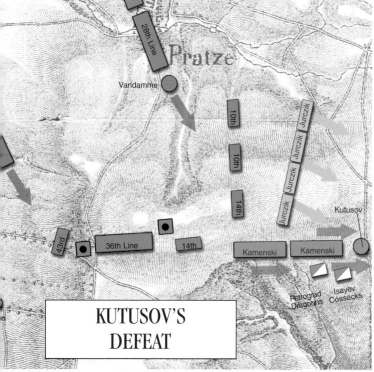

28th Line · Pratze · Vandamme · 10th Jurczik · 10th Jurczik · Jurczik · Jurczik · Jurczik · Jurczik · 14th · Kutusov · 43rd · 36th Line · 14th · Kamenski · Kamenski · Petrograd Dragoons · Isayev Cossacks

**KUTUSOV'S
DEFEAT**

ky, who was too subtle a person to be taken in by this vulgar game.

'*What is much more serious, Excellency*', replied General Intzov, '*is that he is totally immersed occupied with all that pantomime whereas he hasn't given a single order to his men since this morning.*'

It was the Russians who were holding the Plateau; the Austrians who were in the second line where some were being directed towards the Staré Vinhorady, towards which the Vandamme Division was heading, the others to the Pratzenberg.

Between 09.00 and 09.30, Thiébault was sent to the village of Pratzen which normally was not to be attacked, only isolated as it was the hill behind it which was more important. This attack cost the life of Colonel Mazas who broke out at the head of the 1st battalion of the 14th and fell into the ambush set up by a Russian battalion whose men, huddling below the crest which was in front of the village, suddenly stood up and fired their salvo routing the French battalion. Thiébault came to the rescue and took the village in a rush with the three other battalions. Vandamme came up on his side with Ferey's Brigade (46th and 57th). General Repninski tried to get the 1st battalion of the Novgorod back into the fray, but he fell, hit by three bullets. General Berg

who tried to get the Little Russia regiment back into the battle was wounded and captured. The rout of general Miloradovitch was completed in thirty minutes. The Tsar tried to stop them but unsuccessfully. On the Pratzenberg, Morand was having difficulty advancing and Jurczik's Austrians were coming up from the east, drawn on by their bands. For a moment, one general managed to hold the defence of the Pratzenberg. This was Kamenski who belonged to Langeron's column. Following the disorder caused by Liechtenstein, he was late and was present when the French attacked the plateau. Rather intelligently he decided to move up to this rather important point instead of going down to Sokolnitz. He got Colonel Balk, in command of two Saint-Petersburg Dragoons (who were with the Isayev Cossacks attached to their column) to warn Langeron. Flabbergasted, Langeron wanted the cavalry who had brought the message to confirm the surprising and totally unexpected facts they had brought with them, and once this was obtained, leaving Olsufiev to direct operations in Sokolnitz, he went off to find Kamenski.

Vandamme on the other hand was advancing towards his objective, the Staré Vinhorady. The 55th and a battalion of the 43rd (Varé's Brigade) originally a reserve, were now being used to support the attack on the Staré Vinhorady. The other battalion of the 43rd was sent to Thiébault's right which was threatened by Kamenski's turnaround. Kamenski was approaching with his battalions from the Fanagoria and Ryazan Regiments. The other battalion joined up later.

The Allies' general staff was very close to the fighting and Weyrother, like Volkonski (Alexander's aide de camp), had come up to lead Kamenski's men. They had them charge but without success. Thiébault relates:

"*As a result of all movements (which especially during the first hours of the fighting were carried out running, such was the pressure from the enemy on all sides), the 36th had the 2nd battalion of the 14th on its left and my line was perpendicular to General Morand's 10th Light whose right was made up of the 1st Battalion of the 14th in an L-shaped formation.*"

The brigade thus divided, General Morand with his three battalions was given the task of beating Jurczik's Austrians who were advancing to the accompaniment of music. General Thiébault, with the three other battalions, was facing the new masses of General Kamenski whose brigade was part of Langeron's second column, but had not yet started to move down towards Sokolnitz.

On the Staré Vinhorady, Kollowrath's Austrians with General Rottermund were beaten by the 24th Light and the 4th helped by men from Varé's Brigade and especially the 55th; the battalion of the 43rd then went to reinforce Thiébault's right. The Austrians fled in the direction of Aujezd and their artillery was captured. They drew into their flight with them the Guards battalion from the Ismaïlovsky which had been sent to reinforce them by Konstantin at Kutusov's request.

Thiébault received reinforcements in the form of six 12-pounders coming from corps reserve under battalion commander Fontenay. He set up these heavy guns with the tree already there behind an infantry screen. He explains his action thus:

"*I put them on either side of the 36th... ordering Major Fontenay to load the guns with grapeshot and cannonballs and when he objected that this would damage them, I answered that I only needed them for ten minutes or so. I had the guns checked for range fixing them at 15 or 20 toises (90-120 feet); I got them to stack ten grapeshot cartridges and ten cannonballs next to each gun so that they could fire quicker; I renewed my recommendation to the soldiers in person to aim well before firing, to aim at the man's belt and to aim into the centre of the platoons so that there would be no wasted shots. Then having carried on like that until the last moment, I let the huge masses approach within range and suddenly with my nine guns revealed, the whole of my line started the most destructive shooting ever seen...*

"*Imagine my satisfaction when I saw each of these gun shots cutting large swathes in the enemy regiments, and these regiments which were attacking my battalions breaking up into in huge fleeing masses... In avoiding a shock which we were incapable of resisting, I saved my brigade and the Vanguard under Morand; we were able thus to stay on the Pratzen Plateau; losing it would have been as fatal as holding it was, in the end, decisive.*"

Kamenski was pushed back and two hitched up batteries were captured. Langeron who had moved up to Kamenski said that he saw Austrians being chased by the French. It was 11.00. He paid tribute to the Russian conscripts whose firing was rather badly directed as they had almost never been under fire. He admired them for holding out for almost two hours when half their number was already lying on the field. Kutusov got a scratch from a bullet fired from the lines of Morand's 10th Light; his son-in-law was killed trying to rally the fleeing men, just as was general Jurczik. Thiébault was deservedly called the 'Butcher' and his lack of modesty fits in with the rest of his

Bagration

asowitz

Caffarelli

Murat

Suchet

(Panorama de Lejeune. © RMN)

memoirs. He carried out his 'butcher's' job which was indispensable in the confrontations of the time. Moreover at Austerlitz, the French infantry charged with fixed bayonets quite decided not to give any quarter; their general had said *"Don't leave anything behind you"*, particularly as the wounded Russians tried to reload their rifles and shoot once the French had passed them by. The Russians had fought the Turks and were quite used to cruel fighting.

Varé's Brigade came on stage with the 43rd which came up to reinforce Thiébault with its 1st Battalion (the 2nd was marching with the 55th against Miloradovitch's battalions). Langeron related that in the Staré Vinhorady sector the front line was crushed in less than thirty minutes through the fault of the general who pranced around in front of the Tsar.

Ledru des Essarts who was in command of the 55th wrote to his brother and gave the following details:

"My dear friend, I escaped from the dangers of the battle of Austerlitz. You will no doubt like to have some details of what my regiment did during that famous day.

"The first Division of Marshal Soult's corps, commanded by General Saint-Hilaire (which included the 55th), *had been chosen by the Emperor to begin the attack and was to cut the enemy in the middle. On the 2nd, at dawn, it marched in a column towards the heights of Pratzen. I went off to the left with my corps and with the 2nd Battalion of the 43rd regiment to capture a six-gun battery which was on our flank and was doing us a lot of harm; it was defended by two Russian regiments. In a flash my Brigadier (Varé) and my three battalion commanders were put out of action. I took over command. I hastened the pace whilst keeping up our terrible shooting. The enemy was pushed out and we captured his artillery. The two regiments we had chased out ran off in disorder and rallied three hundred paces behind a mass of 4 000 men holding heights with eight guns. I did not hesitate to*

Below: **Napoleon was everywhere all at once, giving out his orders, seeming already to know the different phases of the battle.** *(RR)*

Above: **The Pratzen Plateau, in winter in the fog as it must surely have appeared to the eyes of the Emperor's infantrymen, a few moments before the famous sun.** *(© Garnier)*

attack even though the enemy was twice as many as us. Getting the battalion to fire as we advanced, we took the position as quickly as the first.

Almost all the artillerymen were killed at their posts and this second lot of artillery was captured by our regiment. This advantage cost me dearly because thanks to the grapeshot and the bullets, I lost 300 men and my horse. We reached the heights.

"I expected to be heartily welcomed by Russian bayonets, the famous Russians!, but they were already fleeing towards the village of Pratzen. Our volleys were knocking them down in their hundreds and the ground was littered with their dead. I was going to enter Pratzen and destroy this column entirely when the Cuirassiers of the Russian Imperial Guard galloped up to save them, and charged me. I formed up quickly in a mass although the Tirailleurs went forward to kill a few. They did not dare attack me and it was then that Marshal Soult arrived with General Vandamme's Division. He complimented me in a most flattering manner and I went and joined General Saint-Hilaire, who was half a league away, ready to attack the Castle of Sokolnitz; there, my regiment took 400 prisoners in the park. Until then the soldiers had killed without mercy and had not wanted to take anybody in reaction to the Russians' cruelty. At about four o'clock when the leftovers of the enemy were backed up against the lake at Menitz, the Emperor passed near me, called out to me, and was kind enough to say how satisfied he was with my regiment's conduct and to give me details of the results of the battle.

"You will read all this in the official reports. The French Army has never been covered in glory like this. The 55th has lost 344 men of which 18 officers; my two battalion commanders and eight captains have been seriously wounded. I have just reached Vienna, a rather favourable garrison; I intend to rest a while as I am very tired. I am housed in a very beautiful inn where the town pays for six people at mealtimes, two servants, a carriage and tickets for the theatre, all for me.

"As you can see, I am not too unhappy. Send me your news. I embrace you and our sister…" Ledru des Essarts.

This letter gives a good account of the cruelty of the fighting, without pity, in the infantry attacks, which the Russians started by shouting horribly. These men had all been 'drugged' at the beginning by a good dose of alcohol; and the French, just as 'drugged', were jealous of the reputation which showed off the so-called superiority of the Russians. The famous saying about the 'Mujiks' was confirmed at that moment: 'You don't just kill a Russian, you have to push him for him to fall.'

At Staré Vinhorady, the 9 Russian battalions put there by Miloradovitch and which were on the right of Pratzen with a strength of about 4 500 men from the leading regiments, were attacked by Vandamme with Ferey's Brigade (57th and 46th) which arrived head-on, whereas Varé's Brigade with the 55th and one battalion from the 43rd attacked them on their left flank. The line was crushed in half-an-hour. The 1st battalion of the Novgorod Regiment was almost entirely destroyed (related by Colin in his precious article in the Historical Review). General Repinsky was wounded three times and General Berg who was trying to rally his Little Russia Regiment was captured. Rottermund's Austrians, with the Salzburg Regiment and two battalions from Kaunitz and Auersperg reached the Staré Vinhorady. Vandamme got the 4th and the 24th Light to attack them; the French went into the attack without firing, using their bayonets. The Austrians were routed and fled towards Aujezd. Their artillery had already

been taken. In their flight, they carried along with them the leftovers of the beaten Russian battalions as well as the Ismaïlovsky Regiment which Konstantin had sent them. The rest of the Russian Guard called back by Kutusov moved down towards Vandamme's Division; the plateau was free.

After the decisive conquest of the plateau, Napoleon came over to the Staré Vinhorady, which had fallen at 11.00. From there at midday, Napoleon could follow the whole of the battle's development. He was followed by the Guard and Soult was there with the General Staff. The Guard had followed him but the Grenadiers under Oudinot were kept near Turas to help Davout if necessary. Levasseur's Brigade which had been left in front of Kobelnitz advanced towards Thiébault's right thus completing the line of attack. The first corps divisions had crossed the Goldbach at Girzikowitz and were now starting the climb with on the right, Drouet who had divided his battalions (advancing by half battalions), and Rivaud, more to the left towards Blasowitz.

This account together with Thiébault's shows us how complex the fighting on the Pratzen was and how it led to the destruction of what was the fourth Allied column, in spite of Kamenski's intelligent return, even though he was obliged to fall back on Krenowitz to Kutusov. The Ryazan Regiment had two of its flags taken. Weyrother and Volkonski, two of the Tsar's aide de camps, tried to rally all the battalions retreating towards Krenowitz but to no avail.

The Allies only had one solution left for holding the centre of the line. This was the Russian Guard which moved up into the line.

THE RUSSIAN GUARD ATTACKS

Grand-Duke Konstantin got his regiments to advance towards the Pratzen and towards Blasowitz where the beginnings of a crack were starting to appear. Bagration was being attacked at this point. The Allied right wing risked being cut in the centre and pushed back towards Olmutz which was isolated. The effort by Lannes and Murat, whose right held by Caffarelli was advancing and attacking, and pushing the Allied right wing towards into a position where it would have to retreat.

The Russian Guard deployed to the south-west of Blasowitz had its infantry drawn up in two lines with in front:

The Preobrajensky and Semenovsky Regiments with a company of artillery between them. Behind were the Ismaïlovsky Regiment and the Chasseurs of the Guard. At the rear, the Cuirassiers and the Hussars formed a third line.

In reserve were the Life Guards, the Cossacks of the Guard and finally the Grenadiers of the corps. Konstantin who led a dissolute life, ill treated his servants to the point of killing them for the slightest fault was only a novice as generals went, and felt

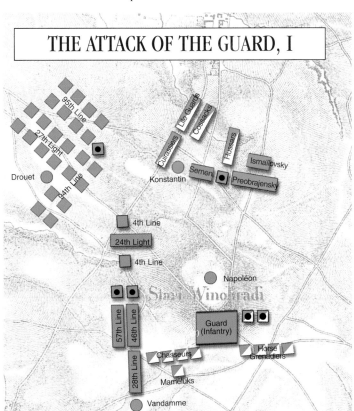

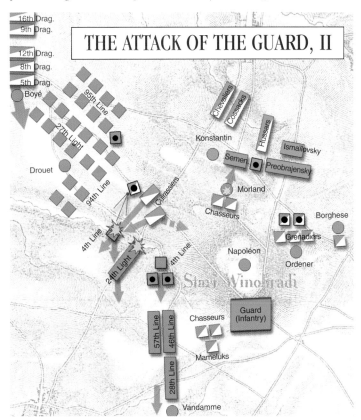

very isolated. He lent on the linchpin at Blasowitz which he got the Chasseurs of the Guard, a battalion of the Semenovsky and three cannon, to occupy. Liechtenstein's cavalry (from the fifth column) was also gathered together near Blasowitz, having finally reached its original step – off point. Kutusov asked for reinforcements for the centre and Konstantin sent him a battalion of the Ismaïlovsky; but this battalion which headed for the Staré Vinhorady got dragged into the flight of the Austrian battalions from the fourth column. The Cavalry of the Guard had to intervene.

THE GREAT CHARGE AT AUSTERLITZ

It was Vandamme's left, a little isolated between Blasowitz and Pratzen, which took the brunt of the attack together with the 4th and the 24th of the Line themselves also isolated to the north of the Staré Vinhorady. This was even more so when Napoleon moved the remainder of Vandamme's division towards the right, which the division of the first corps began to replace coming up from Girzikowitz after crossing the Goldbach. Drouet was on the right and Rivaud on the left. Konstantin threw his infantry into a charge but got them to start too far away. Making contact after a run-up of more than 300 yards, they were very quickly stopped. It was the Cavalry of the Guard which had to intervene.

Captain Vincent, Vandamme's aide de camp, seeing Russian cavalry coming passed in front of them and alerted his general. He had seen a mounted artillery battery setting itself up in front of the cavalry lines but was a victim of their first salvo. Bigarré went off to find the 1st battalion of the 4th which was very exposed. He reached it and got it to form a square. A first squadron was in full charge against it. It was the 1st Squadron of the Cuirassiers of the Russian Guard under Colonel Ojarovsky. The charge was welcomed with a salvo which pushed it back. But the second squadron followed quick on its heels and surprised the battalion which had lost two standard-bearers killed by the artillery. It was Sergeant-Major Saint-Cyr who held the flag which was taken off him by the men of the 3rd Company of this 2nd Squadron led by Lieutenant Khmelev and Guards Lazonov, Ushakov, Omeltchenko who wounded him twelve times and took the flag off him.

This charge routed the 4th and the 24th Light who ran away turning round all the time. These episodes made Bessières say to his aide de camp César de Laville: *"this is going to be a cavalry affair!"* He explained afterwards that those fleeing from infantry did not turn round whereas when the cavalry was behind them, they did because they were frightened of being caught up with at any time.

From the height of the Staré Vinhorady, Napoleon saw the disorder and asked Bessières to order up the cavalry of the Guard to stop the gap in the front line. Bessières had four squadrons of Chasseurs à Cheval of the Guard, 375 cavalrymen under the

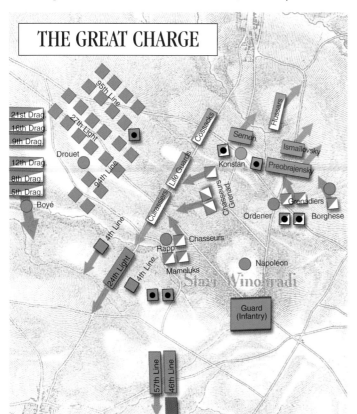

THE GREAT CHARGE

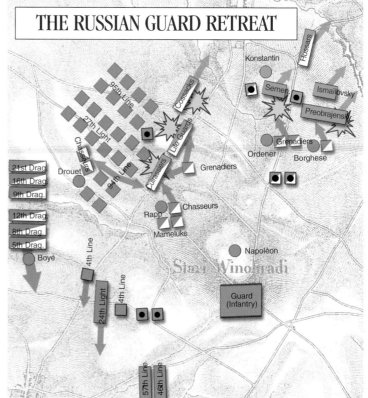

THE RUSSIAN GUARD RETREAT

Above: ***At the height of the fray, the Mameluks next to the Chasseurs à Cheval charge the Cavalry of the Russian Guard.*** *(J. Girbal, Author's Collection)*

Right: ***The death of Morland at the head of his Chasseurs, killed by a bullet from a Semenovsky Regiment infantryman.***
(© painting by Rigo 'le Plumet' for Histoire & Collections)

command of Colonel Morland together with 42 Mameluks and six officers. Grenadiers à Cheval, the 'Black Horses', the 'Invincibles'. Commanded by Ordener, there were 706 of them. Two hundred and forty-eight had been left on the way. Prince Borghese, Pauline's husband, commanded a squadron of this black cavalry.

The Gendarmes d'Elite were not present at Austerlitz.

Bessières who was sparing of his soldiers' lives, at first only sent two squadrons of Chasseurs under Morland supported by three of Ordener's squadrons on the right. In spite of their courage, they were pushed back by the Semenovsky Regiment which had rallied. Morland was killed.

He was replaced by Doguereau with a flying battery of the Guard (with 8 guns). He fired on the infantry of the Russian Guard. The men from the 24th Light and the 4th gradually rallied and helped the cavalry. The standard of the 5th reserve Cuirassier squadron was taken and the Russian cavalry put to flight. In fact this standard was nothing else but a colour pennant of the Guards' reserve squadron which appears in Verillon's book. It was said that it was the standard of the Life Guards which had been taken but this was not so as the standard of the Life Guards was a vexillum with a silver shaft. This was always left behind as was the regimental standard of the Cuirassiers of the Guard who had made up the first wave.

The Russians had the Life Guards charge supported by the Cossacks of the Guard. As the outcome of the skirmish was still uncertain, the Emperor sent Rapp to put a

bit of order over there. Napoleon's aide de camp, unleashed, set off at the head of the Mameluks which he had formed earlier. A second wave of French cavalry was launched, carried away by Ordener with the last squadron of the Grenadiers — magnificent, experienced horsemen — with Dahlmann leading the last two squadrons of the Chasseurs. Prince Borghese covered Ordener's right with his squadron. Doguereau installed one of the Guard's flying batteries with eight guns and shot at the Foot Guards.

At the same time, General Drouet made his regiments advance. Their fire caused the attackers to break. His battalions separated into two halves, were spaced out and the cavalry of the Guard was able to seek refuge between their squares and behind their withering fire directed against the Russians who wanted to chase the cavalry of the Guard. The latter, once rested, took up the charge again. With Werlé, the 94th was first in line, the 95th was in the second line and the 27th Light in the third; this regiment was commanded by Frère. Their artillery was set up. The Chasseurs of the Guard sheltered behind Drouet's infantry used their carbines against their would-be pursuers.

Rapp was engaged too far away and was in danger; he was saved by Daumesnil helped by two Mameluks, Lieutenants Chahin and Daoud Habaiby. Prince Repnin, squadron commander of the Life Guards was captured with 200 of his cavalry. Five hundred Russians of the Guard were left on the battlefield. Drouet's advance completed this victory. Rapp led the captured Prince and the standards taken by the cavalry of the Guard to the Emperor as is shown on the magnificent painting which Napoleon commissioned and which shows all the details. The French cavalry charged against the Semenovsky and Preobrajensky regiments which Daumesnil was showering with shot from his cannon. The Russian Guard fell back towards the Grenadiers in position near Krenowitz which was soon taken by the 27th Light.

This famous episode is but a brief fight for the glory of the Life Guards which 'made the beautiful ladies in St-Petersburg cry', because all the officers of the Guard were sons of Russian noble families. These bright young things certainly had courage but they did not have either the technique or the experience of the old warriors of Napoleon's Guard who were professionals of great quality. This remark was just as valid for the relative quality of the two arms, be it the French infantry trained perfectly at Boulogne at shooting and manoeuvring and encouraged by the presence of the Emperor, or the cavalry, very highly-trained by highly experienced cadres of whom many had gained experience in Egypt. The camp at Boulogne at least served the purpose of forging a professional, properly trained army which was far better than the novices which opposed it.

Morland was mummified by Larrey and sent to Paris in a cask of rum. When he was taken from the cask, his moustache and beard had grown down to his feet. Napoleon had thought of having a statue of each of the principal heroes of Austerlitz made and placed on the Pont de la Concorde. This idea was replaced by giving their names to streets near Austerlitz Bridge.

The second wave of Russian cavalry was launched against Rapp and Ordener (4th and 5th Squadrons of the Life Guards and Cossacks of the Guard). The standard of the 5th squadron (reserve) of the Life Guards in the end was the only standard taken in this maul, but the casualties among the Life Guards were very high. Danilevsky gave the figures of 16 officers and 200 cuirassiers killed or wounded as well as 300 horses. Only 18 survived this giants' struggle. Prince Repnin and several wounded officers were captured. The Hussars of the Russian Guards managed to disappear into a small valley where they hid, according to Langeron. The infantry of the Russian Guard had to resist the charges and the blows of Doguereau's artillery. It retreated as much as possible in order towards Krenowitz. The Grenadiers du Corps were not able to stop the retreat.

I have searched for the service records of a great number of French cavalrymen who took part in this great cavalry fight. They are to be found among the other combatants listed in this book. The losses on the French side were relatively light. The Grenadiers lost 6 officers wounded, three cavalrymen killed and 18 wounded. 99 horses were lost. The Chasseurs lost their colonel, Morland and captain Thervay; 18 officers and 5 chasseurs were wounded. 151 horses were killed. Only three Mameluks were wounded.

The Russian Guard fell back. The Allies' centre had been broken. Drouet had reached the top of the Pratzen and threatened the village of Krenowitz and the road to Austerlitz; but Bernadotte was still holding back and did not want to take any risks by moving his troops too far forward. He finally had Frère's 27th light take Krenowitz, pushing out the infantry of the Russian Guard. They entered Austerlitz which had been abandoned by the Allies.

Napoleon was going to sleep in the palace the following night, in the bed in which the Tsar had slept the night before. On the evening of the 2nd, Napoleon slept at the Posorzitz post office. The Tsar, ill and depressed, found only Czernitchev, who went out to find Kutusov and bring him back. Alexander's carriage could not be found – it was found three days later. The wounded and the laggards were abandoned, as was all the equipment. Only Bagration, who had joined him, tried to put some order into the chaos.

Dahlmann. *(RR)*

MURAT AND LANNES
AGAINST BAGRATION'S CORPS

The enemy's centre was in full flight. It was scarcely 1 p.m.

The first essential objective was

It was Caffarelli's Division which was marching on Lannes' right wing. It emerged in front of Blasowitz, coordinating its movements with those of Vandamme whose 4th and 24th Light made up the far left. At about 10.30, Lannes could see the progress made by the centre towards Pratzen and got Caffarelli to attack Blasowitz with the 13th Light leading, followed by the 30th. The 17th, 51st and 61st followed in the second line. Blasowitz was held by a battalion of the Semenovsky Regiment and the Chasseurs of the Guard, commanded by Saint-Priest (an émigré who was killed in 1814); they only had three cannon. The 13th Light was to the fore, preceded by four companies of Tirailleurs. The 2nd Battalion charged into the village and made 300 prisoners and captured the three cannon.

*Below: **The French troops deployed and endlessly marched up and down the Austerlitz battlefield. It was above all thanks to his infantrymen's legs that Napoleon won the battle.** (RR)*

Colonel Castex was killed during the attack. The 51st followed and blocked 250 runaways, 450 prisoners were taken. Kellermann drove off the Allied cavalry and took a battery.

Liechtenstein wanted to get rid of this threat and it was General Essen II who started off too soon and charged with Konstantin's 10 squadrons of Uhlans. They ran into Kellermann's cavalry who very cleverly fell back behind the infantry, moving through and between the battalions. Coming up against the infantry, the Uhlans were decimated and suffered heavy losses. The larger part of the regiment was forced to pass through Caffarelli's and Suchet's men and got shot at from both sides, leaving a quarter of their number on the field. Essen II was killed and General Miller-Zomzelski was seriously wounded and captured. The fleeing Uhlans rallied over towards the Posorzitz post office.

Kellermann was happy hat his trap had worked so well, went through the gaps between the French battalions and charged several times. The third charge was very effective and Colonel Burthe of the 4th Hussars, who had been captured very briefly, was freed. Against Dolgorukov who was in command of this linchpin, Kellermann supported by Sébastiani and the 3rd and 6th Dragoons and followed by Walther's Division, pushed back Uvarov's Cavalry. The 5th Chasseurs acted brilliantly and their chief, Corbineau, managed to get through the Russian lines and seize a flag. His horse was killed and two chasseurs had to come to his rescue. Here is the text of their citations:

Fortier, Chasseur: *"Captured a flag right in the middle of an enemy battalion, at the moment when the colonel wounded the standard-bearer and grabbed the flag; he helped the colonel rejoin the French Army."*

Tassu, Chasseur: *"Prevented the Colonel from being captured by placing himself between him and the enemy, when after hitting the standard-bearer, his horse was killed and he fell among the enemy ranks; he was wounded defending the Colonel but managed to recover him, dragging away him by his horse's tail; he had tried to pull him up with him but the Colonel did not have the time to get on."*

Bagration tried to attack in the direction of the Santon with some Cossacks, Marioupol Hussars and the 5th Russian Chasseurs. But even though they managed to get a foothold in Bosenitz, the 17th Light fell back towards the big battery on the Santon where the enemy was stopped by the artillery fire coming from the 18 guns. Anglès, the battalion commander, went forward again with the 2nd battalion of the 17th Light, supported by Treillard's and Milhaud's cavalry, themselves covered by Roger's Dragoons. They retook Bosenitz and pushed the attackers back towards Sitwitz.

To reduce the enemy cavalry, Murat used Nansouty's Cuirassiers who made some magnificent charges just as though they were on manoeuvres, and enabled Holubitz to be taken. The Carabiniers attacked first followed by the Cuirassiers. The 3rd Cuirassiers got carried away beyond the bridge and had to be brought back out. Uvarov's cavalry was dispersed and his artillery lost. Leaving Blasowitz, the 13th Light drove off the charges by Russian dragoons and Caffarelli's regiments took Holubitz and Kruh. All enemy cavalry attempts at charging were repulsed by this infantry, and Ulanius' 6th Dragoons were driven back out of the villages.

Lannes was with his powder-blackened, open-necked, hatless men with two days' stubble on their chins; he was terrible. He pushed forward his advantage, and Dumont's Brigade with the 30th and the 17th crossed the Olmutz road and passed the post office at Posorzitz. The Allied cavalry was beaten by Nansouty's and d'Hautpoul's Cuirassiers. Having seen the rout of the centre, Bagration knew that the battle was lost and so decided to fall back in good order, in stages towards Rausnitz. Frierenberger, the Austrian major turned up at the opportune moment, bringing a battery of 12 guns from Olmutz which enabled Bagration to set up a position in front of Rausnitz. Frierenberger was decorated for his action with the Order of Maria-Theresa. The 5th Chasseurs distinguished themselves.

Towards his left wing he had Dolgorukov (who was still holding Holubitz and Kruh) with the remainder of the 6th Chasseurs. Behind him Uvarov had got together an impressive number of cavalry with the Elisabethgrad Hussars, the Kharkov and Tchernigov Dragoons, together with the Marioupol and Pavlograd Hussars, and the Tver and Saint-Petersburg Dragoons in reserve, of which two squadrons were attached to Langeron. He tried to charge but was driven off and Nansouty's Cuirassiers, lined up as if on parade, broke up this cavalry of Liechtenstein's. Caffarelli's men in the 30th, 17th and 61st drove the chasseurs out of Holubitz and Kruh; the Archangelsk Regiment sent to the rescue of the 6th Chasseurs was annihilated. The Pavlograd Hussars formed the last cavalry screen.

With the cuirassiers, Kellermann's cavalry and Walther's Dragoons cleaned up the field; Kellermann had a leg broken by a bullet and their general was also wounded. The most far-righted of Suchet's regiments (34th, 40th and 88th) had contributed to the destruction of the Russian cavalry. Very worn down by d'Hautpoul's Cuirassier charges, the Pskov and Old Ingria Regiments were dispersed by Suchet's charges.

Bagration fell back by stages to Rausnitz, thanks to the reinforcement given by the 12 guns which arrived from Olmutz. Leaving Liechtenstein to look after Blasowitz, Konstantin replied to Kutusov's urgent calls from the centre, and marched towards the south.

It was Murat who had overall command of the left wing. Once the villages in the linchpin area had been taken, Bagration cut off from the rest of the Russian Army and falling back towards Rausnitz, Murat stopped the chase, consolidating his positions at Holubitz and Kruh. He now controlled the post office at Posorzitz.

He thought it possible that Napoleon might need reinforcements from among his cavalry, as he had already done with Boyé's Dragoon Division.

Bagration who was thought to be retreating towards Olmutz, ended up by being able to reach Austerlitz, the Tsar and the army for which he made a safer rearguard than Miloradovitch and the debris he had tried to regroup. Caffarelli was furious and wanted to push on even further. Thus, on this so-called *"cavalry plain"*, the Allied forces were routed by Nansouty's and d'Hautpoul's Cuirassiers' decisive attacks.

Bagration nevertheless retreated in good order, from position to position; but he lost his cannon and his infantry had been tried a great deal. Murat's attack slowing down and then stopping gave him the possibility to rally a bit.

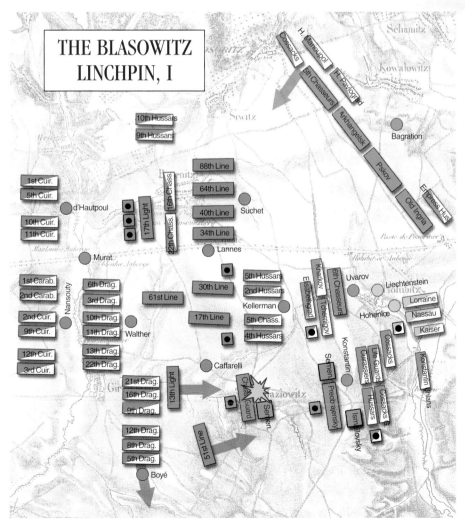

THE BLASOWITZ LINCHPIN, I

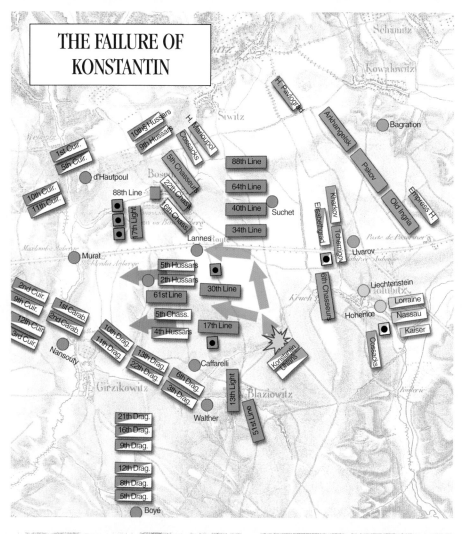

THE FAILURE OF KONSTANTIN

THE LIECHTENSTEIN'S RETREAT

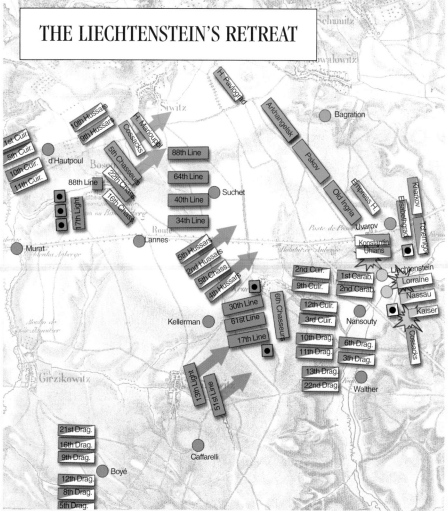

THE BLASOWITZ LINCHPIN

- **It was only after 9.00** that Murat and Lannes marched forwards, seeing the progress made by the centre. They went to meet Bagration.

- **Caffarelli's Division** marched towards Blasowitz, behind Kellermann's Division.

- **Konstantin** placed the Guard in a position to dominate the Blasowitz valley with the Semenovsky and Preobrajensky Regiments in the front line and the Chasseurs and the Ismaïlovsky Regiment from which one battalion was sent to Kutusov to reinforce him after he had asked for it. He had moved forward with the Guard and sent the Chasseurs of the Guard and Semenovsky battalion with three cannon in Blasowitz which was under threat.

- **Behind them, the Gardes du Corps** and the Hussars of the Guard. Further back the Life-Guards and the Cossacks of the Guard. Right at the back towards Krenowitz, the Grenadiers du Corps made up the last barrier.

- **Liechtenstein's Cavalry** finally got into place where it was supposed to be. It included Hohenlohe's Austrian Cavalry and Uvarov's, Essen II's and Shepelev's Russian Cavalry. They were more than 5 000 gathered together towards Kruh and Holubitz.

- **General Essen** started his charge against Kellermann too early. He led Konstantin's Uhlans (10 squadrons) against Kellermann's 4 regiments. They were driven off, but Essen pulled his squadrons back between the infantry squares of Caffarelli's Division and Suchet's 34th Regiment. The Uhlans rode all along the sides of these regiments which totally shot them up. They left a quarter of their strength on the field.

- **Coming out of his trap Kellermann** went over to the attack but the 4th Hussars was encircled and Colonel Burthe captured. On the regiments' third charge, Burthe was freed and 2 cannon were captured. The Uhlans fell back to rally over near Holubitz. General Meller-Zakomelski was wounded and captured, Essen II mortally wounded.

- **At Kutusov's request,** Liechtenstein sent Hohenlohe to charge against the 4th of the Line and the 24th Light who were on the northern slope of the Staré Vinhorady. This charge was hindered by the vines and was unsuccessful for the Cuirassiers.

- **At about 10.30 Lannes** attacked Blasowitz with the 13th Light which ran through the village. Colonel Castex was killed, but the village was taken. The 51st which took part in the attack blocked the runaways' escape and 450 men were captured with 5 cannon. A charge by Uvarov and Essen was unsuccessful.

- **Murat then got Nansouty** to advance and charge first with the carabiniers who broke through the first line. Then the 2nd and 3rd Cuirassiers broke through the second, driving back the enemy which was sheltering beyond the bridge at Holubitz. The 3rd Cuirassiers got carried away but were brought back.

- **Caffarelli's Division** went up to attack Holubitz and Kruh with the 30th, 17th and 61st which dislodged General Ulanius' 6th Chasseurs. Kellermann started charging again with Walther. On the Olmutz road, Yachvill's battery was in position, supported by the Empress' Dragoons commanded by Witt, but which did not move to help him. Above this, Bagration put the Archangel, Pskov and Old Ingria under the command of Dolguruki into the line. There were also the Pavlograd and Marioupol Hussars together with the 5th Russian Chasseurs.

- **Bagration tried** to make a diversion by threatening the Santon and the 5th Chasseurs entered Bosenitz; but they were very quickly kicked out by the 2nd Battalion of the 17th Light helped by Treillard and Milhaud's cavalry.

- **Suchet** made his line move forward. General Valhubert had his thigh blown of by a cannonball, but he refused to be evacuated and died on the battlefield. According to Suchet, the 34th, 40th and 88th "covered the battlefield with 2 000 dead, they took 16 cannon and a great number of prisoners."

- **Kellermann charged** above Kruh but his leg was broken by a bullet. Walther's Dragoons charged and the Gene-

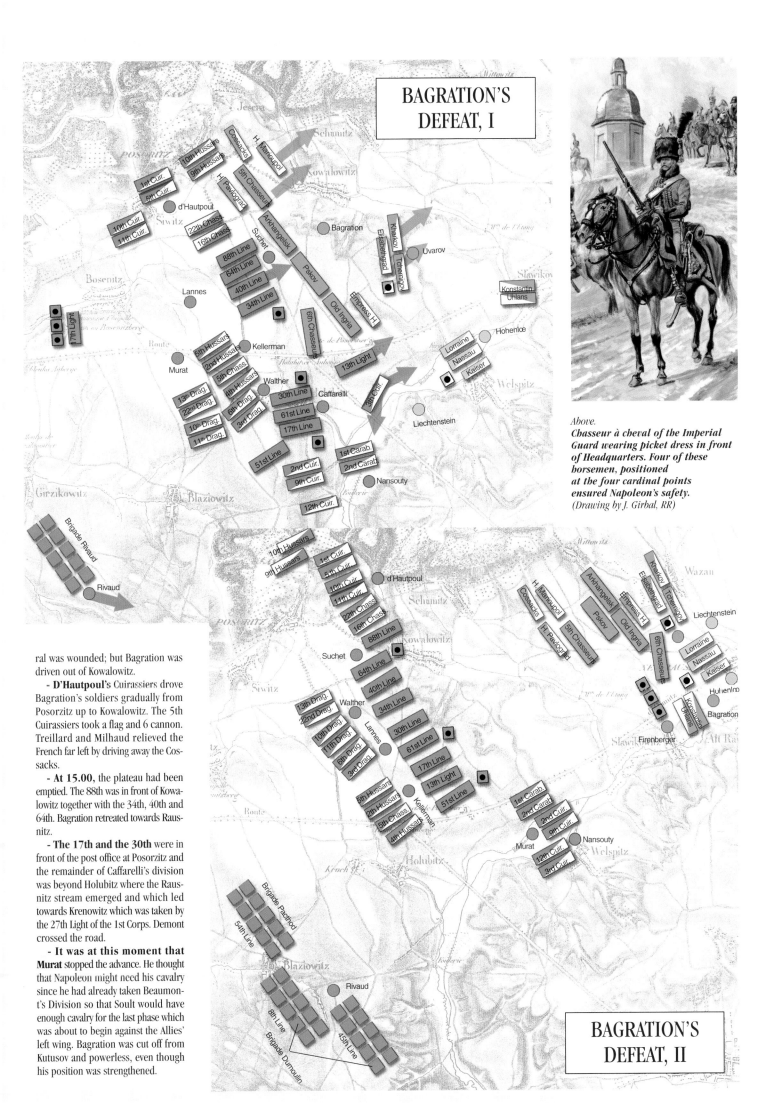

Above.
Chasseur à cheval of the Imperial Guard wearing picket dress in front of Headquarters. Four of these horsemen, positioned at the four cardinal points ensured Napoleon's safety.
(Drawing by J. Girbal, RR)

ral was wounded; but Bagration was driven out of Kowalowitz.

- **D'Hautpoul's** Cuirassiers drove Bagration's soldiers gradually from Posorzitz up to Kowalowitz. The 5th Cuirassiers took a flag and 6 cannon. Treillard and Milhaud relieved the French far left by driving away the Cossacks.

- **At 15.00,** the plateau had been emptied. The 88th was in front of Kowalowitz together with the 34th, 40th and 64th. Bagration retreated towards Rausnitz.

- **The 17th and the 30th** were in front of the post office at Posorzitz and the remainder of Caffarelli's division was beyond Holubitz where the Rausnitz stream emerged and which led towards Krenowitz which was taken by the 27th Light of the 1st Corps. Demont crossed the road.

- **It was at this moment that Murat** stopped the advance. He thought that Napoleon might need his cavalry since he had already taken Beaumont's Division so that Soult would have enough cavalry for the last phase which was about to begin against the Allies' left wing. Bagration was cut off from Kutusov and powerless, even though his position was strengthened.

59

THE CRUSHING
OF THE ALLIED LEFT WING

1. The Recapture of Sokolnitz

Buxhoewden's first three columns were driven back into the infernal triangle of Sokolnitz, Telnitz and Aujezd beyond the lakes. The Emperor left the Staré Vinhorady to come up to the southern point of the plateau of Pratzen, near to Saint Anthony's chapel. The 1st Corps had to relieve Soult's in the centre and push on to Krenowitz. Without worrying about his right wing, letting Bernadotte's corps replace Soult in front of Krenowitz and Austerlitz, Napoleon came over to supervise the crushing of this mass of enemy troops caught in the trap. Soult's corps was brought back towards the south to help Davout. Boyé's dragoon division was also recalled to take part in this glorious finale.

Saint-Hilaire had Levasseur on his right and came down towards Sokolnitz driving back the debris of Austrian troops who for a moment had been reinforced by two battalions of the Kursk Regiment brought up by Langeron. These two battalions were crushed, *"one half was killed, the other captured. The cannon and the flags were captured,"* as Langeron admitted and then added:

"Count Buxhoewden saw the march and the defeat of those two battalions and could not emerge from his physical and moral immobility. This general was at that moment on a hillock to the south-east of Sokolnitz. He was quite proud of his little success at Telnitz and he was now strutting about on the hillock; he was motionless and gave no orders. His face was crimson and he appeared not to have full control of his faculties. I told him what had happened at Pratzen, that we had been turned and surrounded by the enemy. He replied rather rudely 'General, you seem to see the enemy everywhere!'

"I replied, telling him, with scant respect, the truth: 'Count, you are no longer in a state to see anything anywhere. A captain from Austrian headquarters, called Jurczik, expressed himself in more forceful terms."

He said that Count Buxhoewden had been totally drunk for some time now. At that moment, Kutusov's order to retreat came over. Colin states that, in his opinion, the means for gathering intelligence available to the Allied generals no longer existed and that the rout had begun.

Saint-Hilaire emerged at Sokolnitz followed by Vandamme and Boyé's dragoons supported by Varé's and Levasseur's Brigades. Friant had rallied his heroes and attacked in three points. The survivors of the 33rd, 11th and 15th Light were grouped to the north-west of the village and attacked the little bridge over the Goldbach. The remainder of the 3rd and the 108th helped the men of the 48th who were still holding the south angle of the village to come up with the 26th along the stream.

Langeron states: *"I pulled the 8th and Viborg Regiments who were with General Olsufiev and Colonel Laptiev out of the village towards Telnitz. The enemy had already broken through and surrounded Przybyszewski and with it the Perm Regiment and a battalion of the Kursk Regiment, mine. Their shooting was terribly effective."* Not having enough men with whom to counter-attack, Langeron placed his men to the south of the village with the cannon of the Viborg Regiment. At that moment the French attack stopped and the general was able to go off to find Buxhoewden who never forgot Langeron's remarks and caused the latter's disgrace; Langeron was the ideal dogsbody and scapegoat.

Shut up in the village to the north were the 7th Russian Chasseurs, the Perm, Galitz and Butyrsk Regiments then General Wimpfen in front of the Goldbach with two battalions from the Narva and the Azov and Podolia Regiments.

Saint-Hilaire's columns rushed towards the village. Wimpfen was wounded and was caught by the dragoons; Seletkow tried to replace him. Thiébault reached Sokolnitz with his 36th which joined up with the 48th. Friant overwhelmed the Russians who were on the plain in front of the wall of the park. The 36th and 48th took the castle and the park and drove back the

enemy on to the hill to the north-west of the village. It was there that General Thiébault was seriously wounded leading the attack against a battery.

Legrand and Saint-Hilaire sent the 14th, 43rd and 10th Light to cut off the retreat of the enemy who had been driven north-west from Sokolnitz and those who were trying to reach Schlapanitz after crossing the Faisanderie. Oudinot's grenadier regiments were directed towards this area as possible reinforcements.

The latter from Dupas' Brigade were those which had been divided and entrusted to Duroc to relieve Oudinot who had been wounded recently. Other elements tried to seek refuge in the Faisanderie, but surrounded and attacked, they surrendered. Przybyszewski with Seletkow and Strick tried to escape but were pursued by the 36th and the 48th, including among them Lochet, bent on capturing those generals. But he was overtaken by Franceschi who appeared with his 8th Hussars and captured them.

2. The Capture of Aujezd

Vandamme had stopped near Saint-Anthony's Chapel to wait for his artillery to catch up with him. He overlooked Aujezd and on that side the slopes were steeper. First he sent a battalion of the 28th to block the escape route from Aujezd to Hostizeradeck and towards Austerlitz. The battalion carried

out its mission by blocking the eastern exit of the village. The 3rd Dragoon Division was behind Vandamme who was still waiting for his artillery.

Buxhoewden was given the order to retreat and actually decided to react. He gathered his forces in front of Aujezd and Telnitz and lined up a 24-gun battery under Sievers. The infantry gathered up the remainders of the Kiev, Yaroslav, Vladimir, New Ingria, Bryansk, Vyatka and Moscow Regiments, and the battalions of the 7th and 8th Chasseurs. Buxhoewden had the cavalry he had managed to recover - consisting of Prince Moritz Liechtenstein's Szekler Hussars, O'Reilly's Chevau-Léger with Stutterheim and some Cossacks - to cover them. Outside Aujezd, Buxhoewden crossed the bridge which was in a bad state and which was reserved for cattle. He crossed it with his suite and two of his battalions; however, an Austrian battery which followed destroyed the bridge, effectively blocking the way for the other survivors. Buxhoewden was able to rally Austerlitz by following the left bank of the Litawa.

Vandamme who was under pressure from the artillery had Boyé's Division char-

61

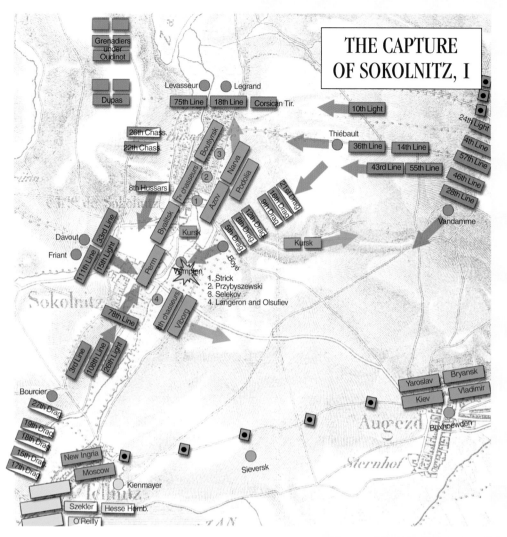

THE CAPTURE OF SOKOLNITZ, I

1. Strick
2. Przybyszewski
3. Selekov
4. Langeron and Olsufiev

THE CAPTURE OF SOKOLNITZ

- **Soult's corps** helped Davout. It was Saint-Hilaire's Division which came down off the Pratzen Plateau and attacked Sokolnitz from the east.

- **Thiébault's Brigade** marched in the centre towards the castle, supported by Morand and the 10th Light on the right and by Waré's Brigade (43rd and 55th), and not by Levasseur's Brigade on the left. This brigade attacked the castle and captured 400 prisoners as Ledru mentioned. The castle was taken by Thiébault with the help of the Pô Tirailleurs. General Müller who was found wounded was captured.

- **Further north, Levasseur's Brigade** (18th, 75th and Corsican Tirailleurs) opposed the Russian runaways who tried to escape towards Kobelnitz. Dupas' Brigade from Duroc's and Oudinot's Grenadiers was marching in support.

- **To the west,** Friant's Regiment had joined Davout behind the stream located beyond the village and attacked with the 15th Light in the lead; they captured the little bridge which led to Sokolnitz. In the village itself Lochet was still holding on to its southern part and attacked, supported by the 26th Light which moved along the Goldbach.

- **Przybyszewski** with Generals Selekov and Stryeck was driven out by these attacks towards the neighbouring heights to the south-west. It was Franceschi's 8th Hussars who took their surrender, depriving General Lochet of this reward.

- **Langeron left** the last battalion of the Kursk Regiment and the Perm Regiment surrounded in the northern part of the village. He only managed to get the 8th Chasseurs and the Viborg Regiment out; he positioned them outside Sokolnitz in the direction of Aujezd where he joined Buxhoewden. He took two battalions of the Kursk Regiment and sent them to the Pratzenberg; unfortunately this was too late and they fell into the hands of the French and were destroyed.

- **General Wimpfen** remained on the left bank of the Goldbach with the Narva, Azov and Podolia Regiments. He was attacked by Boyé's Dragoons on their way to the south. He was wounded and captured with part of his troops.

- **When he emerged from Sokolnitz** Castle, Thiébault attacked a Russian battery with the 36th of the Line. The battery was taken but the general was seriously wounded.

ge the line; but the charge was a bit listless and annoyed Napoleon who sent Gardane to get things under control again. Then Digeon arrived with one of the Guards' mounted batteries and reinforced Soult's artillery which had set itself up. The French attacked and occupied Aujezd: the enemy was thrown out towards the lakes or to Telnitz. Some wanted to reach Satchan and tried to use a dyke which led there directly, but it was half under water and ice which did not resist the weight of the horses and the cannon, which fell through it. It was not very deep and the men managed to get out.

The 4th helped by the 28th and the 24th Light got their revenge in Aujezd. Bigarré, disheartened by the loss of his Eagle, captured Colonel Soulima of the 8th Chasseurs and managed to take two enemy flags. At the time he thought he had recovered his Eagle, but it was in fact one of the 24th Light's Eagles, picked up by the men of the 4th. It was claimed later that evening.

3. The Capture of Telnitz

Once Buxhoewden had left, Dokhturov was in command. The only way out for him was the road from Telnitz to Menitz. A line of defence was formed up in Telnitz to allow the other remaining troops to fall back; they had to use however a very narrow dyke going straight to Satchan along which only two men could move at a time; it was also half-submerged and covered with ice. General Levis sacrificed

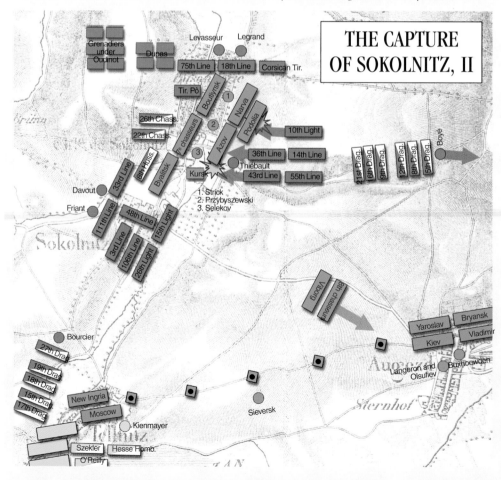

THE CAPTURE OF SOKOLNITZ, II

1. Strick
2. Przybyszewski
3. Selekov

himself by staying in Telnitz. Some of the cavalry wanted to try a charge, but they were driven back by the Dragoons and Chasseurs of the Guard which had just arrived.

Davout sent Friant and Bourcier's Dragoons towards Menitz which made the last defenders of Telnitz abandon this ever-so-coveted village which Vandamme now occupied. Langeron described the retreat thus: *"You had to have witnessed the confusion there was during our retreat* (or rather our flight) *to get an idea. There were not two men of the same company still together, everything was so confused: the soldiers threw away their rifles and no longer listened to their officers, neither to their generals. These shouted out after them but to no avail, and ran like them. The two Saint-Petersburg Dragoons and the hundred Isayev Cossacks lost their horses in the Menitz lakes when the ice gave way. I was among the unfortunate who tried to escape the victors and, to add to everything, I was on foot."* After the bridge at Aujezd broke up, he left his horse.

Dahlmann and two squadrons of the Guard pursued the fleeing troops and captured 1 200 of them to the south of Menitz. Dokhturov and only the Moscow Regiment were in relative good order and were able to carry out a proper retreat and reach the Allies at Czeitsch on 3rd December. Langeron accompanied these fleeing troops who were however in fairly good order.

He explained: *"I joined the runaways; we marched or rather we ran all night. The remainder of the troops, except for the rearguard under Prince Bagration was in the same situation... everybody was fleeing... Nobody was in his proper place: the corps, the divisions and the regiments; everything was topsy-turvy and nobody had anything to eat. We fed on what we looted in the neighbouring villages or off the wounded who were too tired or exhausted. We did not stop anywhere; we covered 60 kilometres in forty hours and in that lapse of time, many officers, generals and soldiers had nothing to eat. If the enemy had chased us - and I do not see why they did not do so - they would have cut down or taken another 20 000 men."*

The Russians had reached Czeitsch; Merveldt covered them at Gœding but Davout and Gudin caught up with him. The Tsar, ill and exhausted, slept on straw in a hovel at Urchitz. From there he reached Czeitsch. Czernitchev found Kutusov for him and brought him during the night. The Tsar then took the remnants of his army back to Russia.

Liechtenstein was sent by the Emperor of Austria to seek a meeting with Napoleon to discuss armistice terms; he had the Tsar's agreement. The meeting took place at the windmill at Spaleny on 4th December. The windmill had been looted and the Emperors talked around a big fire lit by the Guard. During the talks, the Emperor of Austria said that the *"English were dealers in human flesh"*; he said a great deal of bad things about the Cossacks, promised not to start war again and accepted all Napoleon's conditions. He lost several bits of land. De Ségur witnessed what was said. Peace was decided, the agreements completed and Napoleon's conditions accepted.

In just the same way as after the battle of the Moskova, the Russians tried to trick public opinion by singing the praises of the soldiers and handing out

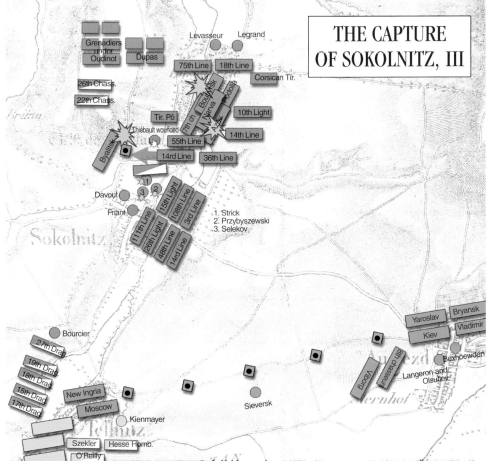

THE CAPTURE OF SOKOLNITZ, III

1. Strick
2. Przybyszewski
3. Selekov

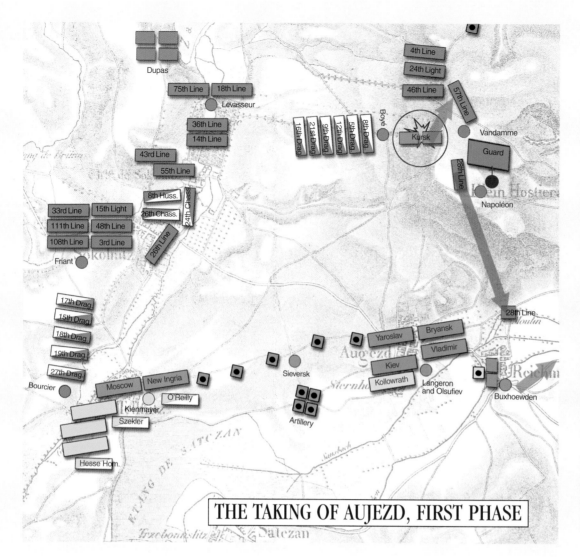

Map labels:
Dupas
75th Line · 18th Line
Levasseur
36th Line
14th Line
43rd Line
55th Line
8th Huss.
26th Chass.
24th Chass.
33rd Line · 15th Light
111th Line · 48th Line
108th Line · 3rd Line
26th Line
Friant
17th Drag.
15th Drag.
18th Drag.
19th Drag.
27th Drag.
Bourcier
Moscow · New Ingria
Kienmayer
O'Reilly
Szekler
Hesse Hom.

16th Drag. · 21st Drag. · 9th Drag. · 12th Drag. · 5th Drag. · 8th Drag.
Boyé
Kursk
4th Line
24th Light
46th Line
57th Line
Vandamme
Guard
28th Line
Napoléon
Klein Hostier

Sieversk
Yaroslav · Bryansk
Vladimir
Kiev
Kollowrath
Langeron and Olsufiev
Artillery
28th Line
Reichm
Buxhoewden

THE TAKING OF AUJEZD, FIRST PHASE

THE TAKING OF AUJEZD

- **It was Vandamme** who got into line to the right of the Saint-Anthony Chapel. He was waiting for his artillery and Boyé's Dragoons. He sent a battalion from the 28th to block the Aujezd – Austerlitz road.

- **The 4th, 28th of the Line and the 24th Light** were got together. The 46th and 57th with Boyé's Dragoons annihilated the two Kursk Regiment battalions heading for the Pratzenberg. Half the Russian troops were killed and the other captured with its flags.

- Buxhoewden was still in front of Aujezd with his four regiment reserve; the fleeing Austrians and the Russian artillery pool (42 cannon). He got Sievers to set up a battery with 15-20 guns which drove off Boyé's dragoons' first charge which Napoleon deemed too soft; Gardane was sent to change this lack of determination.

- **When he received the order to fall back, Buxhoewden,** his following and two battalions crossed the Litawa over a rotten bridge. An Austrian battery following behind them broke up the bridge, thus cutting off any possibility of retreat to those already engaged in Aujezd and under attack by Vandamme. Buxhoewden was able to fall back on Austerlitz.

- **The attack on Aujezd** was led by the 4th, the 24th Light and the 28th of the Line, followed by the 46th. Bigarré got his revenge by capturing two flags and Colonel Soulima of the 8th Russian Chasseurs. The artillery pool and 4 000 men were captured.

---

rewards: Konstantin's Uhlans got silver trumpets and the standard of the Gardes du Corps were given an inscription commemorating the capture of the 4th of the Line's flag. Napoleon, almost drunk with victory, only took an interest in

Above. ***Franceschi and his 8th Hussars capturing the Russian Generals Przybyszewski, Seletkow and Strick.*** *(Water colour by J. Rousselot, RR)*

Following Page, Top. ***Drama! The Russian artillery batteries were too heavy and broke the ice, cutting off the retreat for the Allies near Menitz (RR)***

the pursuit on the following morning and even then without knowing really which way the Allies had gone. Towards Olmutz, the pursuers only found a lot of wagons and baggage. Although late the order was given. Davout, the quickest, took part in the chase and came across General Merveldt's detachment and did not want to believe in the armistice which the general insisted was in effect. Davout was with Friant, Klein, Lasalle and their dragoons; Gudin arrived. Merveldt sent an officer to the Tsar who returned bearing a paper signed by the Tsar himself; Savary came up to confirm that armistice discussions were planned at the windmill at Spaleny. Austria paid a heavy tribute. Bavaria became a kingdom and got the Tyrol and the Voralberg in the Anspach region back. Wurtemberg became a fully-recognised kingdom and Baden became a Grand-Duchy. Venice, Frioul and Dalmatia were attached to the Kingdom of Italy.

Finally the contributions were fixed at 85 million. Peace was signed at Presburg, on 16th December without either Russia or England taking part.

THE MYTH OF THE LAKES

A rather Dantean picture has been painted of thousands of Russians, surrounded and cut off from any retreat and stuck on the shores of the lakes which they tried to cross on the ice whilst under fire from French artillery which helped to break the ice too and drown them.

In fact, the ice did break but under the weight of the Allies' cannon; but all the men could stand up in the water. They were able to get out and about 2 000 prisoners and the artillery pool left on the shores were taken. Suchet was responsible for recovering the Russian cannon. Helped by the locals,

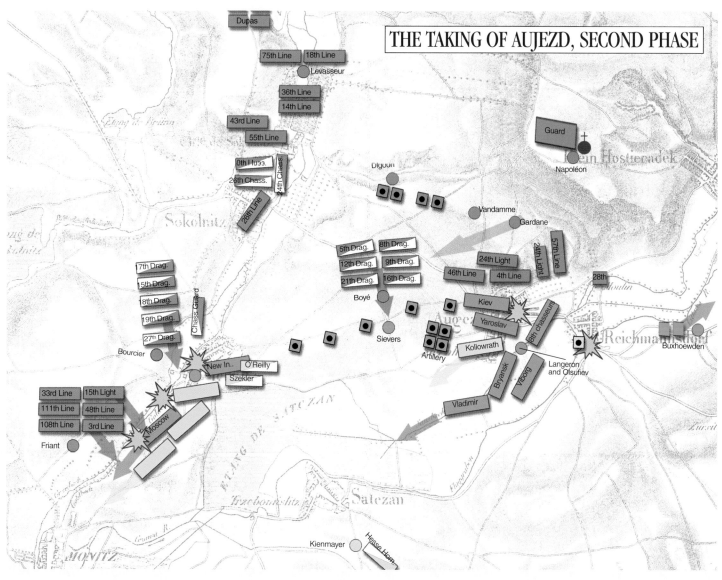

THE TAKING OF AUJEZD, SECOND PHASE

Dupas

75th Line   18th Line

Levasseur

36th Line

14th Line

43rd Line

55th Line

0th Huss.

26th Chass.   24th Chass.

26th Line

Digoun

Vandamme

Gardane

Guard

Napoléon

Klein Hostieradek

5th Drag.   8th Drag.

12th Drag.   9th Drag.

21st Drag.   16th Drag.

17th Drag.

15th Drag.

18th Drag.

19th Drag.

27th Drag.

Chass. Guard

Boyé

Sievers

Artillery

Kiev

Yaroslav

Kollowrath

Bryansk   Vfborg

Vladimir

24th Light

46th Line   4th Line

24th Light   57th Line

28th

Moulin

Reichmannsdorf

Buxhoewden

Langeron
and Olsufiev

6th chasseurs

Bourcier

New In..   O'Reilly

Szekler

33rd Line   15th Light

111th Line   48th Line

108th Line   3rd Line

Moscow

Friant

Sokolnitz

Aujez..

ETANG DE SATCZAN

Satezan

Trzebounitz

MONITZ

Kienmayer   Hesse Hom..

65

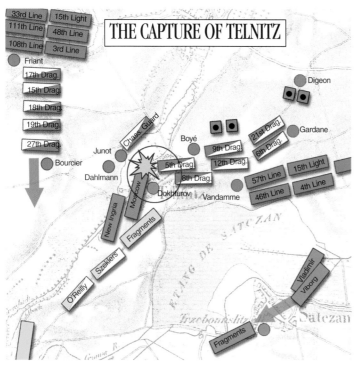

THE CAPTURE OF TELNITZ

Labels on map: 33rd Line, 15th Light, 111th Line, 48th Line, 108th Line, 3rd Line, Friant, 17th Drag., 15th Drag., 18th Drag., 19th Drag., 27th Drag., Bourcier, Junot, Chass. Guard, Dahlmann, Boyé, 9th Drag., 21st Drag., 8th Drag., Digeon, Gardane, Moscow, 5th Drag., 12th Drag., 8th Drag., Dokhturov, 57th Line, 15th Light, Vandamme, 46th Line, 4th Line, New Ingria, Fragments, Szekers, O'Reilly, Vladimir, Viborg, Fragments

once the lakes had been emptied, 38 cannon were found and the corpses of 130 horses. Nothing was found in the lake at Menitz. All eye-witness accounts agree on this point. Several local enquiries were carried out. For the lake at Satchan, there were only two dead Russians, 140 horses and 18 cannon.

Marbot who had come on a mission to headquarters as an aide de camp to Marshal Augereau with his friend Massy, witnessed this last episode and was perhaps exaggerating a bit when he described the scene where he helped rescue a Russian on a slab of ice; he entered the water followed by an artillery officer called Boumestain. Naked in the icy water, they succeeded in landing the Russian on his ice block in front of the Emperor.

Warmed up and cared for, Marbot recovered quickly without any problems. He speaks of ropes thrown to the Russians in the water of the vast pond at Satchan. The rescued Russian asked to serve in the French Army and finished up in the Polish Lancers of the Guard where Marbot met him later, still grateful.

THE FLAGS CAPTURED AT AUSTERLITZ

They have been studied in the book by General Andolenko. There were 29 coloured Russian Flags and 16 Austrian ones. For the Russian ones, not all were complete; for some there was no shaft, for others there was only the shaft, the flag having been torn off and kept by prisoners who brought them back later. In all

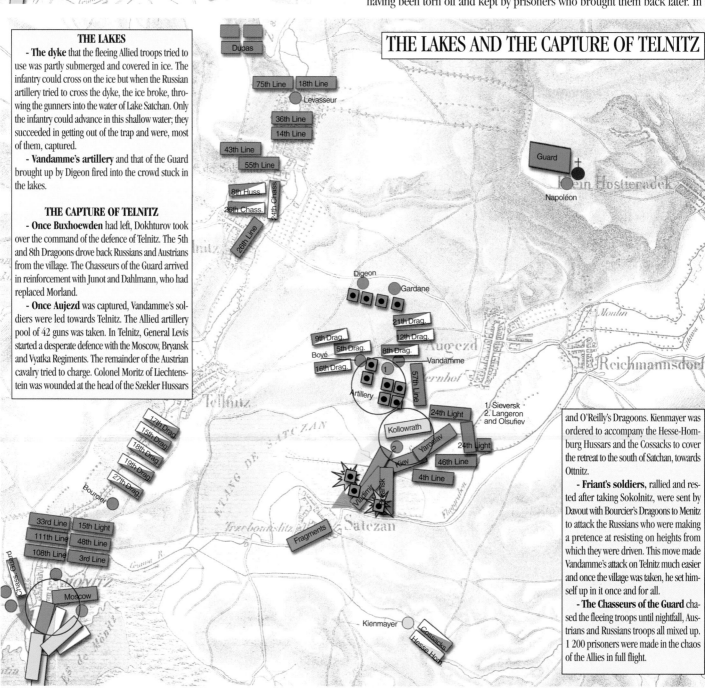

THE LAKES AND THE CAPTURE OF TELNITZ

Labels on map: Dupas, 75th Line, 18th Line, Levasseur, 36th Line, 14th Line, 43rd Line, 55th Line, 8th Huss., 26th Chass., 24th Chass., 26th Line, Digeon, Gardane, 21th Drag., 9th Drag., 12th Drag., 5th Drag., 8th Drag., Boyé, Vandamme, 16th Drag., 57th Line, Artillery, 1, 24th Light, Kollowrath, 2, Yargelav, 24th Light, Kiev, 46th Line, Vladimir, 4th Line, Fragments, Satczan, Telnitz, 17th Drag., 15th Drag., 18th Drag., 19th Drag., 27th Drag., Bourcier, 33rd Line, 15th Light, 111th Line, 48th Line, 108th Line, 3rd Line, Chass. Guard, Moscow, Kienmayer, Cossacks, Hesse-Hom., Guard, Napoléon, Reichmannsdorf

1. Sieversk
2. Langeron and Olsufiev

THE LAKES

- **The dyke** that the fleeing Allied troops tried to use was partly submerged and covered in ice. The infantry could cross on the ice but when the Russian artillery tried to cross the dyke, the ice broke, throwing the gunners into the water of Lake Satchan. Only the infantry could advance in this shallow water; they succeeded in getting out of the trap and were, most of them, captured.

- **Vandamme's artillery** and that of the Guard brought up by Digeon fired into the crowd stuck in the lakes.

THE CAPTURE OF TELNITZ

- **Once Buxhoewden** had left, Dokhturov took over the command of the defence of Telnitz. The 5th and 8th Dragoons drove back Russians and Austrians from the village. The Chasseurs of the Guard arrived in reinforcement with Junot and Dahlmann, who had replaced Morland.

- **Once Aujezd** was captured, Vandamme's soldiers were led towards Telnitz. The Allied artillery pool of 42 guns was taken. In Telnitz, General Levis started a desperate defence with the Moscow, Bryansk and Vyatka Regiments. The remainder of the Austrian cavalry tried to charge. Colonel Moritz of Liechtenstein was wounded at the head of the Szekler Hussars

and O'Reilly's Dragoons. Kienmayer was ordered to accompany the Hesse-Homburg Hussars and the Cossacks to cover the retreat to the south of Satchan, towards Ottnitz.

- **Friant's soldiers,** rallied and rested after taking Sokolnitz, were sent by Davout with Bourcier's Dragoons to Menitz to attack the Russians who were making a pretence at resisting on heights from which they were driven. This move made Vandamme's attack on Telnitz much easier and once the village was taken, he set himself up in it once and for all.

- **The Chasseurs of the Guard** chased the fleeing troops until nightfall, Austrians and Russians troops all mixed up. 1 200 prisoners were made in the chaos of the Allies in full flight.

Above.
The Flags captured at Austerlitz were the last elements of the legend which was started the following day in the Grande Armée's bulletin, by the Emperor himself.

19 insignia were brought back by prisoners. This was the case of the Butyrsk Regiment, saved by Master-Sergeant Izmailov, who escaped from Brünn. Three others were saved like the white flag, by Master-Sergeant Kokurin and kept by Sergeant Mostowski whilst in captivity.

- One of the Kursk Regiment's by Master-Sergeant Svirtchevski.

- One of the Perm's by Master-Sergeant Karlukov. Two others were saved including the Colonel Flag saved by Colonel Kuznetzov.

- One of the Narva Regiment's ripped from the shaft by Garilenko. Two others were saved and two lost.

- The Arkhangelsk Regiment lost a flag taken by Squadron commander Jacquemin of the 5th Cuirassiers.

- One of the Azov Regiment's was famous. It was given to soldier Tchaika by Sergeant Staritchov who was dying. It ended up at Kaluga, the sergeant's birthplace. The Tsar got involved with the municipality to improve the lot of the family; a plaque was erected on the wall of the hero's house, his name was given to a street, and the flag was put in the Kaluga regional museum. At Austerlitz the regiment nevertheless lost three flags.

- One of the Podolia's ripped from its shaft by Master-Sergeant Letzik.

All these men were rewarded by a promotion (to officer cadet) or by 100 roubles. Thus Kutusov reported that twelve flags had been brought back in this way, which reduced the exact number of flags taken to 18 instead of the thirty announced after the battle.

Where the emblems of the Russian Guard were concerned, it seems that the standards of the Life Guards and the Gardes du Corps were sent to the rear before the charges; thus none were taken. So probably the only one captured was that of the Life Guards (5th Reserve Squadron) which appeared in Verillon's book. For the French what was important was the Eagle and the number of the regiment above it, not the material of the flag itself.

---

1. Langeron, a former Colonel and second-in-command of the Régiment du Médoc in 1786 was an émigré. He entered Russian service, served against the Swedes and against the Turks. After his disgrace, he sought refuge with the Duke of Richelieu in Odessa. He recovered his rank in 1807 and served with Tchitchagov at the Berezina then in 1813, he accompanied 5 000 men to Bautzen and to Katzbach. In 1814, he blocked Mainz and then Soissons, Reims and Laon. He captured Montmartre. In 1815 he blocked Alsace and died of Cholera in 1831.

Andolenko gave a final figure of complete flags captured of: 3 from the Azov Regiment, one from the Arkhangelgorod, two from the Narva, five from Polodia, two or five from the Kursk and one from the Perm, a total of 14 to 17, without counting the shafts. He also said that on the famous painting, Baron Gérard reproduced the paintings using the ones which were at the Invalides as models, whereas the flags taken at Austerlitz had been entrusted to Notre-Dame, where they disappeared after the fire in 1851.

From the vaults of Notre-Dame, 47 Russian and Austrian flags had been hung, but many were only shafts. In his report, Davout said that: *"For Friant six flags had been taken by his men, but that two soldiers who did not attach enough importance to them as they were only 'poles', must have broken two of them and thrown them away."*

Back in Russia, the Tsar punished the generals who were responsible. Przybyszewski was imprisoned, disgraced, and reduced to the ranks for ten years. Langeron was relieved of his command without the promotion he had hoped for. It is highly likely that the fact that they were foreigners had something to do with their disgrace.

Langeron received the following letter: *"As the consequences of the 2 December were particularly unfortunate for the column which was under your Excellency's command, and His Majesty being dissatisfied with the way in which the column was led, he grants you, through my good offices, permission for you to ask to be retired."*

Langeron tendered his resignation.

Langeron's column's losses were 5 senior officers, 39 officers, 1 684 men and 6 cannon. Przybyszewski lost 5 280 men out of 7 563.

The bitterness which clearly appears in Langeron's memoirs of Austerlitz is quite understandable. In them he denounces the real culprits responsible for the defeat and justified his leaving the attack on Sokolnitz to rejoin Kamenski.

Two battalions from the Novgorod Regiment which had been routed in front of the Tsar were punished: the regiment became the '43rd Chasseurs' (without a flag), the officers were deprived of sabre knots and the soldiers of their sabres, and the length of service was increased by five years. This punishment was rescinded in 1810 because of their brilliant action against the Turks.

On St-Helen, Napoleon said several times that the Russians at Austerlitz fought more energetically than at Borodino. The lack of unity and the mistakes made by the commanding officers slowed down the manoeuvres, causing a disaster for the Allies.

Miloradovitch and Buxhoewden have a heavy responsibility to bear.

All you will have to say is "I was at the battle of Austerlitz",
for people to answer "There goes a brave man."

The Brave Men.

THE EMPEROR'S HOUSEHOLD

The details of the functioning of the household are to be found in the memoirs of Menneval and Baron Fain. What strikes one at first, is the capacity for work and organisation that was Napoleon's, even though he used very simple formulae. He surrounded himself with efficient men who understood their role perfectly well.

First there was the Grand Maréchal du Palais **Du Roc** (Duroc), gentleman cadet in 1789; he was a student artilleryman at Chalons. He was an émigré and came back to the School in 1793. He was in the Army of Italy as a Second-Lieutenant, served at Toulon and was promoted Captain in 1794. Aide de camp to Bonaparte in 1796 he followed him to Egypt. He was brigade commander in 1799, wounded at Aboukir and was sent several times on special missions. General in 1801, he was named Governor of the Tuileries and Major-General in 1803. Grand Maréchal du Palais and Grand Aigle of the LH in 1804. He shared command of Oudinot's Grenadiers at Austerlitz. In the Emperor's name, he signed the Treaty of Posen with the King of Saxony as well as the Treaty of Renunciation of Charles IV to the Spanish throne. He was at Essling and Wagram and signed the armistice at Znaim. Couronne de Fer in 1809. He went to Russia and was appointed Senator in 1813. Present at Lutzen and Bautzen, he was killed with Kirgener, hit by a cannonball on 23 May 1813 near Gorlitz.

His Deputy Maréchal des logis des Palais was **Count Ségur D'Auguesseau,** the son of the Marquis. In America, he commanded a regiment with his name in 1782 (SL). Ambassador in Russia in 1789, then to Berlin in 1792, he was wounded in a duel. Elected Deputy for Isère in 1801, he became Grand Master of Ceremonies in 1804, then Count in 1808 and Senator in 1813. Peer of France in 1814, he served in 1815 and was sacked as a peer then reinstated in 1819. He was Grand Officier du Palais at Austerlitz.

He had an aide de camp called **Jacquinot**, born in Melun, wounded at Hohenlinden, Colonel with the 11th Chasseurs in 1806, wounded at Jena, General in 1809. He fought at Raab then at Wagram with Montbrun. He was in Russia with Bruyère's Division. Wounded at Denewitz in 1813, he was at Waterloo, then became cavalry inspector. CR de SL and Gd Cx of the LH in 1844. He died in 1848.

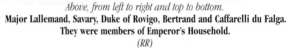

Above, from left to right and top to bottom.
Major Lallemand, Savary, Duke of Rovigo, Bertrand and Caffarelli du Falga.
They were members of Emperor's Household.
(RR)

Duroc was helped by **General Macon,** commissaire for war then Battalion Commander with the 61st of the Line. He was senior Adjudant of the palace of the government in 1802, General in 1803, Ct LH, attached to the Emperor, Governor of the Grand Palais at headquarters at Austerlitz. Governor of Leipzig in 1806, he was rapidly considered to be an intriguer by his peers. He died of illness at Leipzig in 1816.

The Marquis of Caulaincourt, son of the Senator, had the rank of Second-Lieutenant in 1789. He was his father's aide de camp and Captain with his uncle d'Harville. Volunteered in 1792, Captain with the Army of the Cotes de Cherbourg and aide de camp to Aubert-Dubayet whom he followed to Constantinople in 1796. He commanded the 2nd Carabiniers in 1799. Wounded twice he became Bonaparte's aide de camp in 1802. He organised the arrest of the Duke of Enghien in 1804. He was appointed Grand-Ecuyer and Major-General in 1805. Grand Aigle of the LH, he was on the headquarters staff of the army at Austerlitz. He replaced Savary as Ambassador to Russia in 1807; Duke of Vicence in 1808. He returned from Russia in December 1812. He was promoted Maréchal du Palais on the death of Duroc.

He was minister of Foreign Affairs from 21 March to 8 July 1814; he was made a Peer of France by Napoleon. Outlawed in July 1815, he returned in August 1815 and was retired. He died in 1827.

Napoleon's aide de camps were **Junot** called the '*Tempest*', the first aide de camp. He was born near Alésia, studied law, volunteered for the Cote d'Or; he became famous for his action at Toulon with Bonaparte who named him Aide de camp. He was promoted to Colonel in Italy, he went to Egypt and was made a General when he returned He was Governor of Paris were he committed excesses which caused him to be removed; he was therefore sent to Arras where he formed the reunited Grenadiers who were commanded by Oudinot. Displeased at not having been appointed Marshal; he was dismissed again. Sent to Parma to put down a rebellion, he was made Governor of Paris again where his excesses started all over again; he fell under the influence of Caroline Bonaparte. He was sent to Portugal and thanks to the convention of Cintra, he was able to bring his soldiers back. He returned to Portugal with Masséna but under his command. In Russia he was thought to be incapable at Valutina, letting Gudin do all the work and get killed. His mental illness started and he was useless at the Moskova. Nominated to Illyria, he turned up at a ball organised by him wearing only his decorations; He returned to Burgundy where he committed suicide on 29 July 1813, a victim of tertiary syphilis (called General paralysis). On 1 December before the battle of Austerlitz, he had just arrived from Lisbon after a 700-league march to reach the battlefield.

He had several aide de camps, among which:

Bardin: aide de camp to Junot while he was Governor of Paris in 1800. He commanded the Pupilles de la Garde in 1811. He retired as Honorary Marshal of the Camp in 1823.

Lallemand, François. Served at Rivoli, he was a Guide in Egypt; Captain and aide de camp to Junot in 1799, Major in the 18th Dragoons in 1805 and Colonel of the 25th Dragoons in 1806, he was made a Baron then General in 1811. He was in Spain until 1813, then Chief of Staff of the 11th Corps in Saxony. He served in Hamburg with Davout and returned in 1814. Learning of the return of Napoleon from Elba, with Lefebvre Desnoettes to raise his troops but failed. Arrested but then released, he was made Lieutenant-General on 30 March, Second-in Command of the Chasseurs à Cheval of the Guard, he was wounded at Waterloo. He accompanied Napoleon to Rochefort but was arrested and sent to Malta. Condemned to death in his absence, he left for Smyrnia, then Egypt. He went into exile in Texas where he founded the Champ d'Asile which failed. Fallen upon hard times he failed in New York and returned to France in 1830. He was Lieutenant-General then Peer of France in 1832, GdOLH in 1835, Inspector of Saint-Cyr, he died in 1839.

Caffarelli du Falga. Brother of the General who died in Egypt. He was in the 15th Dragoons as cavalryman, wounded in 1793, Colonel of the 9th Light, General in 1802, Governor of the Tuileries, Major-General in 1805, aide de camp to Napoleon. At Austerlitz he replaced Bison wounded leading Davout's 1st Division, but went over with Lannes to the left wing. Grand Aigle of the LH 1806. He was in Spain but returned to be aide de camp to the Emperor in 1813. He accompanied Marie-Louise and the Aiglon to Vienna. He served during the hundred Days, retired in 1816. Peer of France in 1832, he retired once and for all in 1832 and looked after the return of Napoleon's ashes in 1840. It was his brother who had lost a leg and wore a wooden one.

Savary. He was Squadron Commander in the Army of the Rhine. Aide de camp to Desaix, he went to Egypt and at Marengo where he brought back the mortally wounded Desaix. He subsequently commanded the Gendarmerie d'Elite and took part in the kidnapping of the Duke of Enghien. Aide de camp to napoleon at Austerlitz, he went to the headquarters of Tsar Alexander before the battle. Major-Gene-

STAFF OFFICERS

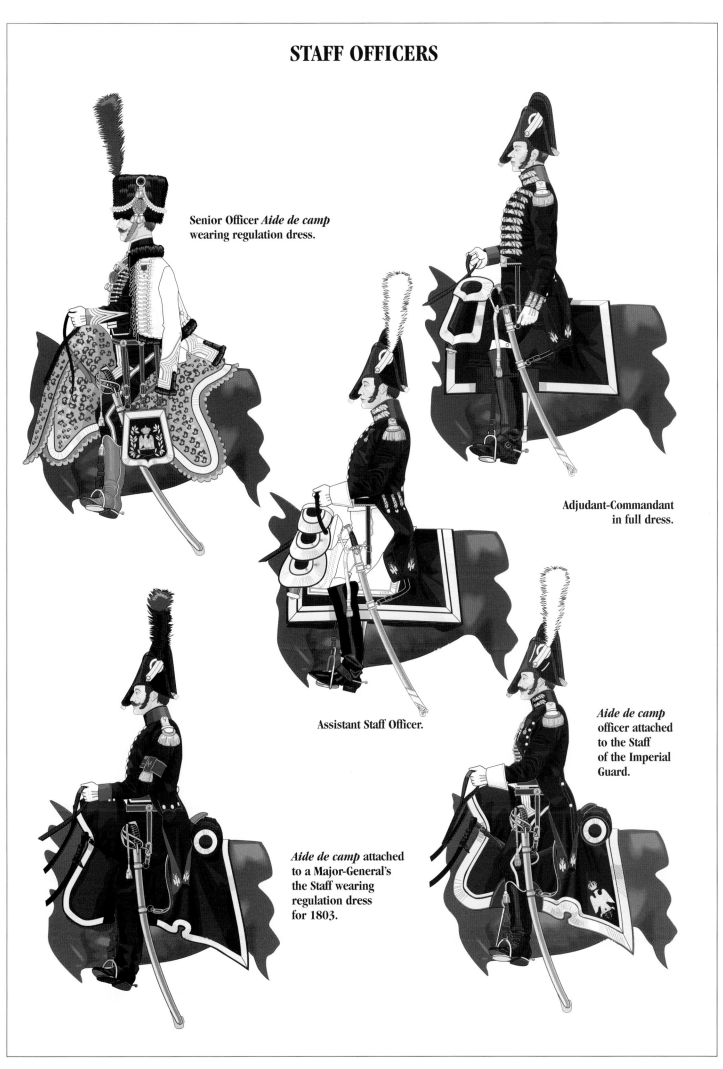

Senior Officer *Aide de camp* wearing regulation dress.

Adjudant-Commandant in full dress.

Assistant Staff Officer.

Aide de camp officer attached to the Staff of the Imperial Guard.

Aide de camp attached to a Major-General's the Staff wearing regulation dress for 1803.

ral. After Jena, he chased the Prussians with the 7th Chasseurs and the 1st Hussars. He replaced Lannes in 1807 in front of Ostrolenka. GdCxLH, he was sent to Russia where Caulaincourt replaced him. He was appointed Governor of Prussia after Friedland. He was made Duke of Rovigo in 1808. He was sent to Spain then he was present at Eckmühl in 1809. He was Minister of Police in place of Fouché who had been dismissed. He was a victim of Malet's conspiracy but freed. He was inactive during the first Restoration; he was appointed First Inspector during the Hundred days and also Peer of France. He wanted to follow Napoleon into exile, but was shut up in Malta instead. He escaped to Smyrna. Condemned to death in absentia, he stayed in Graz and then returned to Smyrna. Acquitted in 1819, his rank was restored to him. Retired in 1823, he left for Rome. Appointed Commander in Africa in 1831, he died in 1833.

Lemarois: commanded the gunners in 1793, he was at Toulon in 1793; aide de camp to Bonaparte. He was at Lodi, wounded at Roveredo, present at Arcola, but could not follow Bonaparte to Egypt because of his wounds. He returned to Bonaparte when he came back from Egypt. He was at Marengo where he was made General in 1803. He was at Austerlitz and Jena where he was wounded. He was Governor of Warsaw, Deputy for the Manche in 1807. Count in 1808, Gd OLH. He disapproved of the attack on Russia and was left behind as Commandant of the Grand-Duchy of Berg; Governor of Magdeburg in 1813, he capitulated on 28 May 1814. He commanded at Rouen in 1815 and was retired afterwards, retired in 1832; he was not re-elected.

Rapp. Born at Colmar, aide de camp to Desaix in 1796, he had already been wounded many times. He followed him to Egypt. At Marengo, he held his dying commanding officer. Aide de camp to Bonaparte he was entrusted with organising the squadron of Mamelukes in 1801. General in 1803, second in command of the Grenadiers à Cheval in 1805, he was made aide de camp to Napoleon at Austerlitz. Wounded during the great charge, he captured Prince Repnin and was made Major-General on 25 December. He was present at Jena and wounded at Golymin, he left arm broken by a bullet. Appointed Governor of Danzig, Couronne de Fer and Count in January 1809, he took part in the recapture of Essling with Mouton. He disapproved of Napoleon's divorce and of the Russian Campaign, but nevertheless took part as aide de camp to the Emperor. He was wounded four times at the Moskova. Gd Cx of the Réunion in 1813. Besieged in Danzig he surrendered on the condition that he could return with his France, but the conditions were not respected and he was sent to the Ukraine. He returned to France in 1814. GdCx LH in 1814. In 1815, he rallied to Napoleon and was in command in Alsace. Deputy and Peer of France, he escaped to Switzerland, returned in 1817, Peer of France in 1819, First Chamberlain to Louis XVIII in 1820. Cr SL in 1821. He died of cancer of the pylorus in the same year. He was wounded twenty-two times.

Mouton. Count of Lobau, born at Phalsbourg. An exemplary soldier, he was in Italy and became aide de camp to Joubert in 1797. He was the hero of the siege of Genoa where he was wounded twice. General in 1805, aide de camp to Napoleon on 6 March, he was at Austerlitz, Jena and Eylau. Cr of the Couronne de Fer, seriously wounded at Friedland, he was made Major-General in 1807. He was with Bessières at Medina de Rio Seco then came back to the Emperor. Mentioned in despatches at Eckmühl, he was very brilliant at Essling where he was wounded. He was at Wagram after which he was covered with gifts; Count in 1810; he was in Russia from which he returned with Napoleon from Smorgoni. Peer of France in 1815, aide de camp at Waterloo. He was captured. GdCxLH in 1830. In 1831, he was re-elected Deputy and made a Peer of France. He died in 1838.

Lebrun, son of the arch-treasurer, was aide de camp to Napoleon in Italy in 1800. With Desaix at Marengo, he held him in his arms, dying. Colonel in 1804, he was with Napoleon at Austerlitz. Colonel of the 3rd Hussars at Jena; he took several Saxon flags. He charged at Eylau; General in 1807. Major-General in 1812, he was with the Emperor at Waterloo and then placed on the non-active list. Duke of Plaisance and Peer of France after the death of his father on 16 June 1824, GdCxLH in 1833, retired in 1848, Senator in 1852, Gd Chancelier LH in 1853 and, Military Medal, he died in 1859.

Bertrand. Pupil at the Mézières School then served at the Embassy in Constantinople in 1796. He served in Italy in 1797. He was at Toulon in 1798, wounded in Egypt, General in 1800. Aide de camp to Napoleon in 1804, he took part in the capture of the bridge at Vienna and took part in the Battle of Austerlitz. He was at Jena and Spandau in 1806, Danzig in 1807, he was made a Major-General at Friedland;

Count in 1808, he was present at the siege of Vienna in 1809 at Essling. GdCxLH and GdCX of Baden, he replaced Marmont in Illyria. He commanded the 4th Corps in 1813. Grand Marshal of the Palace in November 1813. He took part in the French Campaign in 1814 and followed the Emperor to Elba. After Waterloo he accompanied the Emperor to St-Helena and was with him when he died on 5 May 1821. He was condemned to death in absentia then reinstated. He presided over the return of the ashes on 30 November 1840 and died in 1847. He lies next to Napoleon in the Invalides.

General Clarke was a cadet in 1781, Captain in the Hussars in 1784, then Major with the 2nd Cavalry with the Army of the Rhine, promoted to General in 1793. Councillor of State, he was also secretary to Napoleon's cabinet in 1805 and 1806. Governor of Berlin and Prussia, he replaced Bernadotte in 1807 as Minister of War. Gd Aigle LH, Peer of France, Minister of War instead of Soult in March 1815, he followed the King to Gand and was made a Marshal of France in 1816.

As his aide de camp there was:

Henry Count of Turenne was Napoleon's Chamberlain and Master of the Wardrobe until 1814. He was wounded at Austerlitz. He refused to serve the King. A peer during the Hundred Days, struck off and then reinstated in 1831.

Above, from left to right and top to bottom. **General Clarke; the future Count of Lobau, Mouton; Rapp; Napoleon's aide de camp at Austerlitz and Girardin d'Ermenonville, Berthier's aide de camp.**
(RR)

Gardane. Born in Marseilles, he commanded the 9th Chasseurs in 1796. General in 1799, Equerry cavalcadour to the Emperor in 1804, he was Governor of the Pages. He was at Austerlitz, Jena and Eylau. Appointed Ambassador to Persia in 1807, he was made a Count in 1808. He was with Masséna in Portugal and was suspended for not having carried out his mission properly; he was re-instated in 1814. He went over to Napoleon in 1815. Retired the same year, he died in 1818. He is not to be confused with General Gardane who was with Masséna in Italy.

Durosnel, a Scottish Gendarme in 1763, commanded the 16th Chasseurs in 1799 and became Equerry cavalcadour to Napoleon in 1801. He was with Milhaud at Austerlitz and was made a General in 1805. He was with Lasalle in 1807 and was made a Count in 1808, Equerry in Spain, and Napoleon's aide de camp in 1809 and Governor of the Pages. He was wounded and taken at Essling. He commanded the Gendarmes d'Elite in Russia, was aide de camp during the Hundred Days. He was put on the non-active list in 1815 and retired in 1806. He was elected Deputy and re-elected. He was Louis-Philippe's aide de camp in 1832 and GdCxLH, Peer of France in 1837. He died in 1849.

Defrance was a Colonel in the 12th Chasseurs and Equerry to Napoleon, whilst keeping the command of his regiment which was with Vialannes and therefore no present at Austerlitz. He was with Gudin, near Vienna. He was appointed General in 1805 and commanded the Carabiniers.

Thiard. An émigré with the army of Condé, he returned to France in 1801. Napoleon's Chamberlain, he succeeded in getting the alliance with Saxony. Exiled until 1809, he defended Paris in 1814 and was elected Deputy in 1815. Maréchal de camp, he lost Royal favour as he was implicated with Didier's Bonapartist conspiracy in Grenoble in 1816. He was elected Deputy again in 1820.

BERTHIER'S HEADQUARTERS

Major-General Berthier, the Prince of Neuchatel had the following aide de camps:

Girardin d'Ermenonville, the son of the Marquis: officer cadet in the Navy in 1790. He went over to the cavalry in 1793. He was Berthier's aide de camp in 1803 then appointed Colonel in the 8th Dragoons. Wounded at Friedland, Baron in 1808, Count in 1810, he was appointed General in 1811, went to Russia, Major-General in 1814. He served with Grouchy in 1815, GdOLH in 1825, he died in 1855. He was very brilliant at Austerlitz: sent to Thiébault, he took part in the whole of the battle against Kamenski's troops, then on the dykes and the lakes.

Edouard de Colbert-Chabanais. He was a volunteer in the William Tell Battalion, then in the 3rd Dragoons; he went to Upper Egypt and became Berthier's aide de camp in 1805. Wounded at Austerlitz and mentioned in the report, he became a Colonel with the 7th Hussars in 1806. General in 1809, he was at Raab and was wounded at Wagram. He went to Holland and became a Colonel in the 2nd Lancers of the Guard. He took part in the Russian Campaign, was appointed Major-General in 1813. He was brilliant during the whole of the French Campaign and Waterloo. Wounded at Quatre-Bras, he charged at Waterloo. Inspector of Cavalry; GdOLH in 1828, he was wounded by Fieschi's bomb in 1835. He served in Africa, GdCxLH in 1837. he went into the Reserve Corps and died in 1853.

Lejeune. Born in Strasbourg, volunteer in 1792 at the Compagnie des Arts in Paris, engineering assistant, he was also a famous military painter. Second-Lieutenant in the Sappers in 1797, Berthier's aide de camp in 1800, he was made a Battalion Commander after Austerlitz; he took part in the siege of Danzig. Wounded at Saragossa with Lacoste, Colonel in 1809; he took part at Essling, Wagram. Baron, he was captured in Spain, wounded and his escort killed. He was sent to England and freed in 1811. He served in Russia with Berthier. He designed the new uniform for the Major-General's aide de camps. He replaced Romoeuf as chief of staff to Davout. General in 1812, he was at Dennewitz, Hanau and retired in 1813. He was with Harispe in Spain in 1823, GdOLH in 1841, died in 1814.

Dalton. Born in Brive. Hoche's aide de camp in

Above, left to right: **the first Aide-Major-General Andréossy and General Reille.**
(RR)

1795, he became aide de camp to Berthier in 1800 and then he was with the 5th Dragoons. Adjutant-Commandant with Berthier in 1805, he took part in Austerlitz and was mentioned in the report. Colonel of the 59th at Jena, he was also at Eylau and Friedland? General in 1809, he was with Morand in Russia. He was seriously wounded at Smolensk, and allowed to return to France. Commanded Ehrfurt in 1813, besieged and surrendered in May 1814 with the honours of war. He returned on half pay. He served during the Hundred Days, was then placed on the non-active list. Lieutenant-General in 1821, he served in Africa in 1831, GdOLH in 1833, retired in 1848. He died in 1848.

Le Camus, Baron of Monlignon, called 'Camus'. Volunteered in 1792, he served in the headquarters of the Army of the Rhine. He was with Berthier from 1802 and was in command of the headquarters. He went over to Mortier on 7 November 1805. General in 1806, he came back to Berthier as Assistant-Major-General. He was in Spain, wounded in 1813; he served in Champagne in 1814 with Victor then Gérard. Wounded in the knee at Craonne, he was put on the non-active list. He was pensioned off in 1825. He was not at Austerlitz on 2 December 1805.

Bailly de Monthion was Turreau's aide de camp from 1793 to 1796. He was on the Grande Armée's staff in 1805, at Ulm, Hollabrünn and at Austerlitz. He was mentioned in the report, Adjutant-Commandant under Pannetier at Heislberg and Friedland. Governor of Tilsitt. He was with Murat in Spain, made a Baron and assistant to the Major-General in 1809. He followed Murat to Berlin and to Russia; Major-General in 1812, he replaced Berthier after his departure with the Emperor and became assistant Chief of Staff again in 1813. He was a Peer of France in 1833, GdCxLH in 1843 and retired in 1848.

Charles Louis le Lièvre, Comte de la Grange, wounded at Marengo, aide de camp to Berthier on 12 September 1805; he was Squadron Commander of the 9th Hussars at Eylau. He was in Madrid in 1808, at Eckmühl, at Regensburg. He was sent to parley at Vienna, he was wounded. He served at Essling and Wagram and became the Emperor's Equerry and Count in 1810. General in 1812, he was in Russia with the Valence Cuirassiers. He was mentioned in despatches at Hanau, took part in the French Campaign, fought at Laon and at la Fère-Champenoise. Lieutenant-General in 1814, Peer of France in 1832, GcOLH in 1836, he was pensioned in 1848; Senator in 1859, he died in 1864.

Charles-Eugène de Montesquiou-Fézensac, aide de camp to Berthier, he was appointed on December 1804 as aide de camp to Davout (like his brother Anatole-Augustin, the future General, faithful companion of Louis-Philippe). Napoleon's ordnance Captain in 1806, LH in 1807, he was made a baron then Chamberlain to the Emperor in 1801. Colonel in the 13th Chasseurs in Spain, he was killed at Ciudad-Rodrigo, 12 December 1810.

Talleyrand-Périgord, Louis, aide de camp, Squadron Commander in 1807, died in Berlin of fever in 1808, mentioned in the report.

Talleyrand-Périgord, Alexandre, Edmond, Duc de Dino: Cavalry Lieutenant in 1805, also mentioned at Austerlitz. He was captured in Russia and returned in 1814, the year he was appointed General. He was disgraced by Napoleon during the Hundred days; Lieutenant-General in Spain in 1823, CrLH in 1831. A gambler, he had married Dorothée de Biron, the very beautiful Princess of Courlande. After ten years with her husband, she became the Duke of Benevent's good genius and lived with him in England for four years. She played an important role in Vienna. After the death of the Prince, she took the title of Duchess of Talleyrand, then after the death of her sister, that of princess of Sagan in 1845.

These two officers both charged on the Russian infantry with the Cavalry of the Guard. Louis wrote on 3 December: *"I'm at last happy: this morning I took part in a good bayonet charge, then I was under fire; in the evening we charged, Edmond and myself with a squadron of the Guard; we were welcomed by grapeshot at thirty paces and enemy infantry. We took it very well and then we worked on it. Edmond was his usual quiet self."*

De Noailles, Alfred, son of the former member of the Assembly who died in Cuba in 1804. Seconded to Berthier's Staff, he was mentioned in despatches.

The first Aide-Major-General was **Andréossy**, born at Castelnaudary, First-lieutenant in the artillery in 1784. He was commander of the bridge crews in Italy in 1796. He was at Arcola, General in 1797.

He went to Egypt and was Berthier's Deputy in 1805, mentioned in the report. Count in 1809 and Gd Aigle LH, Deputy in 1827.

His aide de camp was **Guérin**, Artillery School, Andréossy's Deputy and his aide de camp in Egypt, Battalion Commander in 1804, LH, killed by a cannonball in front of Neiss in 1807.

Andréossy had a Deputy, d'**Hastrel de Rivedoux**, a great friend of General Guyot. He was born in Canada, gentleman cadet in 1781 with Army of the Rhine then in the Army of the West. He was brigade commander with Masséna in Zurich, Adjutant-Commandant under Andréossy with the General Staff. He did not hold his boss in high esteem and wrote to his friend: *"My General is a confirmed thief, whose principal concern is himself, not even thinking of me. If he was given any money he'd keep it and once again I would miss the opportunity to get make my fortune!"*

The second Aide-Major-General was **Mathieu Dumas**, an aristocrat, son of a treasurer of France. Second-Lieutenant in 1780, he was Lafayette's aide de camp in 1789. He brought back Louis XVI back from Varennes, was made Maréchal du Camp in 1791. Deputy then President of the Legislative Assembly, threatened in 1792, he escaped to Switzerland and came back after 9 Thermidor. Elected to the Conseil des Anciens, outlawed on 19 Fructidor, he left for Hamburg and returned after 18 Brumaire Chief of Staff to Davout in 1804, Major-General in 1805, he was the second Aide-Major-General in September 1805. He was at Ulm, Elchingen, Austerlitz where he was mentioned in despatches. He was sent to Naples in 1806, became Minister of War under Joseph Bonaparte and followed him to Madrid. Deputy Chief of Staff in 1809 with Berthier, he was at Essling and Wagram. He was made a Count and Intendant-General of the Grande-Armée in 1812. He was with Prince Eugène until 1813. He was captured at Leipzig and returned in 1814. Councillor of State, he served during the Hundred Days, pensioned in 1815. Deputy for Bernay, re-elected in 1830, he was made a Peer of France in 1831. Blind, he died in 1837.

The deputies were **Pannetier**, Comte de Valdotte. Volunteered in the Ain in 1791, wounded and appointed Captain at Rivoli, he was Adjutant-Commandant in 1801, Berthier's Deputy in 1805, and in command at Brünn. He was mentioned for his work with the wounded. CtLH, Count 1808, captured at Baylen, he was returned. In 1814, he was ordered to take 10 000 men to Lyon. Lieutenant-General with Suchet in the Army of the Alps, he retired in 1825 and again in 1834.

Reilles was born at Antibes, volunteered in the 2nd Var then aide de camp to Masséna at Toulon. Mentioned in Switzerland, he was Squadron Commander and succeeded in getting to Genoa to join up with Masséna. General in 1803, the Major-General's Deputy on 17 September 1805; on 7 November, he replaced Valhubert at the head of the second brigade of Suchet's Division. Valhubert took over the third brigade of the Division. After Austerlitz, he took Becher's place in 1806 and commanded the 34th and 40th regiments. He was promoted Major-General and Chief of Staff of the 5th Corps. He was at Ostrolenka, then returned to Masséna on 24th February 1807. Appointed aide de camp to Napoleon on 13 May 1807, Couronne de Fer, Count in 1808 with numerous endowments. He was at Girone, and then retur-

Napoleon and his staff during the battle of Austerlitz: staff officers, orderlies, aide de camps, Generals and Marshals. The Emperor never moved around without a real cohort of people ready to transmit his orders to all the fighting troops. (© RMN)

THE EMPEROR HOUSEHOLD ON CAMPAIGN

When Campaigning, Napoleon established his quarters according to the circumstances. In big towns, it would be in a real castle, but on the battlefield, he could pitch a tent or just as easily occupy a tumbledown building. This was the case at Austerlitz.

The tent was made up of two communicating parts, the bedroom and the office. The sides were double and between them there was a sort of corridor which served as store room. This corridor was occupied by the valet and the Mameluke and where the luggage, the mattresses and the leather bags for the tents were left there during the day. The little metal bed was six-feet long, three wide and four high. Its metal structure was very light being made of steel rods which could be adjusted very precisely. They were slipped into two leather sheathes. Green silk curtains covered the bed. Small folding items of furniture were used in the office. Everything was foldable and wrapped up in leather bundles which were carried by mules.

At Austerlitz, there is doubt about where exactly the Emperor's camp was situated. Some talk about a tent; others about accommodation being found in the inn in Kandia. This fact is still carved on a low rafter. It would seem that the tent mentioned was nothing else than a little cabin made up by the Sappers of the Guard on the hillock at Zuran a round cabin with an opening in the centre of the roof enabling a fire to be lit called the *'Emperor's Hillock'*. But just next door there is the Kandia barn where, carved on a rafter, is the statement that Napoleon spent three days there. This barn was no doubt arranged by the sappers so that meals could be taken; they had made a big table. It was there that they had supper on 1 December, and so well described de Ségur. Zuran (287 m above sea-level) corresponds well with the spot from where the Emperor would have the sort of overall view of everything that he would want.

Napoleon says that he slept on straw for three nights. Constant was Surprised that there was no tent for the Emperor. He had not been able to set up the normal metal bed; he put a bearskin over the straw and worried about whether it was good enough. In 1809, according to Heudelet and Slovak, it was here that Napoleon made a small pilgrimage with his secretary Mounier and Captain de Galbois, Berthier's aide de camp. For other witnesses, especially Marbot and his friend Massy [1] who had come up to bring him the flags captured by d'Augereau's Corps, the Emperor had slept during the nights preceding the battle on straw in a barn, maybe that of the inn, or in his cabin. This is what Napoleon himself said: *"I slept on straw for three nights"*. This is also what Constant reported. Some insist that he slept in his 'sleeping' carriage where he could work and where he could shelter if it rained. On the night of 1 December, he slept, at last, in a bed in the castle of the lords of Konice, at Austerlitz. He slept in the bed where Alexander had slept on the previous night. De Ségur described supper with the Emperor on the evening of 1 December, before the battle and spoke of a tumbledown building or a barn. His description of this supper is very precise, describing the role of Junot who had just arrived from Lisbon, giving news of literature and the theatres from Paris, which led Napoleon to talk about Corneille, finishing by *"you have to want to live and know how to die."* The Emperor evoked his mirage of the East and his failure at St-John of Acre.

_____

(1) Massy was born in Corrèze like Marbot. He was wounded as a young Captain, he was wounded twice more in Italy. He became d'Augereau's aide de camp like Marbot in 1803. Major in the 44th, he was mentioned in despatches at Eylau and became Colonel in the 4th of the Line in 1811. He was killed at the Moskova.

ned to Essling, he commanded the Fusiliers and the Grenadiers of the Guard at Wagram, in support of MacDonald if needed. He was then sent on a mission to Antwerp to watch Bernadotte's behaviour which was become suspicious. Governor of Navarra and then of Aragon, he was at Vittoria, then Toulouse. GdCxLH in 1815 and Peer of France, he fought at Waterloo. He was decorated by Bernadotte with GdCx of the Order of Seraphims of Sweden (the suspect decorating his watcher?); he was a peer again in 1819, appointed Gentleman of the King's Bedchamber. He was made Marshal of France in 1847, Military Medal. He married Masséna's daughter. He died in 1860.

Comte de Montholon-Sémonville, son of the Marquis, employed on the General Staff on 17 September, mentioned in the report on Austerlitz, LH. Commanding Officer of the Squadrons and Berthier's aide de camp in 1807, he was Adjutant-Commandant in 1809, Napoleon's Chamberlain after Wagram. He was appointed Maréchal de camp in 1814 and left with Napoleon for St-Helena. Struck off the officers' list, dismissed without pension when he returned, he was reinstated as Maréchal de camp in 1830. He took part in the second plot led by Louis-Napoleon Bonaparte in 1840. Imprisoned in the Fort of Ham, sentenced to twenty years, disgraced and deprived of his titles and decorations, he was pardoned in 1846. Elected Deputy in 1849, he was made a General in 1853, the year of his death.

Bœrnere, born in Swabia, soldier in 1780, brigade commander at Saint Domingo in 1797, he returned in 1799. He was on the General Staff on 29 September 1805, entrusted with the problem of the prisoners. He was mentioned in the report on the battle. CtLH, General in Westphalia, he served in Spain. Maréchal de camp in 1814 in France, he was pensioned off. Chevalier d'Empire, naturalised in 1817, he died in 1829.

Sarraire, Captain at Genoa in 1800. He joined the General Staff on 17 September 1805, mentioned in the report. LH in 1807, Baron, he commanded a regiment of Puthod's Division at Wagram where he was wounded. He was Colonel of the 8th Light in Illyria where he died in 1810.

René, Lieutenant at the siege of Toulon, Sabre of Honour at Rivoli, he left for Egypt. He was appoin-

ted General in 1801. CtLH, the Major-General's Deputy in October 1805, he was sent to take command at Augsburg on 11 October, so he was not at Austerlitz. Taken by Spanish guerrillas he was burnt alive in a cauldron of boiling oil in 1808.

Blein was an engineer in the Ponts et Chaussées then Battalion Commander in 1799 with the Army of the Rhine. Attached to Berthier's staff he was at Austerlitz and mentioned in the after-battle report, he was promoted to Colonel after the battle. He was at Jena, Somo-Sierra and Madrid, he returned to Austria where he was wounded twice. He was present at Vienna, Essling, Wagram and Znaim. He went to Russia with Oudinot, made a General in 1813 and served during the French Campaign, CtLH, pensioned in August 1815. He was seriously wounded by Fieschi's bomb in 1832, GdLH in 1837, he died in 1845.

Dufresne, Aide-Commissaire in 1792, was Deputy of the Commissioner for War, then Commissaire First Class in 1795 in Italy. LH, he was sub-inspector for reviews, third class, attached to the Major-General in Austria. He was OLH after Austerlitz, second class and then first class in 1807. He was appointed Inspector in 1809. Baron, in Spain, he then went over to the Gendarmerie in 1815. He died in 1818.

Mergez, with the 9th Hussars in 1793, he was aide de camp to Bernadotte in 1799, Deputy on Berthier's staff in 1804, mentioned in the report on Austerlitz. He left for Spain and then was sent to the 2nd Cavalry Corps in Russia. Wounded several times at Winkowo he was captured and returned in 1814; he served in 1815 and was put on the non-active list, pensioned in 1823 as Honorary Maréchal de Camp. He was reinstated in 1830 and finally retired with all his entitlements in 1832.

Parigot, Captain in the 2nd of the Line, was a Deputy on Berthier's staff in 1805. Adjudant-Commandant in 1807, retired as Honorary Maréchal de camp in 1823.

Pascal-Vallongue was an engineer in the Ponts et Chaussées, Battalion Commander in the Engineers. He went to Egypt was made prisoner at Aboukir. Held for four months in a Greek jail, he was freed thanks to Sidney Smith. Colonel in the engineers with Sanson and Andréossy, he was entrusted with the details of the General Staff on 21 September 1805. Mentioned in the report, he was appointed General after Austerlitz. He was killed at the siege of Gaete in 1806.

In Berthier's report published by J. Garnier, there were a lot of 'adjoints' (deputies) and aide de camps mentioned for their action like **Salley, Chateau, Ducondras, Deschales, Alfred de Noailles, Rosily** and **Valmabelle.** He also mentioned Lieutenant **Belle** of the 21st Dragoons, in command of the Elite Company who was on duty at Headquarters. The Elite Company charged towards Telnitz and took some prisoners, Belle having no doubt followed Gardane. There were also two Bavarian Lieutenant-Colonels (**Pocci** and **Daubert**) and a Wurtemberger, Captain Spitzamberg. Berthier finished his praises by evoking the devotion of the Medical Service where Percy and Larrey were especially singled out.

Percy was born at Montmagney-les Pesmes. He was much admired for his many qualities; he was the inventor of the 'wurst' which was not as successful as expected. He only wanted surgeons, leaving the doctors for the civilians. During operations he was much more for keeping limbs if possible than Larrey. GrLH, full of honours, the author of many learned papers, he was elected to the Académie des Sciences. As his sight was deteriorating, he left the army in 1809, and came back to teaching. During the Hundred days, he joined Napoleon and was elected Deputy. After Waterloo he retired to Meaux where he wrote; he died in 1827. He was mentioned for his untiring activity at Austerlitz.

Larrey, trained at Toulouse and then Paris, Baron and CtLH; he transformed the idea of the 'wurst' into flying ambulances which could go

Above, from left to right.
Marbot and Larrey, Surgeon-Commander in the Guard. *(RR)*

as near as possible and pick up the wounded. He 'invented' the techniques of quick and well-ordered amputations which saved so many lives. The fact that there was no real anaesthetic was the justification for the rapidity of his operations. Some soldiers who lost an arm went straight off into battle afterwards. Berthier mentioned him as the Surgeon-Commander of the Guard who was as untiring as Percy, operating on friend and foe alike. Napoleon said of him that he was the most virtuous man that he had ever met; Wellington doffed his hat to him when he saw him passing and declared: "I salute Honour when it passes."

Costes was born near Bellegarde in the Ain, trained in Paris, a friend of Voltaire who was his friend. He was a doctor in Nancy. He fought the greed of the intendants who fed the soldiers so badly. First Doctor in Rochambeau's Corps in America, Mayor of Versailles in 1790, he worked with Berthier. He created military hospitals. Dismissed in 1806 by Napoleon who preferred surgeons, he had to wait for the Restoration to get back into the Medical Service. He re-opened the Val de Grace Hospital. He was CrLH and Chevalier of Saint-Michel. He died in 1819.

Berthier also mentioned **Tabarie** and **Gérard,** divisional commanders at the Ministry of War who did the utmost to help the wounded with General Pannetier who commanded so well at Brünn.

THE ADMINISTRATION

Daru was born in Montpelier. Second-Lieutenant, he resigned to enter the Administration. Commissioner for War in 1789, he was saved by 9 Thermidor. He put order into the Ministry of War with Petiet, the Inspector of Reviews. He was a General Secretary who revealed his great talents, relieving Berthier of all the administrative part, leaving him to bite his nails with the military part. Taken to Italy by Bonaparte, he remained very much attached to him. LH, Councillor of State, Intendant-General of the Military Household and of the Civil List in 1805. He became Intendant-General of Austria after Austerlitz, recovering the stipulated indemnities. When Petiet died, he became Intendant-General of the Grande Armée, member of the Institut and Councillor of State. After Tilsitt, he was Plenipotentiary to Prussia levying the 150 million-worth of indemnities, and then he followed the 1809 Campaign until Wagram. Replaced by Mathieu Dumas in 1812 in Russia, he recovered his position because his successor had fallen ill in Moscow. He was invalided out of the Army in 1813; Senior Administrator of the Army, Minister and Secretary of State, Minister of the Army Administration in place of Lacuée de Cessac, he followed the Empress to Blois in 1814. He was with the Ministry of War during the Hundred Days. In 1816, he was made a member of the Académie Française, then Peer of France in 1819. He was against the war with Spain in 1823 and he denounced the scandals of the *Ouvrard tenders*. Intendant-General of the King's Armies, he was able to give full rein to his love of literature and poetry. He wrote a history of Venice, one of Brittany but his death on 5 September 1829, interrupted his work on the history of the Vendée. Napoleon said of him: *"He allies the work of the oxen with that of the lion"*.

Petiet, Commissioner for War in 1774, he defended Nantes. Minister of War in 1796, he was dismissed in 1979 and became Councillor of State in 1799. Intendant in Boulogne, Ulm and Austerlitz. CtLH, he was made GdOLH and Senator in 1806 and he died six days later of exhaustion.

The Emperor's cabinet was divided into the inner cabinet, next to the bedroom where Napoleon could work alone and the outside cabinet where he received his visitors and the members of his secretariat.

General Clarke was at the head of the secretariat in 1805. He was helped by two former aide de camps: Curvier-Fleury who was Councillor of State under Louis-Bonaparte and Tourné who died in St-Domingo. The secretary of the so-called "Portfolio" was Meneval.

Meneval was chosen to replace **Bourienne (Fauvelet de)** whom Napoleon had dismissed after the so-called Coulon Brothers' affair who had dragged Bourienne down with them when they went bankrupt. Sent to Hamburg, Bourienne (with his personal secretary Enoch) decided to make Bernadotte's fortune with the help of Gérard. He did not forget himself either, on the way. Meneval was Joseph Bonaparte's secretary and held his post until exhausted by the return from Moscow, he was obliged to leave the job, becoming the *"secretary of Marie-Louise's Commands"*.

Beside this first secretary there was **Baron Fain**, the *"archiving secretary"* trained in the Secretariat of State under the Directoire to be Lagarde's cabinet secretary, and seconded to Maret. Fain was made a Baron in 1809, then CtLH in 1811, Master of Requests in the Council of State. He took over from Meneval in 1812. He was recalled by Louis-Philippe in 1830, he wrote his manuscripts and his memoirs which are very precious and useful. He was elected Deputy in 1834, re-elected in 1836. His son remained Louis-Philippe's secretary.

The valets are **Constant** (Constant Wiry called **'Constant'**) was born in Belgium. He was entrusted by his father who was an innkeeper in Saint-Amand les Eaux to the Marquis de Lure who was emigrated. Constant was abandoned and was brought to Paris by Squadron Commander Micheau and placed as a clerk with Gobert. He got a job with Eugène de Beauharnais; then moved over to work for Napoleon in 1800 where he stayed until 1814. After the abdication, he deserted taking silver and jewels with him. Ruined, he got his wife to be granted the Post Office at Breteuil sur Iton in the Eure. He died in 1845.

Roustam was a Georgian offered to Bonaparte by the Bey in Cairo (with another called Ali who was very quickly eliminated); he would sleep in front of Napoleon's door and his role was essentially ceremonial. After the attempt to poison Napoleon at Fontainebleau, he fled terrorised. Ugly rumours about his dreadful deeds were spread around. In 1824 he went to London to make a show of himself in order to earn some money. Louis-Philippe got him the post office at Dourdan. He died in 1845.

In 1811, Napoleon took on another Mameluke called **Saint-Denis** who became the one and only Mameluke after the departure of Roustam and who went to Elba and followed the Emperor to St-Helena where with his friend Marchand, he helped Napoleon as best he could, acting as his secretary. There he married the governess of the Bertrand children. He left very precious memoirs published in 18226.

*Above, from right to left. **Daru the (Quartermaster) Intendant-General of the Military Household and Constant, the Emperor's valet.** (RR)*

He was awarded the Légion d'Honneur by Napoleon III and installed in Sens where he died in 1846.

Thanks to these people who worked in the shadow of the great man, a lot about the way Napoleon worked is now known. He worked with extraordinary power and a fantastic sense of organisation. We also know how the secretaries took down letters dictated by the Emperor, copying them and classifying them as quickly as they could.

Mounier was the son of the former Assembly member who had become Prefet of Rennes and councillor of State and Napoleon supported him after the death of his father, taking him on as assistant secretary in 1809. He accompanied the Emperor who wanted to revisit the battlefield of Austerlitz. This fact was mentioned in Heudelet's memoirs. They were accompanied by Captain de Galbois, then on Berthier's staff.

De Galbois, Lieutenant in the 8th Hussars in 1804, he was with Berthier in 1808 and carried out several missions in Spain and Portugal. From 1812 to 1813 he was with Berthier. He was made a Colonel of the 12th Hussars, he was wounded at Quatre-Bras. Baron in 1813. Maréchal de camp in 1831, Lieutenant-General commanding at Constantine in 1838, GdOLH in 1839, he retired in 1848.

While there was a Campaign, there was an important person, the man in charge of surveying and maps. At Austerlitz, it was **Sanson**, a volunteer from the Tarn, a Captain of Engineers in 1793. Wounded four times in the Pyrenees, Battalion Commander in Italy, he fought at Rivoli and Mantua. He was in Egypt with Andréossy where he replaced Caffarelli as commanding officer of the Engineers. General in 1800, Sabre of Honour in 1802, CtLH, he was appointed director of the Surveying Department of the Grande Armée and served at Ulm and Austerlitz, Jena, Eylau, Heilsberg, Friedland. Major-General in 1807, Count in 1808, he retired in 1815.

With him was **Bacler d'Albe** born at St-Pol in the Pas de Calais. He was wounded at Lyon and Toulon; he was a painter and surveyor in Italy, chief of the Emperor's Topography section in 1804. Adjutant-Commandant in 1807, he followed Napoleon to Spain. He was made a Baron, then General in 1813, OLH. He was on the active list but retired in 1820.

Brousseaud was born in Limoges, Second-Lieutenant at the war depot, surveyor then Captain. Battalion and section commander of the Surveyors on the General Staff, he was wounded at Austerlitz. He continued in Prussia then was made a Colonel at The war depot in Paris. He was in Belgium in 1815, OLH in 1825 retired as Honorary Maréchal de camp in 1834 and CtLH. Grand Prize for Astronomy in 1839.

THE ARTILLERY GENERAL STAFF

Songis des Courbons, pupil in 1779, Battalion Commander in 1793, went to Italy then Egypt where he was in command of the artillery pool. General in 1799, Major-General in 1800, he commanded the artillery of the Grande Armée in 1805. He was Gd Aigle of LH, Couronne de Fer, Count. He returned to Paris for grounds of ill-health and was replaced by Lariboisière in June 1809. He died in 1810.His aide de camp was **Doguereau**, born in Orléans in 1774. After the School at Chalons, he left for Egypt and was made Songis' aide de camp in 1802 and Colonel in 1806. In Spain he was a Colonel and was in command at Pamplona. Captured in 1813, he returned in 1814. Appointed Maréchal de camp during the Hundred Days, he was revoked in 1815 and reinstated in 1821. He was Commanding Officer of the La Fère School until his death inv1826. CrLH in 1807, Baron then Viscount in 1825, he wrote the Diary of the Expedition to Egypt, published in 1904.

Pernety, Chief of Staff. Pupil in 1777, he was at Metz in 1782, then Captain in Italy where he took part at Arcola, Rivoli and Marengo in 1800. Appointed General in 1805, he was at Ulm, Austerlitz, Jena. Major-General in 1807, he commanded the artillery of Davout's 1st Corps in Russia. In 1813, he was present at Leipzig and Hanau. Viscount in 1817, he was Councillor of State, GdCxLH in 1821, Peer of France in 1835 and Senator in 1854.

Sénarmont was at the Metz School in 1784. Promoted to Captain in 1792 he was at Marengo. Deputy Chief of Staff of the Artillery in 1805, he was at Austerlitz. Promoted General in 1806, CtLH in 1807, Couronne de Fer and Baron in 1808, he was appointed Major-General in 1808. He was killed at Cadiz in 1810.

THE ENGINEERS GENERAL STAFF

Marescot was born at Tours, a pupil at La Flèche, he was at Mézières in 1778. Battalion Commander in 17983, he served at Toulon. He was made a brigadier then a Major-General in 1794. He was at the Fort du Bard and Marengo. First Inspector-General of the Engineers, Gd Aigle of LH in 1805, he was at Austerlitz. Captured at Baylen, made destitute and locked up in Paris, he was then exiled to Tours in 1812. He was made a Count with the Restoration and retired in 1815. He was made a Marquis in 1817, Peer of France in 1819, he died in 1832.

Andréossy, the brother of the aide de camp to Berthier began his career at Mezières. General of Engineers at Zurich, he was under the command of Marescot at Austerlitz and replaced him in 1806, CtLH, Baron, in command of Masséna's Engineers in 1804, he retired in 1814.

Above, from left to right. **Maréchal Bessières and his aide de camp Lieutenant Desmichels.** *(DR)*

THE IMPERIAL GUARD

Maréchal Bessières, Duke of Istria was born at Prayssac in the Lot Department. Captain of the National Guard in 1789, he went over the King's Guards in 1792. He was in the Pyrenees then in Italy where he was appointed Commander of the Guides in 1796. Promoted to Squadron Commander on the battlefield of Roveredo, mentioned at Rivoli, he took the flags taken from the enemy back to Paris. He was brigade commander in Egypt. Upon his return, he took part in 18 Brumaire. He commanded the Grenadiers à Cheval of the Guard at Marengo. Commander in Chief of the cavalry of the Guard in 1801, he was made a Marshal and Gd Aigle of the LH in 1805. He was at Austerlitz and Jena, and commanded the Guard in 1807. He charged at Eylau, he was also at Friedland. He received the highest decorations from Saxony, Wurtemberg, and Portugal. He won at Medina de Rio Seco, Somo Sierra, and Madrid. He returned to Austria and was at Essling; he was wounded at Wagram. He commanded the cavalry of the Guard in Russia and the whole Guard in 1813. He was killed by a cannonball near Weissenfels on 1 May 1813. His younger brother was a Colonel in the 11th Chasseurs and was wounded at Austerlitz.

His aide de camps were **César de Laville de Villa-Stellone**, born in Turin. His left hand was hurt in front of Verona in 1799; he became Berthier's aide de camp in 1805, Equerry to the King of Holland. He returned to his job with Bessières in 1809, followed him as Colonel then General in 1812. Appointed Ney's Chief of Staff (OLH), he was with Davout at Hamburg and served with him in 1815. He was put on the non-active list and then retired in 1848.

Lebrun was the third son of the Consul. Second-Lieutenant with the 5th Dragoons, he became aide de camp to Bessières in 1802. He was at Naples in 1803, aide de camp to Bernadotte with the 1st Corps in 1805 and was made a Captain at Austerlitz. He was Squadron Commander in 1807 with the 3rd Cuirassiers then aide de camp to Berthier in 1808. He commanded the 3rd Chevau-Légers in 1812 in Russia. He was killed by a biscayen bullet in October of the same year.

D'Oullembourg was born at Landau the son of a baron. First aide de camp, this Captain of the 11th Chasseurs was wounded in 1793. He was with Bessières in 1805. Colonel of the 1st dragoons in 1806, he was wounded again at Jena. General in 1807 (4th and 14th dragoons), he was at Friedland. He was with Doumerc in 1811. He was in Russia and was made CtLH in 1814. He was promoted to Honorary

Lieutenant-General in 1817 on his retirement.

Louis de Seganville was born at Lavaur in the Tarn. A Guide in 1796, aide de camp to Bessières in 1800, he was made a Colonel in 1808. Baron in 1810, OLH in 1813 and commanded the 2nd Hussars. He fought in the Jura then was elected Deputy. He was retired after the Hundred Days and was pensioned as Honorary Maréchal de camp in 1823.

Leinsteinschneider was born at Sarrelouis, volunteered in 1791, Italy in 1796 with the 1st Hussars. He was appointed Squadron Commander and Bessières' aide de camp in 1805. He took part in the Spanish Campaigns then in Russia and became Chief of Staff of the Cavalry of the guard then Adjudant-Commandant in 1813. OLH, he died in Mainz in 1813.

Desmichels was born at Digne Guide in Italy, he then fought in Egypt was then appointed Second-Lieutenant with the Chasseur à cheval of the Guard in 1803 and finally Lieutenant in 1805. He was an orderly with Bessières at Austerlitz and described the great charge of the Guard, mentioning the merits of the Marshal. Captain and OLH in 1806, he was made Colonel of the 31st Chasseurs in 1811. He was with the 4th Chasseurs at Waterloo. Sacked from 1815 to 1821, he was reinstated and appointed Maréchal de camp in 1823. He was made CtLH in 1826, then Lieutenant-General in 1835, then Baron.

Lapeyrière was born at Cahors. He was with Bessières in 1804 and at Austerlitz. He was a Captain at Eylau. He was in Spain and in Russia with the Marshal. He was appointed Squadron Commander and Chevalier in 1812. After Bessières death, he was in Saxony and France with the 11th Chasseurs. He served in 1815 and was put on half-pay until his death in 1831.

Barbanègre was the brother of the General. He was in the Pyrenees in 1793, in Italy with the 22nd Chasseurs and was wounded seven times in front of Cremona. He was at Arcola and Rivoli. He went to Egypt and was made a Lieutenant with Bonaparte's Guides. Captain with the Grenadiers à Cheval of the Guard, he was awarded the Sabre of Honour at Marengo. Bessières' aide de camp in 1800, he was mentioned at Austerlitz. He was appointed Colonel of the 9th Hussars after the battle on 27 December 1805. OLH, he was killed at Jena and embalmed at Napoleon's request in order to make a statue for the Concorde Bridge project. He was finally buried at Pontacq.

THE ARTILLERY

Couin, an artilleryman in 1780, was wounded at Nancy in 1787, Captain in 1792. he served in Vendée, then in the Pyrenees, then in Italy where, as Squadron Commander, he was in charge the artillery. After Austerlitz, he was appointed General commanding the Artillery of the Guard and CtLH. He was at Tudela with the 9th Corps in 1810 then with the 4th Corps with Drouet in Portugal and finally with Prince Eugène's Corps in Russia. He was in Champagne in 1814 and retired in the same year. He died in 1834

De Pommereul commanded the pool at Austerlitz. He served in the Kingdom of the Two Sicilies as a Colonel on 1787. He returned to service with France as a General in 1796, became Prefet and Councillor of State then Baron in 1810 and finally Director of the Printing Press and the Library. He was made a Major-General in 1811 and named Governor at La Fère. He surrendered in 1814 and retired in 1816.

Louis Doguereau was born at Dreux in 1777. A Pupil at the School at Chalons, he was on the Rhine then in Egypt. He served with the mounted artillery of the Guard at Marengo, LH. He was appointed Squadron Commander in 1803, Major in 1806 then Colonel in 1807. He was wounded in Spain, made a Baron and resigned in 1811. Recalled in 18113, he was appointed Maréchal de camp during the Hundred Days and commanded the artillery of the 3rd Corps in Belgium. Put on the active list, he was appointed Commandant of the School at Metz in 1816, then Douai in 1831. GdOLH, Lieutenant-General in 1832, Deputy in 1837, re-elected in 1839 and 1842, he was made GdCxLH in 1843, Peer of France in 1845. His elder brother was on Bessières' staff.

Jean-Pierre Doguereau, brother of the above was born in 1774 at Orléans. He was at the School at Chalons then went on the Rhine and Egypt, OLH. He was Songis' aide de camp at Austerlitz and Colonel in 1806. He was in Prussia and Poland (CtLH in 1807) then Spain. He was captured at Pamplona in 1813 and returned in 1814. He was appointed Maréchal de camp in 1821, Hereditary Baron in 1822 and finally Viscount in 1825. He commanded the School at La Fère until his death in 1823. He was the author of the Diary of the Expedition to Egypt, published only in 1904.

The following artillery officers were also present.

Chapuis: one of the regiment's children. With the 5th regiment of 'Dismounted' Artillery, a paid gunner in 1780 he took part in the Campaign of Italy. He was at Mantua and promoted to Sergeant in 1799. He was wounded three times; he was awarded a Grenade of Honour in 1803. In Austria in 1805, appointed First-Lieutenant in 1809, Captain in 1812 in Russia. He fought at Danzig in 1813 and was captured. He returned in 1814 and remained at Verdun until 1837, when he retired. He was entrusted with the

Court Martial and the medical Councils.

Joblot was a gunner with the 7th Foot artillery and with the 4th Mounted in 1797, received a Sabre of Honour in 1804. He was Adjudant Second-Lieutenant with the 7th bis artillery train; he was at Ulm and Austerlitz and was made a Lieutenant in 1806. He took part at Wagram, and in the Russian, Saxon and French Campaigns with the 4th squadron of the artillery train. He remained loyal to the King in 1815 and was appointed Squadron Commander in 1817. He retired in 1824.

Molard was child of the Regiment, paid in 1774 at Toul-Artillery. He was awarded a Grenade of Honour in 1803, for Kehl and Hohenlinden. He was a Lieutenant in 1804, was present at Jena, Friedland. He was a Captain in Russia. OLH. He was made prisoner I, 1812, returned in 1814 was active during the Hundred Days in the Rhine, he was pensioned off, then reinstated in 1831 then finally retired permanently in 1833.

Couin was born in 1763 and served in 1791. He was wounded at Arcola, then went to Egypt and commanded the artillery of the Guard in 11803. CtLH, General in 1806, Baron, he then commanded the cavalry's artillery reserve under Bessières at Wagram. He was in Portugal and Italy with Prince Eugène in 1812. He fought in Champagne with Grouchy, retired in 1814, then in 1832.

Couin was born in 1776, brother of the above. He went over to the Guard in 1801. LH. He was Senior Captain in the Mounted artillery of the Guard in 1806. He went to Spain and Portugal and Russia. He was Battalion Commander in the Artillery in 1813. OLH. He was mentioned during the French Campaign and was billeted in Lyons during the Hundred Days. He retired in 1824 with the honorary rank of Colonel.

Prinet was with the artillery train. He was awarded a Grenade of Honour in 1803. He was at Ulm and Austerlitz and was made Second-Lieutenant. He fought at Jena, Eylau and Friedland. He died in Spain in 1810.

Devarenne was born at Joigny, volunteered for the 5th du Pantheon; he was part of the Strasbourg teams in 1796. He was an Artillery Lieutenant of the Guard (LH) and served at Ulm, Austerlitz. He retired in 1806.

Digeon was a former pupil of the Chalons School and was with the 5th 'Dismounted' then Second-Lieutenant on the Rhine. He left for Egypt where he was wounded. On his return he entered the Guard and was mentioned at Marengo. He was appointed Senior Captain in 1802. OLH. Mentioned at Austerlitz, he also fought at Jena, Eylau where he commanded the pool. He took part in the Spanish Campaign from 1809 to 1813. Appointed General in 1814, he took part in the French Campaign. CrLH, he did not serve during the Hundred Days and was made a Baron in 1817. GdOLH in 1820, he died of a sudden stroke.

Fournier was a gunnery Sergeant in Italy with the 32nd; he fought at Arcola, Rivoli and in Egypt. He was wounded twice, was promoted to Captain and was awarded a sabre of Honour. OLH. After Austerlitz it was in Spain from 1808 to 1813 that he served. He was retired because of his wounds in 1813.

Lafont came from the School at Chalons. First he was a Lieutenant with the 4th à Cheval, he went over to the Mounted Artillery of the Guard in 1802. LH. He was at Ulm, Austerlitz where he was mentioned in despatches. Lafont was promoted to First Captain in 1806 and took part at Eylau, Friedland then Spain in 1808. He was mentioned at Wagram. He was made OLH and Baron of the Empire. He was present in Russia; he was made a Colonel in 1813. He was made prisoner in 1814 and resigned at the time of the Hundred Days. He became a Maréchal de camp in 1817; he was elected Deputy in 1830. CrLH in 1820.

Léglise was a gunnery Captain in the 26th Light, wounded at Austerlitz by a cannonball. He was made a Captain of the Grenadier of the Guard; he took part at Jena, Eylau and Friedland. He was promoted to Battalion Commander with the Fusilier-Grendaniers. Major Colonel of the Regiment, he was mentioned at Leipzig and became baron before Lutzen and Bautzen. CrLH in 1814. He was Maréchal de camp in Alsace in 1815. He was retired and reinstated in 1829, and finally retired in 1835.

Laurent. Chalons School, Captain second in command in the Pyrenees in 1796. He commanded the 1st 'Dismounted' Artillery Regiment. OLH. He served during the Hundred Days, became director of the Forges in 1816 and Maréchal de camp in 1824.

Faure de Giere was a pupil from Artillery School, then it was Italy and Egypt. He became Battalion Commander then Colonel of the 4th Mounted Artillery. LH and OLH, he was present at Austerlitz; mentioned at Wagram, he became a General in 1811 and served in Russia. He died from exhaustion after the retreat, in February 1813, in Berlin.

Aigouy, a gunner in the artillery company of the 'Homme Armé' section, he was wounded at Marengo defending the regimental flag for which he received a Rifle of Honour; lieutenant after Austerlitz, he was killed at Los Arapiles in 1812.

Boisselier was in the artillery in Italy in 1797; he went to Egypt and was present at Austerlitz, Eylau, Friedland and in Spain. He was mentioned in despatches and was made an OLH for Wagram. He was killed at Reims just after being appointed Colonel.

Carry was a volunteer from the Ain and was in the Guard's Mounted Artillery in 1805 at Austerlitz then at Jena. He was killed at Heilsberg on 10 June 1807.

Gendarmes d'élite à pied

Although the presence of the Gendarmes d'Elite at Austerlitz has not been confirmed, it can be assumed that some of them at least did guard duty around the General Staff Headquarters during the Campaign.

Drummer

Gendarme

André Jouineau © Histoire & Collections 2003

Digeon, officer from the Artillery of the Guard. *(RR)*

Laval was a Captain in the 1st Artillery (LH) and present at Austerlitz. He was an active Bonapartist in 1815 and served two years' prison at Nancy.

THE ENGINEERS

Boissonet was born in the Ardèche, went to the Mézières School fought at Toulon and in Italy, and at Mantua and the Fort du Bard. He was Battalion Commander in the Guard in 1803. OLH He was present at Austerlitz, Putulsk, Daneig, Eylau, Heilsberg and Friedland. He was Major Colonel of the Engineers of the Guard in Russia. He took part in 1813 at Lutzen, Bautzen, Dresden, Leipzig and Hanau before the French Campaign in 1814. He served during the Hundred Days. In 1815, he was sacked then recalled and finished as Honorary Maréchal de camp when he retired in 1824. He retired to Sézanne.

Among the officers present at Austerlitz, the following must be mentioned.
Deponthon. After the School at Metz and Egypt, he was promoted to Captain then ordnance officer to Napoleon in 1806. Mentioned at Austerlitz, he also fought at Jena and Stralsund and then carried out several missions in Russia and Spain. He was a General at Lutzen and Bautzen and commanded the Engineers at Hamburg. CrLH in 1821, he was promoted to Lieutenant-General in 1838 and GdOLH in 1844.

Label, Count of Mézières was born at Bernay. Captain. He came out of Polytechnique in 1796 and became Battalion Commander after Hohenlinden. In 1805, he organised the defence of Brünn, fought at Austerlitz, became a Colonel in Venice and commanded the garrison at Mantua. In 1809, he attacked Raab, fought at Wagram and was made a Baron before commanding St-Omer. OLH, he retired with the rank of Honorary Maréchal de camp in 1826. Cr LH in 1825.

Flayelle. This National Guardsman was a pupil at the Engineers School and became a Captain in 1793. He was at Toulon where he led three assaults against the English redoubt. Wounded, he was promoted to Battalion Commander. He led the main attack against Valenciennes in 1794, was sent to the Pyrenees. He asked to go on a course at the Metz School. He was with Berthier against the Fort du Bard and was awarded two pistols of Honour. He was present at Marengo (OLH), he was mentioned at Austerlitz. CtLH in 1809. He became a Baron and retired in 1822.

Mutel de Boucheville was born at Bernay, went to the Pont et Chaussées School and distinguished himself in Vendée. He was sent to Maubeuge, was wounded there and became battalion Commander in 1795. He was wounded on the Rhine, he fought at Zurich. LH. Member of the Committee of Engineers, he was at Austerlitz. Promoted to Chevalier of the Empire in 1809, he later organised the defence of Hamburg and that of other German towns. He was with the 11th Corps in Russia and became Honorary Maréchal de camp when he retired in 1815.

Above. **the Bivouac of the Guard on the eve of Austerlitz. The old soldiers watch over their 'little corporal's' sleep.** (DR)

THE INFANTRY

The Chief of Staff of the Guard was **Roussel** who served since 1770. He was Furrier to the 10th Dragoons in 1791 and General in the Army of the Rhine in 1799. CtLH in 1804, he was the Chief of Staff to Lefebvre in 1805 with the Guard. He was with Bessières in 1806, became General again in 1807. He died at Heilsberg.

The Grenadiers were under the command of **Hulin**. Enrolled in 1771 he became a Swiss Guard in 1779. Sacked in 1787, he took part in the taking of the Bastille and commanded the winners. In command of the Grenadiers of the Consular Guard, he became a General in 1803 and presided over the sentencing of the Duke of Enghien. He commanded Vienna in 1805, Berlin in 1806 and Paris from 1807 to 1804. He was made a Count in 1808 and was wounded by Malet in 1812. GdCX of the Réunion in 1813, rallied to the King in 1814, he was replaced by Andréossy. Retired in 1815 he was outlawed and went into exile in Holland. He returned in 1819 and died in 1841.

The Chasseurs were commanded by **Soules**. Born at Lectoure, enrolled in 1776, he was with the 51st of the Line, was mentioned at Dego, wounded at Castiglione and then at Arcola. He became Battalion Commander of the Chasseurs à pied in 1800 and won a Sabre of Honour fro Marengo. He was General commanding the regiment and CtLH in 18004. Peer of France in 1814, he did not serve during the Hundred Days. Soules voted for the execution of Ney.

The Italian Guard (one battalion of Grenadiers and one of Chasseurs) was commanded by **Colonel Lechi** who was a General in France's service in 1799. Major-General of a cisalpine division in 1800, he was revoked from the army of Naples for embezzlement. He served in Catalonia and was arrested for abuse of power and misappropriation of public funds. Called back by Murat, he served in Naples in 1813. He finished by fighting against France. He was CtLH and Chevalier of the Two Sicilies. He fought against the Austrians in 1815. He died of Cholera at Milan in 1836.

THE CAVALRY OF THE GUARD

The Grenadiers à Cheval of the Guard, these were the *'Black Horses'*, the *'Invicibles'* and were commanded by **Ordener** was a cavalryman in 1772 with the 4th Chasseurs. He was Squadron Commander in Italy at the battle of Lodi. He was wounded twelve times on 14 August 1799, in Switzerland. He commanded the Grenadiers à Cheval of the Guard from 1803, as their General and was ordered to go and fetch the Duke of Enghien. CtLH in 1804, he was seriously wounded at Austerlitz; he was promoted to Major-General after the battle. He became a Senator because of his wounds and obtained the position of First Equerry to the Empress. Count, Governor of the palace at Compiègne in 1809, he died in 1811.

Ordener, his son was a pupil from the School at Fontainebleau in 1803. He became a Second-Lieutenant with the 24th Dragoons then aide de camp to his father before becoming Duroc's in 11806. LH in 1805, he was Colonel of the 7th Cuirassiers, he was wounded at Polotsk, mentioned at the Beresina and took command of the 30th Dragoons in 1813, OLH the same year. He was wounded in the head at Waterloo. Maréchal de camp in 1831, Lieutenant-General in 1846 and GdOLH in 1848, he died in 1862.

Camille Borghèse, Prince and Duke of Guastalla. He married Pauline Bonaparte and was Gd Aigle LH in 1805, then Squadron Commander of the Grenadiers à Cheval of the Guard, Prince and Duke in 1806; then GdCx of the Couronne de Fer, Colonel of the 1st Carabiniers in 1807, then General in the same year. Promoted to Major-General in 1810, he commanded the reserve army of Italy in 1813. He surrendered in 1814 and handed over the Piemont to the Austrians, he left French service and returned home where he died in 1832.

Prince Aldobrandini Borghèse, the brother of Camille was also Squadron Commander of the Guard and served at Austerlitz and was no doubt with the Chasseurs à Cheval since it was there that a Borghèse was mentioned by some in the descriptions of the great charge, but there is still enough confu-

sion about this. Colonel of the 4th Cuirassiers in 1808, First Equerry of the Empress in 1810, he became a General in 1812 and Gd Cx of the Réunion in 1813. He was appointed Lieutenant-General without remuneration at his own request in 1830, and died in 1839.

Oulié was born at Cahors and was with the Champagne Cavalry Regiment from 1780 to 1783. Squadron Commander of the 22nd Chasseurs, he went over to the Grenadiers in 1799. He was decorated with the LH and appointed Major in 1804. CtLH in 1805. He was with the Army of the North in 1806 then became Colonel of the Gendarmerie in 1814, retired as Maréchal de camp and died in 1827.

Duclaux was born in the Lot. He was first of all a cavalryman with the 22nd Chasseurs in the Pyrenees; then became a Guide in 1796 then Lieutenant in Egypt where he was wounded at Heliopolis. He was in the Grenadiers à Cheval in 1802 and became Commander of the Squadrons in 1805. OLH, Baron in the years that followed, was at the Battle of Wagram as Colonel of the 11th Cuirassiers. He got a frozen nose in Russia, fought in Saxony, wounded at Leipzig, he was put in command of the Department of the Forests, then in the Meuse during the Hundred Days, retired in 1825.

Duvivier was born at Mons and fought with the 5th Hussars then went over to the 3rd Dragoons in Egypt; Second-Lieutenant with the Grenadiers à Cheval in 1802; First-Lieutenant in 1804, he was made Captain Adjutant-Major with the Polish Chevau-Légers in 1807. Wounded at Wagram, Major in 1811, he went to Russia where he was wounded. In 1813 he was a Colonel in 16th Chasseurs then the 3rd Hussars in 1814. He went into Dutch service and served with Wellington at Waterloo (8th Hussars). He was Lieutenant-General in Belgium in 1830, retired in 1842.

Blancard, the son of the Assembly member, served with the 11th Cavalry Regiment, recaptured the regiment's standards in 1793 and saved two cannon near Rome, but had his arm broken in two places; he won a Sabre of Honour and a promotion to Captain in 1800. He was in the Grenadier à Cheval of the Guard in 1804, Squadron Commander in 1805 at Austerlitz; Colonel with the 2nd Carabiniers at Friedland before being made Baron in 1810. he was wounded at the Moskova and Winkowo; General in 1813, he was in the Moselle in 1815. Blancard was wounded at Waterloo and put on the non-active list during the Second Restoration, he was pensioned off in 1825 before being recalled in 1830. He finished his career ad Lieutenant-General in 1835. Retired in 1848 and died in 1853.

Farliat was born at Lyons was on the Italian Campaign, entered the Grenadiers à Cheval of the Guard in 1801, LH, he was at Austerlitz and became a veteran in 1806, he died in 1837.

Fanard was admitted into the Grenadiers à Cheval of the Guard in 1801. LH, he was at Austerlitz and was retired in 1807.

Grandjean was the brother of the General and was born at Nancy; trooper with the 8th Dragoons, Second-Lieutenant with the Guides in Italy, he was admitted into the Grenadiers à Cheval in September 1805. He was wounded at Eylau. Promoted to Squadron Commander in 1807, he was wounded at Medina de Rio Seco before becoming Colonel of the 8th Cuirassiers. OLH and Baron of the Empire, he served in 1809 and was then wounded at the Moskova. He retired as he was an invalid but took command of the 2nd Cuirassiers during the Hundred Days. Wounded at Waterloo, he retired in 1816.

Grosselin was wounded in the Campaigns in the West and entered the Grenadiers à Cheval of the Guard and won a Rifle of Honour at Marengo. Maréchal des Logis- Chef at Austerlitz, wounded at Eylau, he was made a Second-Lieutenant Standard-Bearer. Promoted to Captain in the 1st Cuirassiers in 1811, he took part in the Russian, Saxon and French Campaigns. He fought at Waterloo. He retired in 1815.

Guillaume was with the 5th Dragoons at the Battle of Bassano, Lieutenant in 1800, First-Lieutenant in the Grenadiers à Cheval in 1801, he was mentioned in despatches and promoted to Captain at Austerlitz. He was at Essling and Wagram. OLH. He became Major in the 7th Dragoons in 1811. He retired because of his wounds in 1813. He died in 1830.

Jacob, born in the Moselle, was with the Grenadiers à Cheval of the Guard in 1804; standard-bearer, LH, he fought at Ulm and Austerlitz. First-Lieutenant in the Velites at Jena and Friedland, he retired in 1811.

Joannes was wounded seven times in 1795, captured, exchanged, wounded again at Fleurus; he entered the future Grenadiers à Cheval of the Guard in 1799. He was at Marengo (LH) then Austerlitz. Seriously wounded at Eylau, he was also present at Essling, Wagram (OLH) and in Russia and in Saxony. He was wounded at Hanau and was made a Colonel of the 2nd Chevau-Légers for the French Campaign. CrLH in 1821, Maréchal de camp in 1823 in Spain, he finally retired in 1834.

Jolivet, aide de camp to Hoche, Captain in the 14th Dragoons, he was wounded in Egypt. Squadron Commander in the Grenadiers à Cheval of the Guard in 1804 (OLH), he fought at Ulm and Austerlitz. He went over to the Dragoons of the Guard in 1806 and fought at Jena, Eylau and Friedland. Invalided out in 1809, he died in Toul in 1810.

Jubert was a child of the regiment – 19th Cavalry. He was with the Army of the Rhine and was made a Maréchal des Logis of the Grenadiers à Cheval of the Guard in 1800. He won the LH and the rank of Second-Lieutenant in 1805, First-Lieutenant after Austerlitz. Promoted to Captain at Essling, he was Squadron Commander in the 4th Cuirassiers. He was captured at the end of the retreat from Moscow and died at Vilnius.

Lacoste was born at Romans was with the 6th Dragoons and entered the Grenadiers à Cheval of the Guard. LH, he fought at Austerlitz and went over to the Dragoons of the Guard in 1806. He resigned after Tilsitt.

Lajoye was born at Reims was in the 6th Dragoons, then Lieutenant with the 6th Hussars. In 1800, he went over to the Grenadiers à Cheval of the Guard and fought at Marengo. LH, appointed Adjudant-

THE IMPERIAL GUARD, INFANTRY

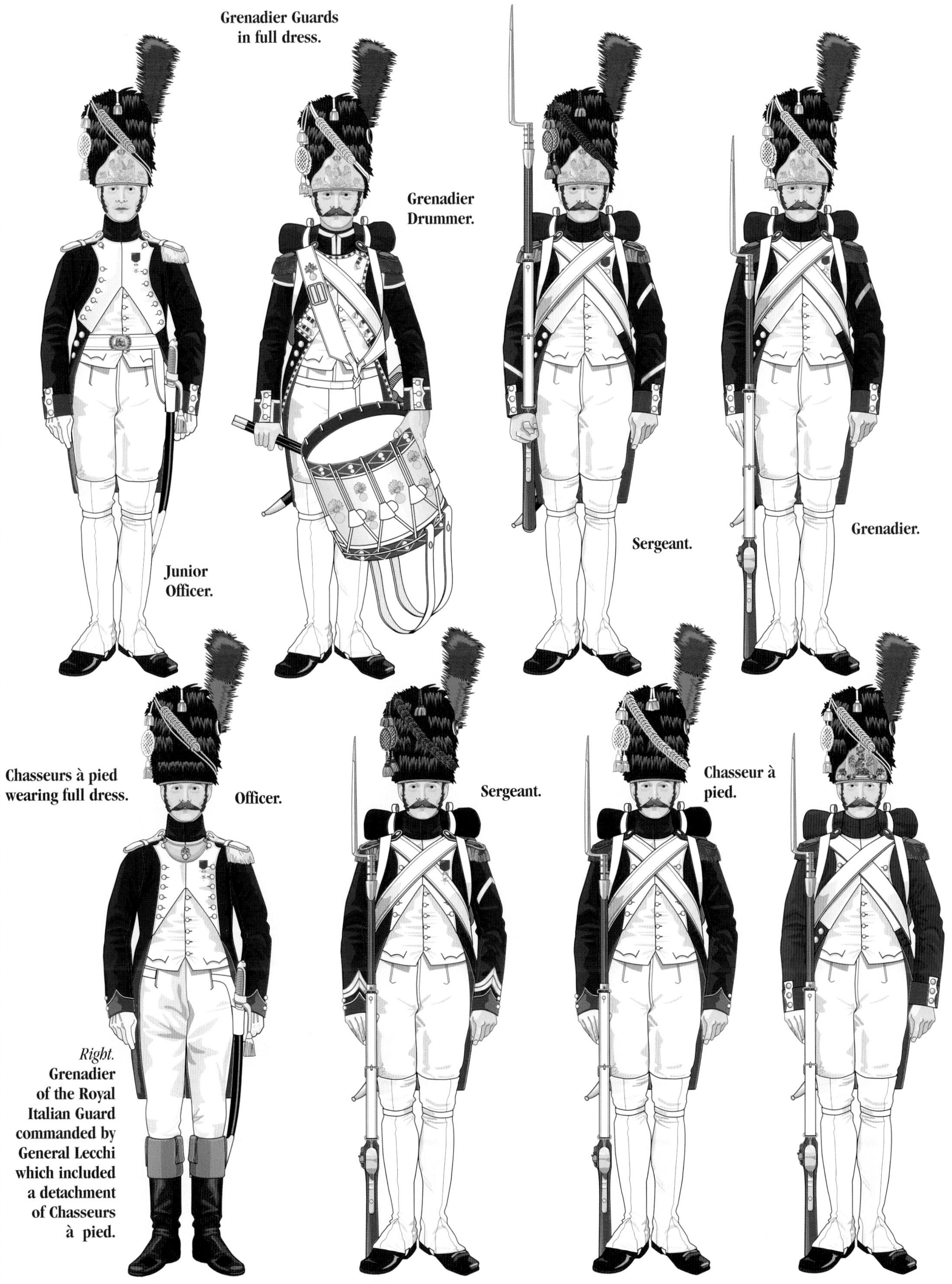

Grenadier Guards in full dress.

Grenadier Drummer.

Junior Officer.

Sergeant.

Grenadier.

Chasseurs à pied wearing full dress.

Officer.

Sergeant.

Chasseur à pied.

Right.
Grenadier of the Royal Italian Guard commanded by General Lecchi which included a detachment of Chasseurs à pied.

André Jouineau © Histoire & Collections 2003

Grenadiers à cheval, campaign dress

Grenadier wearing a round-cloak.

Grenadier wearing an overcoat.

First-Lieutenant in the administration in 1806 then Captain of administration, he became a Major in the 15th Dragoons in 1813, and in the 10th in 1814. He served during the Hundred Days, was put on half-pay and retired in 1818 to Avize in the Marne.

Lambert was born at Carpentras and served in 1790 . Grenadier in the Guard in 1800, he charged at Marengo. LH, he was at Austerlitz and Wagram. He was endowed after Austria. He took par in the Russian Campaign and quit active service because of his frostbite in 1813.

Lambinet was a Grenadier à Cheval in 1800, he died from his wounds in 1806.

La Huberdière: trooper with the 10th Chasseurs, he became Second-Lieutenant with the Grenadiers à Cheval in 1800. He commanded a company of Velites attached to the regiment and became a Major in 1809. He went over to the 9th Cuirassiers in 1811. Colonel of the 10th Cuirassiers, he took part in the Saxon and French Campaigns. He was made a baron in 1813, CtLH in 1832, and retired in 1833.

Lapersonne was born in the Calvados; he was in the Guides in Italy then in the Grenadiers à Cheval in 1800. He was at Marengo, LH; he fought at Ulm, Austerlitz, Jena, Eylau, Friedland and in Spain, at Essling and Wagram. He took part in the Campaigns in Russia, Saxony and France and finished up as a Captain at Waterloo. OLH.

Lapostol was born at Lons-le-Saunier and entered the Grenadiers à Cheval in 1802. LH, Gendarme in Spain, Captain at Besançon. OLH. He was caught in that town during the Hundred Days. He commanded the 1st Battalion of Light Infantry in Africa; he left the army in 1835.

Lefebvre, volunteer in the 1st Battalion of the Lombards, went over to the Carabiniers in Italy in 1797, joined the Grenadiers à Cheval in 1800 and was at Marengo, LH. He was mentioned at Ulm and finished up as a Second-Lieutenant at Wagram. He died on 25 August 1809 from his wounds.

Daubigny was with the Armies of the North and the Rhine, and then joined the Grenadiers à Cheval in 1800. He was promoted to Maréchal des Logis after Austerlitz. He went into the Dragoons of the Guard in 1806, fought at Jena, Friedland and Wagram and retired in 1810.

Delaporte was a Guide in Italy and in Egypt joined the Grenadiers à Cheval in 1800. He was mentioned at Marengo; he was Second-Lieutenant Standard-Bearer in 1802 (LH), First-Lieutenant in 1806, wounded at Eylau, promoted to Captain after Essling, fought at Wagram, made OLH and Baron in 1810, and took part in the Russian Campaign. He was made Squadron Commander in 1813. Wounded seven times and captured, he served at Craonne, had his horse killed under him and was wounded again. He was wounded three times at Waterloo. Sacked in 1816, he was nevertheless Colonel of the 11th Dragoons from 1830 to 1836. CrLH in 1831 and Maréchal de camp in 1836, he retired to Saran in the Loiret.

Dujon, the Hero of Capua, was a Second-Lieutenant in the Grenadiers à Cheval in 1801. He won a Sabre of Honour in 1803. OLH. Captain at Ulm and Austerlitz, he was seriously wounded at Eylau. Squadron Commander at Essling and Wagram, he was made a baron in 1810. Colonel of the 4th Cuirassiers in 1812, he took part in the Campaigns in Saxony and France in 1814. CrLH, Maréchal de camp in 1815, GdOLH in 1825, he retired in 1830.

Dupont was born at Chaville, was a trooper in the 12th Chasseurs, and joined the Grenadiers à Cheval in 1801. LH. He was with the 12th Chasseurs in 1807 then went into the Gendarmerie in 1810.

Dupré was mentioned at Mondovi with the 20th Dragoons, went to Egypt and joined the Grenadiers à Cheval in 1802. He was wounded at Austerlitz which obliged him to resign in 1806.

Beaugeois was born at Verdun, was with the 21st dragoons then the Grenadiers à Cheval. He was at Marengo, LH. He was promoted to First-Lieutenant as a reward for his courage at Austerlitz. Retired in 1809.

Bergeret was in the Grenadiers à Cheval of the Guard in 1799, was mentioned at Marengo, LH, was in Spain in 1808, took part at Essling and Wagram as a Second-Lieutenant Standard-Bearer. After the Russian Campaign, he died at Fulda Hospital on 25 March 1813 from his wounds and exhaustion from the retreat.

Blanchet was in the 5th Dragoons and was wounded twice, obtaining a Sabre of Honour at Marengo in the Grenadiers à Cheval of the Guard. Wounded at Eylau, he was a First-Lieutenant with the 1st Cuirassiers in 1811. After Russia, he was Adjudant-Major in 1813, then Captain AM at Waterloo. He was sacked and retired in 1815.

Bourde of the 13th Hussars was with the Army of the Rhine, went to Italy, then Egypt and joined the Grenadiers à Cheval in 1800. First-Lieutenant in 1805, he was noticed at Austerlitz, LH in 1805, OLH in 1806 and was killed at Eylau.

Carlier de la Garde campaigned in the Alps, in Italy, Helvetia and joined the Grenadiers à Cheval in 1800. He was at Marengo. LH. Second-Lieutenant with the 6th Cuirassiers, he was wounded at Essling. OLH He rejoined the 12th Cuirassiers in Russia as a Captain, then Squadron Commander in 1813. Seriously wounded at Leipzig, he died after an amputation.

Colin was a child of the regiment in the 9th Dragoons, was in the Chasseurs or Grenadiers à Cheval of the Guard in 1797. He was a First-Lieutenant at Marengo, LH. Made a Captain for his bravery at Austerlitz and retired in 1809.

Bourdon, former Squadron Commander in the Grenadiers à Cheval of the Guard became a Colonel in the 11th Dragoons; he was seen by Bessières who was visiting the wounded at Brünn. Seriously wounded at Hollabrünn, Bourdon died of his wounds. From other sources he died of wounds received at Austerlitz.

Bufquin, a trooper with the 14th Chasseurs then the 20th present at Marengo, he joined the Grenadiers à Cheval in 1800. LH He was Second-Lieutenant in 1805, First-Lieutenant in 1807 and took part in all the Campaigns until 1814. Put on half-pay then retired in 1816.

Burgraff was born at Strasbourg. First of all with the 14th cavalry Regiment, he was Second-Lieutenant with the Grenadiers à Cheval of the Guard in 1800. Second-Lieutenant in 1803, LH, he was then First-Lieutenant at Austerlitz. He fought in Spain and in Russia as a Major with the 23rd Dragoons. He joined the 12th Dragoons and was ennobled in January 1815. OLH, he served in 1823, was mentioned in despatches, became a Colonel and left the Army in 1830 as Honorary Maréchal de camp.

Chamorin fought in the Pyrenees, in Italy, at Arcola and was wounded at Montebello. After Marengo, he became squadron Commander in the 3rd Cuirassiers in 1804 and joined the Grenadiers à Cheval in 1805. He was present at Austerlitz, Jena, Eylau, became Colonel of the 26th dragoons and was wounded at Heilsberg. He served at Friedland, was CtLH in 1808, he was made a Baron of the Empire; he went to Spain where he was killed at Campo-Mayor in 1811 with the rank of General.

Chassin was wounded twice with the 22nd Chasseurs and joined the Grenadiers à Cheval of the Guard in 1800. He was First-Lieutenant in 1803, and retired in 1809.

Clément was in Italy in 1796, at Bassano, then in Spain. He fought at Wagram. He left the Army in 1810. On 19 September 1805, Napoleon created the Velites of the Guard comprising four companies of Grenadiers, commanded by Clément and four companies of Chasseurs à cheval, commanded by Clerc.

Clerc was with the Army of the Rhine, with the 2nd Carabiniers before joining the Grenadiers à Cheval of the Guard in 1801. LH, he retired in 1806 and died in 1809.

Croizier was born at Riom; a Guides Second-Lieutenant on the General Staff in Egypt, he joined the Grenadiers à Cheval (LH) before resigning at the end of 1805 with the rank of First-Lieutenant.

Dièche was a Surgeon 3rd Class in Italy in 1792, 2nd Class in 1796 went into the Guides for the Egyptian Campaign. He became a Surgeon 1st Class in 1799 and joined the Grenadiers à Cheval of the Guard in 1800. He looked after the wounded at Marengo. LH. He was in Austria in 1809, in Russia and in Saxony and OLH in 1813. After the French Campaign, he received half-pay and was retired in 1818.

Diettmann was a Gendarme, Second-Lieutenant in the 6th Dragoons and in the 2nd Carabiniers before joining the Grenadiers à Cheval of the Guard in 1804. LH, he was mentioned at Austerlitz. It was as a Major in the 5th Chasseurs that he was accidentally killed while instructing new recruits in 1807.

Forfert was in the 11th dragoons, became a Guide, was wounded at Zurich, then joined the Grenadiers à Cheval in 1802. LH, mentioned at Austerlitz, wounded at Eylau, he left the Army in 1810.

Flament, a trooper with the 5th Chasseurs, was with the Army of the North and was wounded three times. He joined the Grenadiers à Cheval of the Guard and charged at Marengo; He took part in the Russian, Saxon and French Campaigns. He retired in 1814.

Foederlé was born at Colmar, served in the 10th Chasseurs and fought on the Rhine and in Italy; he joined the Grenadiers à Cheval in 1799, LH, fought in Spain, at Wagram, in Russia and disappeared during the retreat.

Gadois, a Brune Guide, Grenadier à Cheval of the Guard in 1801, retired in 1809.

Gautrot, wounded at Verona joined the Grenadiers à Cheval of the Guard at Marengo. LH. He left the Army in 1809.

IMPERIAL GUARD, CAVALRY

Grenadier à Cheval of the Guard. Rather than wearing full dress, the troopers wore the Campaign Dress, the traditional dress of the Grenadiers whilst campaigning.

Trumpeter in the Grenadiers à cheval of the Guard. He is wearing a black bearskin hat, as Lucien Rousselot shows on one of his plates given over to the regiment.

Trumpeter in the Chasseurs à cheval of the Guard.

Chasseurs à Cheval of the Guard. The dress worn here was worn by the Chasseurs Regiment during the great charge against the Cuirassiers of the Russian Guard. The coat was worn saltire-wise to give added protection against sabre blows.

Mameluke. The squadron of Mamelukes was attached to the Regiment of the Chasseurs à cheval of the Guard.

André Jouineau © Histoire & Collections 2003

Gazeau, was in the 8th Cuirassiers, LH, Grenadier à Cheval of the Guard in 1804, he retired in 1809.

Guillot or **Guyot** was wounded in front of Cambrai in 1794, was with the 2nd Carabiniers in 1798. He joined the Grenadiers à Cheval of the Guard in 1800. Wounded at Austerlitz, he joined the Dragoons of the Guard in 1806 and retired in 1808.

Hardy was born in the Aisne. He went from the 3rd Dragoons to the Grenadiers à Cheval in 1797. He was at Marengo, LH. He was Second-Lieutenant Standard-Bearer at Austerlitz. Mentioned at Jena he was killed at Eylau.

Hardy was born at Valenciennes, was in the 17th Dragoons, then the Grenadiers à Cheval in 1803. He was made a Squadron Commander

Above. ***Morland who was killed at the Battle of Austerlitz and Daumesnil who saved Rapp's life during the battle.*** *(RR)*

after Eylau, retired as a Major in 1816 and died in 1831. Hardy left the 14th Dragoons for the Grenadiers à Cheval in 1802. LH, wounded at Eylau, he fought at Wagram and disappeared during the retreat from Russia.

Hueber was born in Switzerland and was a Swiss Guard before becoming a Grenadier of the Consular Guard in 1799. LH, he was at Austerlitz and left the army in 1808.

Klein, *aka* **Conrad** was with the 1st Carabiniers, with the 14th Chasseurs before joining the Grenadiers à Cheval in 1804, LH. He received 10 sabre wounds and one shot at Austerlitz. He returned to the 14th Chasseurs, he was second-Lieutenant in 1812; he was wounded twice at Leipzig. He was captured but returned in 1814, was put on half pay and retired in 1816.

Leroy, Grenadier à Cheval, captured a standard at Marengo and was awarded a Rifle of Honour; he retired in 1808.

Meistrelet was a Grenadier à Cheval of the Guard, mentioned at Marengo and received a Rifle of Honour, he retired in 1806.

Ochard obtained a rifle of Honour at Marengo. OLH with the Grenadiers à Cheval, killed in 1808.

Picard of the 15th Dragoons fought in Italy and in Egypt, joined the Grenadiers à Cheval in 1800, received a sabre of Honour at Marengo. Second-Lieutenant Standard-Bearer in 1805, he was retired in 1807.

Prévost was a trooper with the 5th Dragoons. In 1796 he saved the life of Colonel Milhaud and received a Sabre of Honour. OLH Grenadier à Cheval in 1800, he went into the service of Louis Bonaparte in Holland 1806.

Raulet, of the 3rd Chasseurs became a Guide in Egypt and joined the Grenadiers à Cheval in 1801. Mentioned at Marengo, he was promoted to Second-Lieutenant and obtained a Rifle of Honour at Austerlitz where he got his leg broken. He was in Spain in Napoleon, served in 1809, went to Russia and was invalided out in 1813. He served again in 1814, retired again and died in 11834.

Riss, trumpeter in the 14th Dragoons in Egypt, he went over to the Grenadiers à Cheval in 1805. He received a trumpet of Honour and died in 1808.

Rossignol was with the 12th Chasseurs in 1793, then Captain in 1800 with the Chasseurs of the Guard. He was Squadron Commander in 1805 and was Nansouty's Chief of Staff in Russia. Wounded and captured at Viasma, he returned in 1814, retired in 1824.

Norbet, *aka* **Schmidt,** this trumpeter in the Grenadiers à Cheval of the Guard charged while blowing his trumpet, then fought brilliantly. He received a Trumpet of Honour at Marengo.

Thiebaud with the 28th Dragoons in Egypt, he received a Rifle of Honour in 1803, joined the Grenadiers à Cheval of the Guard and he retired as Marechal des Logis in 1808.

It was related that at one moment of the great charge at Austerlitz, the Grenadiers à Cheval were not all present: there were only 706 of them spread out among 4 squadrons. 248 were left on the way. Very careful research has been done to trace those who were present at Austerlitz using the *'Fastes de la Légion d'Honneur'*, the Légion d'Honneur that all those who are mentioned here received. Only six officers were wounded, three troopers were killed and eighteen wounded. 99 horse were lost.

For such a fight, the casualty figures are not at all high compared with those of the Allies. They show the superior quality of these veterans over the young Russian nobles. The greater number of the wounded received bayonet wounds, courtesy of the infantry of the Russian Guard. There were stars of the Grenadiers à Cheval of the Guard, who only joined after the end of the battle, and who were appointed in December 1805; such was the case of Lepic and Chastel.

THE CHASSEURS À CHEVAL AND THE MAMELUKES

The Colonel-General was still **Prince Eugene** to whom everybody was answerable.

Apart from that, they were still commanded by **Morland.** A trooper with the 11th Chasseurs in 1791, he was with the Armies of the North and the Rhine. Morland became Squadron Commander in 1801. He was a Chasseur à Cheval of the Guard in 1802 and appointed Major in 1804. OLH, died from his wounds at Austerlitz; he was embalmed by Larrey and recalled to Paris in a barrel of rum. When this was

opened it was found that his moustache had grown very long. His body was returned to the family.

Mourier was born in Limoges and was a Captain in the Chasseurs à Cheval of the Guard in 1802. Promoted to Colonel of the 15th Chasseurs he was made a Baron then a General in 1811. CtLH, wounded at the Moskova, then at Berezina, he left the army in 1826, then again in 1832.

Dahlmann was born at Thionville joined up in 1777, wounded in the Pyrenees; he took part in the Italian and Egyptian Campaigns. Captain with the Grenadier à Cheval in 1800, he was made Squadron Commander with the Chasseurs à Cheval of the Guard in 1802. OLH. At Austerlitz, he replaced Morland as Colonel Major. He was present at Jena, he was made a General in 1806 before being wounded at Eylau. He died from his wounds.

Daumesnil, born at Périgueux, he was wounded in the Pyrenees then went to Italy. One of Bonaparte's Guides in Egypt. He saved the life of his General twice and captured the Pasha's standard at Aboukir. He was Captain in the Chasseurs à Cheval of the Guard at Austerlitz. He saved Rapp. He was appointed Squadron Commander and OLH in 1806. On 2 May 1808, he was at Madrid, was wounded at Eckmühl, then at Wagram where he lost his left leg. He was made a Baron, then a General in 1812. Commandant of Vincennes; he gathered together all the equipment and on 31 March 1814, he refused to surrender. He did not surrender to Blücher either. He went into retirement in 1815. He found his old job again in 1830 but he refused to hand over the Ministers of Charles X locked up in Vincennes. Lieutenant-General in 1831, he died of cholera in 1832.

Guyot was born in the Jura and joined the Army of the Rhine. He fought in Vendée and in Italy. Captain in the Chasseurs à Cheval of the Guard, he was Squadron Commander at Austerlitz, and Major at the end of December, Couronne de Fer and Colonel Second in command of the Regiment after Essling. He was in turn promoted to General in 1809, Chamberlain in 1811. He left for Spain and obtained the CtLH and the rank of Major-General in 1811. He commanded the Chasseurs à Cheval of the Guard in Russia and in Saxony – he was wounded at Lutzen – and replaced Walther at the head of the Grenadiers before fighting in France in 1814. He was wounded twice at Waterloo and retired in 1816. He was recalled in 1830 but retired for good in 1833. He died in 1837.

Thervay was a Captain, killed at Austerlitz.

Thiry was in the Army of the North, then in Italy. He received a Sabre of Honour in 1802. Squadron Commander in the Chasseurs à Cheval of the Guard in 1805, he was wounded twice at Austerlitz and once again at Eylau. He was promoted to Major then General in 1809. CtLH, he was wounded three times at the Moskova. He took part in the Campaigns in Saxony, Champagne and served in Paris in 1815; retired the same year and definitively in 1818.

Beurmann was born at Nancy in 1777, was a child of the regiment, then on half-pay with the Salm Infantry Regiment; he was Second-Lieutenant (valid from 18 years old on) in the 62nd of the Line. Kléber's aide de camp at Mainz (following the 1st Chasseurs), he was promoted to Captain and aide de camp to Mortier in 1799. He then joined the Chasseurs à Cheval of the Guard in 1800. He was sent on missions to St-Petersburg with Duroc. Squadron Commander in 1802, he received two bayonet wounds at Austerlitz. Colonel of the 17th Dragoons in 1806, then baron, he was wounded twice in Spain. General in 1811; CtLH in 18112, In Saxony in 1813, wounded, he commanded the rearguard up to Metz which he then defended. He committed suicide there with two pistol shots on 13 April 1815.

Clerc was born at Lyons, volunteered in 1792, wounded three times in 1793, twice in 1795; he was appointed Second-Lieutenant with the Grenadiers à Cheval of the Guard and mentioned at Marengo. Captain-Adjutant-Major in the Chasseurs à Cheval of the Guard, he became Squadron Commander in 1803. He commanded the Velites Chasseurs à Cheval. He was at Ulm, at Austerlitz where he charged with 100 men against a Russian column and captured 8 cannon. OLH in 1806, he was made a Baron, he became Colonel of the 1st Cuirassiers in 1809. He took part in the Russian and Saxon Campaigns; he was wounded at Hanau. Maréchal de camp in 1814, he did not serve during the Hundred Days. Vicount in 1818, CrLH in 1829, he was retired in 1830. He was Inspector of Remounts until 1839 then was put on the Reserve List afterwards.

Clerc was also born in Lyons. He was a trooper with the 13th Chasseurs, had three horses killed under him in Italy and was wounded twice. He was Lieutenant with the Chasseurs à Cheval of the Guard then Captain-Quartermaster, LH; became subsequently Sub-Inspector of the Reille division.

Barbanègre. The brother of the General became a Chasseur à Cheval of the Guard in 1800, wounded at Austerlitz; he was appointed First-Lieutenant on 27 December 1805. OLH in 1809, he was a Captain in Russia and fought at Waterloo. On half-pay, he retired to Pontacq in 1829.

Borde was a trooper with the 3rd Chasseurs, became a Guide in Egypt, won a Rifle of Honour and was wounded twice at Austerlitz. First-Lieutenant, he was wounded several times at Eylau. He was

Wagram. OLH in 1811, he retired in 1813 after the Russian Campaign.

Bureaux-Pusy was a Lieutenant with the Chasseurs à Cheval of the Guard in 1801, he received two bayonet wounds in the right arm at Austerlitz and became a Captain in the Dragoons of the Guard in 1806. Mentioned at Jena, Friedland, given an endowment, he left for Spain; he was called back to Wagram; Colonel of the 13th Hussars. At Leipzig in 1813, then the 12th dragoons which became the 17th for Waterloo, he was sacked then recalled in 1816 into the 3rd Dragoons. He died in 1822.

Bohn, trooper in the 13th Dragoons in 1793 — where he was wounded — he became a Lieutenant with the 1st Hussars in 1793 in Italy. At Roveredo, he captured 500 Austrians, 16 cannon and 7 flags. Squadron Commander with the Chasseurs à Cheval of the Guard in 1805, he got his CxOLH after Austerlitz. He served in Spain in 1808 and died at Raab from his wounds. He was Chevalier of the Empire.

Bourbier, trooper in the 5th dragoons, became Squadron Commander and joined the Chasseurs à Cheval of the Guard in 1804. Mentioned at Austerlitz, he became Colonel of the 11th Dragoons in December 1805. He was killed at Eylau.

Francq was born at Auxonne, enrolled in 1782, he was a trooper with the 5th Chasseurs then with the 11th before becoming a Lieutenant in the Chasseurs à Cheval of the Guard. OLH, he was made Squadron Commander for his action at Austerlitz. Colonel of the 10th Cuirassiers in 1809, he retired in 1812. Baron in 1810, this title was made hereditary in 1818.

Cavrois was born in the Somme; Second-Lieutenant in the 22nd Chasseurs, he was First-Lieutenant in the Chasseurs à Cheval of the Guard. Promoted to Squadron Commander and OLH for Austerlitz, he became Colonel of the 20th Chasseurs in 1809, and baron in 1810. Convicted of negligence for having received bad horses, he was put in the guardhouse for a month. Chief of Staff in 1813, General in 1814, he was wounded at Brienne; he served in 1815 was put on the non-active list and died in 1820.

Callory, born at Cambrai, wounded in 1796 and then in 1797, was with the 11th Chasseurs. Second-Lieutenant in Italy, he became a Guide then a Chasseur à Cheval of the Guard. He was First-Lieutenant in 1803. He was present at Marengo, Ulm, and Austerlitz; he was made a Captain, OLH in 1810. He became Major in the 22nd Chasseurs, he was wounded at Bautzen in 1813. Dismissed, he was called back as Colonel of the 6th Chasseurs in Spain. CrLH in 1828, retired in 1830.

Chapellier was born in the Ardennes. Trumpet-major in the 14th Chasseurs in 1801, he joined the Chasseurs à Cheval of the Guard in 1801. LH. Retired in 1806.

Basse, in 1793, had his right leg broken by a shell burst and was wounded twice more before joining the Chasseurs à Cheval of the Guard in 1802. LH. Second-Lieutenant for Austerlitz, he was appointed First-Lieutenant for Eylau. He disappeared somewhere in Russia.

Bonnet was born at Etampes, this Brigadier-Trompette in 1795 was in the 5th Mounted Artillery; he joined the 3rd Hussars and fought in Italy. Wounded at Savona, he joined Bonaparte's Guides and was mentioned at Castiglione. After Bassano and Arcola, he joined the Chasseurs à Cheval of the Guard at Marengo where he won a Trumpet of Honour for his exploits. Mentioned at Austerlitz, wounded near Jena, he became a Second-Lieutenant in Russia in 1813. He took part in the French Campaign and left the army in 1815.

Doumenge was with the 10th Hussars in Italy in 1796 and joined the Chasseurs à Cheval of the Guard in 1800. LH. He was in Russia and Saxony and was promoted to Major in 1813 with the 1st Cuirassiers. He served during the Hundred Days and was retired to Allemans (Dordogne) in 1816.

Delor was with the 12th Hussars before joining the Chasseurs à Cheval of the Guard in 1802. LH. Maréchal des Logis-Chef after Austerlitz, he was in Spain in 1808. Adjutant for fodder supply then Second-Lieutenant in 1807, he was in Russia and became a First-Lieutenant in 1813. Retired in the same year he was recalled to go to St-Domingo with Fontagnes. Promoted to OLH and Squadron Commander in 1817, he joined the Gendarmerie in 1831. He retired in 1833.

Krettly was born at Versailles, was in the French Guards in 1789 and became a musician in the National Guard in Paris. He was a trumpeter with the Guides in 1798, he was in Egypt, saved Dahlmann on Mount Tabor and was mentioned at Marengo. He received a Sabre of Honour. While saving an officer at Austerlitz he was riddled with wounds. Second-Lieutenant Standard-Bearer in 1806, he took part in the capture of 18 Cannon at Eylau. He got several sabre wounds at Friedland and retired in 1808 because of his numerous incapacitating wounds. Garde-General of the Water and Forests Department at Montélimar, he sought refuge in Bruxelles where he gave music lessons. First Flute at the Theatre du Parc; he came back to fight in 1830 and finished his life as a musician at the Theatre de la Gaîté. He died in 1840.

Delaître was with the Army of the West, he left for Egypt as Lieutenant Aide de camp to Kléber in 1798. He was wounded twice at St John of Acre. He was Captain Quartermaster of the Mamelukes when he returned to France, he became Squadron Commander and commanded the Mamelukes after Austerlitz. He was at Jena, Eylau and was made Major with the Polish Chevau-Légers of the Guard in 1807. He took part in the Russian Campaign where he was wounded and captured with Partouneaux at the Beresina. He returned in 1814 and organised the National Guard of the Marne during the Hundred Days. Put on the non-active list in August 1815, he became Inspector of the Gendarmerie in 1818. CrLH in 1820. He commanded the School at Saumur in 1831 and died in 1838.

Deville was born at Soissons, was with the Army of the Rhine, in Mainz, in Vendée. From the 7th Hussars he went over to the Chasseurs à Cheval of the Guard in 1801. LH. Maréchal de Logis Chef after Austerlitz, he followed Napoleon into Spain and became Second-Lieutenant in 1809, then First-Lieutenant in 1811. He was a Captain during the Russian Campaign; he was appointed Squadron commander

in 1813 in the 5th Cuirassiers. Wounded at Quatre-Bras, he was on half pay before joining the 15th Dragoons in 1823, then the 4th as Lieutenant-Colonel. CtLH in 1830, he retired to Metz in 1837.

Chatrousse was in the 14th Hussars, a Brune Guide and Chasseur à Cheval of the Guard in 1804. LH, he was killed in a duel in 1806.

Louis Sève known as the '*Younger*' (his brother was also in the Guides in Italy but he left the regiment to join the Gendarmerie in 1811) was awarded the LH in Year XII was wounded at Austerlitz and was captured at Benavente. He returned in 1811, was OLH in 1813 and died in Hospital in hospital in Paris in 1815.

Fonnade was born in Haute-Garonne, a hero of Italy and Egypt – he received a Sabre of Honour at Aboukir – he was the Mamelukes' standard-bearer in Russia. He was with the Lancers of the Guard at Waterloo where he was wounded. He left the army in 1806 and died in 1827.

Abdalla d'Asbonne was born at Bethlehem was Guide-Interpreter for the Headquarters in Egypt; he was wounded and his horse killed at Heliopolis. Second-Lieutenant in the company of Mamelukes, he distinguished himself at Austerlitz, his horse was killed and he received seven sabre wounds at Golymin. At Eylau his horse was killed and he broke his arm in the fall. Squadron Commander in 1811, it was with the Guard that he left for Russia and in Saxony where he was wounded at Dresden. He lost another horse and was wounded again at Hanau. He lost another horse during the Hundred Days. Dismissed and retired in 1828, he was recalled in Africa as aide de camp to Boyer at Oran. OLH in 1832, he retired to Melun in 1836.

Adet was born at Montreuil and became a Guide in Italy where he was wounded three times and joined the Chasseurs à Cheval of the Guard as Second-Lieutenant Standard-Bearer in 1803. LH, He was First-Lieutenant after being wounded by a shot which went through both his thighs and his lower abdomen at Austerlitz. Retired in 1808, he died in 1810.

Chaïm was a Georgian. His horse was killed and he received six sabre wounds, three lance wounds and two shots at Heliopolis, he was left for dead and cared for by Larrey. At Austerlitz he took a canon and saved Rapp but received three bayonet wounds. LH, he lost a horse and was wounded at Eylau. Promoted to OLH and First-Lieutenant in 1806, he was given an endowment. Wounded at Madrid on 2 May, he saved Daumesnil, his horse was killed at Benavente; he became Captain -Instructor in 1813. In 1815, he was Squadron Commander and Aide de camp to Lefebvre-Desnoettes. He retired to Melun in 1815.

Assant was a Lieutenant then Captain (administration) in the Chasseurs à Cheval of the Guard. His horse was killed at Austerlitz. LH, he was Squadron commander in the 2nd Regiment of Chasseurs à Cheval of the Guard.

Bocheux was born at St -Quentin, served in Italy, became a Guide in 1797. In Egypt, he took a Battery at Aboukir and joined the Chasseurs à Cheval of the Guard in 1800. He was mentioned at Marengo

Below. **Martinet's Plate N° 158 shows a Mameluke. The exotic uniform of this elite unit did not change at all during the whole of the Empire.** *(RR)*

and received a Sabre of Honour. Bocheux was promoted Second-Lieutenant Standard-Bearer in recognition of his valour; wounded at Austerlitz, he became First-Lieutenant, still a Standard-bearer, for Eylau, and was killed at Benavente.

Bœuf or **Beuf** received a Rifle of Honour for having captured a flag at Marengo; he joined the Chasseurs à Cheval of the Guard.

Charpentier was Squadron Commander in the 8th Chasseurs when he entered the Chasseurs à Cheval of the Guard in 1805. He was shot and wounded at Austerlitz. OLH Colonel of the 3rd Chasseurs after 1806; he was seriously wounded at Wagram and invalided out of the army in 1811.

A Mameluke and his horse, drawn by Swebach in the year 1806. *(RR)*

Eylau, he was also at Wagram and joined the 7th Chasseurs. He was a Captain in Russia and died from his wounds after Dresden.

Chenet was with the 5th dragoons at Bassano and Arcola where he was wounded. At Marengo he was with the Chasseurs à Cheval of the Guard. LH. He left the army in 1806.

Jolly, 11th Dragoons, was wounded at Salzburg joined the Chasseurs à Cheval of the Guard in 1803; he was with the Velites at Austerlitz and was appointed First-Lieutenant after the battle. Promoted to Captain-Adjutant-Major in the Dragoons of the Guard, in 1806, he was wounded at Friedland. Major with the 29th Dragoons (6th Chevau-Légers), he was wounded at Dresden and took part in the French Campaign. OLH in 1814, Jolly was dismissed after Waterloo. CrLH in 1821, Colonel of the 9th Cuirassiers in Spain in 1823, and was at the battle of St-Ferdinand; he died on active service in 1832.

Muzy was born at Villefranche served in Italy became a Guide and went to Egypt. Maréchal des Logis chef of the Chasseurs à Cheval of the Guard at Marengo (LH), he was mentioned in despatches at Austerlitz and Eylau. He was promoted to Captain in 1807 and killed at Wagram.

Beau joined the Chasseurs à Cheval of the Guard in 1802. LH. He was present at Austerlitz, retired in 1806.

Bayeux was in the 11th Hussars of the Army of the West and of Italy! wounded three times, he was promoted to Second-Lieutenant in 1803 in the Chasseurs à Cheval of the Guard (LH) then First-Lieutenant in 1806 (OLH). He served at Wagram and received the Order of Bavaria in 1810. Chevalier of the Empire in 1811, Major, Squadron Commander for the Campaigns in Russia, Saxony – where he was made a Baron – and France, he was present at Waterloo; he was dismissed on the Loire, retired in 1824.

Bagdoune Mustapha was born in Bagdad; he captured a Russian Standard at Austerlitz, it was probably that of the Reserve Squadron of the Guards. He was killed at Dresden.

Renno was born at St John of Acre, saved Rapp at Austerlitz (LH after the battle, saved Daumesnil who was caught under his horse at Madrid and became Lefebvre-Desnoettes' aide de camp.

Schneit was a trooper in the 12th Chasseurs and was wounded twice, became a Maréchal des Logis in the Chasseurs à Cheval of the Guard, First-Lieutenant in 1802, and Captain after Austerlitz and Squadron Commander in 1809. OLH, he was in Russia and was Colonel of the 24th Chasseurs in 1813. Wounded at Leipzig he took part in the French Campaign, served at Waterloo, was put on the non-active list then retired in 1818. He served in Belgium with the 4th Cuirassiers in 1830; CrLH in 1831, Maréchal de camp in 1832, when he retired.

Salame Soliman was born in Bethlehem. LH. He was wounded at Madrid on 2 May; First-Lieutenant in 1813, retired to Melun in 1815. He finished as an interpreter in Africa in 1830.

Lafite Monguinet was born in the Basses-Pyrénées became a Chasseur à Cheval of the Guard, received a Rifle of Honour for Marengo and left the army in 1808.

The Mamelukes only numbered 63 horsemen for the charge at Austerlitz. The Parisian surgeon **Mauban** was the Surgeon-Commander of the Mamelukes. **Bockenheimer** was the Chasseurs'. On 22 December there were only 48 Mamelukes present, so 15 were out of action (?). The losses for the Chasseurs were greater than the Grenadiers à Cheval. Two officers were killed including the Colonel, as well as 9 troopers. Seventeen officers and fifty odd Chasseurs were wounded; 153 horses were lost. Here too the bayonet wounds were numerous. There were only 375 Chasseurs present.

Derat, 11th Chasseurs, joined the Chasseurs à Cheval of the Guard in 1803, LH, and retired in 1806.

Duvernoy was a Trumpeter in 1782 in Conti's Dragoons, Maréchal des Logis in 1794; Second-Lieutenant in 1801 in the Chasseurs à Cheval of the Guard. LH, First-Lieutenant after Austerlitz, he became Adjutant-Major in the Dragoons of the Guard. He was at Jena, Eylau, and Friedland. He was in Spain with Napoleon then at Essling and Wagram where several of his horses were killed. Major in the 6th Cuirassiers in 1812, OLH in 1814, he retired in 1816.

Ebendinger or **Ebnedinger** was in the 10th Chasseurs, received a Musket of Honour and joined the Chasseurs à Cheval of the Guard in 1804. Maréchal des Logis in 1807, he joined the Royal Italian Chasseurs, then to the 32nd Italian Chasseurs as a Captain. Wounded in Russia, he received the Couronne de Fer before being wounded at Dresden and captured. He was at Schelestadt in 1815, retired in 1816.

Chasseraye or **Chasseroy** was born in Eure et Loire, received a Rifle of Honour at Aboukir. He left the army in 1806.

Gauthier was born at Autun, became a Chasseur à Cheval of the Guard in 1804 when he left the School at Versailles. LH Maréchal des Logis after Austerlitz, he joined the Dragoons of the Guard in 1806. He retired after Tilsitt.

Guiod was in the 19th Dragoons of the Army of the West, Second-Lieutenant in the Chasseurs à Cheval of the Guard in 1801 and Captain after Austerlitz; he died of his wounds at Eylau.

Habaiby Yacoub, was born in Syria and was Second-Lieutenant in the Mamelukes. LH, he charged at Austerlitz and received a bayonet wound in the left groin; wounded at Eylau, was at Madrid, wounded three times at Benavente and received an endowment. He retired to Melun in 1814 and died in 1824.

Habaiby Daoud was born in Syria, the brother of Yacoub who raised the first contingent in Egypt. He came to replace his seriously wounded brother in Spain and received the LH in 1814.

Rabusson was born at Ganat, was a Guide at Zurich, Chasseur à Cheval of the Guard in 1800 and was mentioned at Marengo where he received several sabre wounds to the head. He was at Austerlitz and was covered in wounds at Eylau. Captain of the Veterans in 1807, Baron in 1812, Squadron Commander in 1814, Couronne de Fer; he was made Colonel in May 1815. His rank was cancelled, CrLH in 1822. Maréchal de camp in 1826, he retired in 1848, the year of his death. In all he was wounded twenty-two times.

Roul, trooper in the 13th Hussars was a Guide in Italy and in Egypt. LH, joined the Chasseurs à Cheval of the Guard in 1800; Second-Lieutenant after Austerlitz, he was wounded at Eylau. Invalided out of the army he was appointed to the Water and Forests Department then joined the Gendarmerie before becoming Ordnance Officer for the Emperor on Elba. Squadron Commander of the Chevau-Légers of the Guard, he was promoted to Colonel in 1815. Captured at Waterloo, he was struck of the List of officers and dismissed without pay, and exiled.

Vazilier, a Chasseur à Cheval of the Guard, was wounded at Austerlitz. LH, his horse was killed at Benavente, he became a Captain in 1812, wounded and retired in 1815.

Ibrahim was born in Syria and became the Captain of the Mamelukes. LH. He charged at Austerlitz went to the depot at Marseilles after having killed two bully boys in the Halles. Called back for the French Campaign in 1814, he died in 1821.

Legros was born at Autun, trooper in the 10th Chasseurs, one of Bonaparte's Guides in Italy and in Egypt; he joined the Chasseurs à Cheval of the Guard, as Second-Lieutenant Standard-Bearer in 1801. First-Lieutenant in 1805, he was at Austerlitz and died at Eylau.

Lepaumier was born in the Manche, was with the 9th Chasseurs when he freed Lefebvre in 1796. Wounded at Novi, he was in the Chasseurs à Cheval of the Guard before joining the Dragoons of the Guard in 1806. Appointed Second-Lieutenant in 1807, he was wounded in Russia at Malo-Jaroslawetz and invalided out of the army in 1813 to Avranches.

Castel was born at Cambrai, joined the 9th Hussars and was wounded at Zurich, at Moeskirch then at Augsburg (five wounds) where his horse was killed; his horse was also killed at Salzburg. Chasseur à Cheval of the Guard in 1803, LH, he was wounded and lost a horse at Austerlitz. Wounded twice at

Below. All is over; the Emperor receives his opponent surrounded by his headquarters. Note the page boy holding the Emperor's horse, on the right. (RR)

The aide de camps to the Marshal were:

Gérard who was with Bernadotte since 1794, he followed him to Italy as aide de camp, served in the West. He was Adjudant-Commandant with him in Hanover where "they did business together". Wounded at Austerlitz and Lubeck, he was appointed General in 18065, then Chief of staff of the Saxon Corps in 1809 (9th Corps). After Wagram he was given leave of absence. He was in Spain, with Gudin in Russia, then he fought in Saxony in 1813 where he was wounded three times. GdCx of the Reunion. In France in 1814, he replaced Victor, agreed to Napoleon's destitution. GdCxLH then rallied to the Emperor. He was with Grouchy, was wounded at Wavre and retired to Belgium. He returned in 1817 where he was elected Deputy of Paris in 1822, re-elected in 1827 for Bergerac. Minister of War and Maréchal of France in 1830, Deputy for Senlis in 1833, then Grand Chancellor of LH in 1836. Senator in 1852; in 1816 he had married the daughter of General Valence. He died in 1852.

Maison was Mireur's deputy in 1794; he was wounded five times that year. He crossed the Rhine and was with Bernadotte in 1795. He became his aide de camp in 1804; then he was appointed General in 1806. He replaced Léopold Berthier as Chief of Staff of the 1st Corps. He was at Friedland, became a Baron, was with Oudinot in Russia. He was made a Count in 1813, GdCx of the Reunion and Peer of France in 1814. GdCxLH, he followed the King to Gand and rallied to Louis-Philippe, became Maréchal of France in 1829. Minister of War in 1835-36, GdCx of Léopold of Belgium.

Chalopin was killed at Austerlitz.

● **Commanding the Artillery**

Eblé was a child of the regiment, the Auxonne Artillery Regiment; he was a gunner in 1791, a General in 1793. He commanded the Artillery of the 1st Corps in 1805, was appointed Governor of Magdeburg, Minister of War for Westphalia then Baron. GdOLH. Chamberlain to Jérôme, he commanded the bridging teams in Russia. He built the bridges over the Beresina. He was Commander in chief of the Artillery of the Grande Armée in 1813; his title of Count was given to his widow because he died of illness at Koenigsberg in December 1812.

Juvisy joined up in 1774; he was wounded three times in 1796. He was Squadron Commander at Zurich, Hohenlinden. LH in 1805, OLH in 1807. He was retired in 1807, recalled, then went back home in 1809.

For the battle of Austerlitz, Napoleon took the whole of the vanguard and the cavalry off this corps and gave it to Lannes and Murat on the French left wing. They have been put with the 5th Corps in this book. So Bernadotte only had the two basic divisions, which rather annoyed him.

THE 1st DIVISION

Rivaud de la Raffinière volunteered in 1792, was wounded in 1793, was at Arcola and Rivoli, was made a General in 1798. He was wounded at Marengo and became Major-

Above from left to right and top to bottom.
Maréchal Bernadotte, Commander of the 1st Corps; Rivaud de la Raffinière, commanding the 1st Division; Maison, Chief of Staff of the 1st Corps; Eblé commanding the artillery; Drouet d'Erlon commanding the 2nd Division; and Pachtod, General commanding the 1st Brigade of the 1st Division. (RR)

● **The 45th of the Line**

Colonel Barrie volunteered in 1792. Captain in the 20th Light in Italy, he was made battalion Commander then Colonel in 1800. He was in Spain (CtLH), was made a Baron, wounded at Talavera and made a General in 1810. Besieged at Ciudad-Rodrigo, he was taken prisoner; he was given leave of absence in 1815 and retired in 1825.

Only one officer wounded at Austerlitz.

● **The 54th of the Line**

Colonel Phillipon was born at Rouen and was with the 54th in 1803. Appointed OLH and then Baron. It was in Spain that he was made a General in 1810, then Major-General in 1811. He was with the 1st Corps in Russia and replaced the wounded Morand. He retired in 1813.

One officer of the 54th of the Line was wounded.

The division was not really committed by Bernadotte who was being very passive and who did not move very keenly towards Austerlitz.

General in 1802. He was at Ulm, Austerlitz and Lubeck. He was Governor of Brunswick and was made a baron in 1808, then count in 1814. He was suspected of having contacts with the Vendee faction during the Hundred Days so he was given leave of absence. Deputy for Charente-Inférieure, CrSL in 1820, GdCxLH in 1825, he retired in 1825.

PACTHOD'S BRIGADE.

Pacthod, Bodyguard to the King of Sardinia, rallied to France in 1792, was wounded seven times at Toulon. General in 1795, he was at Austerlitz in 1805, then at Friedland. He was made a Baron, then Major-General in 1808. He was in Italy, at Raab and Wagram. Couronne de Fer. He fought at Ragusa in 1812 then in Saxony in 1813. GdOLH and Count, Hero of the French Campaign, naturalised in 1816, retired in 1826, he died in 1830.

● **The 8th of the Line**

Colonel Autié was born in the Hérault, mentioned in the Pyrenees, he fought in Italy, at Bassano and Zurich. He was made a Colonel in 1803, he was mentioned at Austerlitz. He was killed in Spain at Chiclana in 1811.

There were no officers wounded in this regiment.

Douart was wounded 7 times in 1807. LH. Taken at Dresden, but served in 1815. Retired.

Aymard was born at Lézignan and wounded in the Pyrenees. He fought in Italy at Lodi, Rivoli and wounded again ant Novi. Battalion Commander at Austerlitz and Lubeck, he was a Colonel of the 32nd at Friedland. Baron. OLH in Spain, made a General in 1813, wounded at Leipzig and at Hanau; he was with the Young Guard at Antwerp. Retired in 1816, became Lieutenant-General in 1832 and put down the revolt in Lyons. Peer of France in 1834, GdCxLh in 1841, made aide de camp to the King and retired in 1842.

No losses for this regiment.

THE 2nd DIVISION

Drouet d'Erlon was born at Reims, joined up in 1782, made a General in 1799. present at Zurich, wounded at Hohenlinden, made a Major-General in 1803. He commanded the division from September 1805 at Hanover. He was present at Austerlitz, and Lubeck. He was Chief of Staff to Lefebvre in Danzig during the siege. Made a count in 1809, he went to Portugal with Masséna, and to Spain at Vittoria and Toulouse. GdCxLH in 1814, he acquitted Exelmans and plotted with Lefebvre-Desnoettes. He was at Waterloo, Peer of France in 1815, he sought refuge in Munich; sentenced to death in absentia, but pardoned by Charles X for the Coronation, he became Governor-General of Algeria in 1834-35. Maréchal of France in 1843, he died in 1844.

His Chief of Staff was **Fornier d'Albe** who was in Egypt as aide de camp to Menou. Wounded at Ulm (CtLH), he was made a General after Wagram. He was in Paris in 1815; retired in 1825.

FRERE'S BRIGADE

There is only one regiment in this brigade during the battle.
● **The 27th Light**

Colonel **Charnotet** was born at Annecy and became Colonel of the regiment in 1803. OLH after Austerlitz. Retired as a General in 1807, he was made a Baron. He commanded the Nord Department at Arras during the Hundred Days and was retired definitively in 1819.

Soulès received a Sabre of Honour in 1803 for taking 30 prisoners at Salo in Italy. He was Second-Lieutenant at Austerlitz then took part at Jena then retired in 1807.

Herbez-Latour (LH) was at Austerlitz, wounded at Lubeck, appointed Colonel of the 101st in Spain. He was wounded and captured at Salamanca, but returned in 1814. Trapped in Neufbrisach during the Hundred Days, he was retired in 1823, the appointed Honorary Maréchal de camp in 1824. Recalled to Besançon in 1830.

Savoye volunteered in the Allobroges and was one of the first on the bridge at Lodi. LH. He was in Spain where he was wounded in 1811. Aide de camp to Desaix, he was made Battalion Commander in the 8th Light. He was at Lyons in 1814, at Waterloo and so retired in 1816.

Martinet only mentions three officers being wounded in this regiment which was not engaged very much.

WERLÉ'S BRIGADE

Werlé joined up in 1781, became a General in 1803 in Hanover. He was at Lubeck and in Spain where was killed at Albufera in 1811.
● **The 94th of the Line**

Colonel Razout was born at Toulon; he was in Italy with Masséna then became aide de camp to Joubert and took part in 18 Brumaire. Appointed Colonel in 1803 and General in 1807, he was wounded in Spain. He was with Oudinot at Wagram, Major-General in 1811 and was wounded in Russia. GdOLH. Count in 1813, he was captured at Dresden but served in 1815. He was Morand's judge and died in 1820.

De Grométy was born at Toulon this child of the regiment became a Captain AM in the 94th in 1800. Mentioned in despatches at Hochstadt, he was sent by Moreau with the flags to Napoleon. Commanded the 2nd Battalion of the 94th Light, he was wounded at Austerlitz. Major with the 95th in 1807, he was taken prisoner at Baylen and escaped from the hulk ship the Vieille Castille. Appointed Colonel of the 40th in 1812, he returned to Spain and was with the Young Guard in 1813. He was at Waterloo, retired in 1822, he was pensioned off in 1828. He was Maréchal de camp in 1831. CrLH in 1821.

Delamarne was Swiss, Adjudant-Commandant in 1807, he was retired in 1810. Naturalised in 1814, he served in 1815 and retired the same year.

Four Officers from this regiment were wounded at Austerlitz.
● **The 95th of the Line**

Colonel Pécheux was Colonel in 1803, he was at Austerlitz, Lubeck and Friedland. He was appointed General in 1810, and Major-General in 1813. He was in Hamburg with Davout and fought in Spain in 1823. GdOLH in 1825.

Meylier was at Austerlitz. Colonel of the 12th Light at Essling, he was wounded there. He was wounded also at Wagram. He retired to the Gironde in 1812.

Only one officer from this regiment was wounded, even though it helped the Cavalry of the Guard at the moment of the great Charge.

DAVOUT'S 3rd CORPS

This was the heroic corps par excellence.

The Marshal's aide de camps were the following.

Bourke, born near Lorient was of Irish origin. He was in Cochinchina from 1788-90. Wounded at St Domingo, he returned in 1793 and set sail for Ireland where he was captured. Returned in 1799, he was the first aide de camp to Leclerc at St Domingo in 1802; wounded, he came back in 1803, to become Davout's first aide de camp at Austerlitz. Wounded at Auerstaedt, he was at Eylau. Made a Baron, he was at Wagram. General in 1809, he was with Reille in Spain, wounded twice. He was Governor of Wesel which he managed to keep. He defended Givet during the Hundred Days. Inspector of the Infantry, Commanded a Military Division, he served in 1823, CrSL and Peer of France in the same year. GdCxLH in 1826, GdCx of the Order of St Ferdinand, he was on the reserve cadres list in 1839.

Davout, Louis, brother of the Marshal, he became his aide de camp in 1795. He was in Egypt and was a Colonel in 1805. He was at Austerlitz, Auerstaedt, Eylau; CtLH in 1807, Baron. He took part at Wagram, was made a General in 1811. He was unemployed during the Hundred Days and he was given leave of absence in 1818. Napoleon III gave the family the right to use the Title of Duke of Auerstaedt.

Maréchal Davout, the exceptional commander of the heroic 3rd Corps. (DR)

Falcon was born at Castelnaudary and was a Captain-Aide de camp to Davout in 1802. He was at Austerlitz (LH); made a Baron, he was Colonel of the 46th in 1813. He was killed in Silesia on 29 August 1813.

Trobriant, Lieutenant was sent to Bernadotte during the Battle of Auerstaedt. He made a report criticising Bernadotte and what he says has been bitterly discussed since.

Marès was Captain of the gunners in the Hérault Volunteers, Battalion Commander in the Engineers in 1794, then arrested and reinstated in 1795. Brigade commander in 1799, he was Adjudant-Commandant in 1803. He was Friant's Chief of Staff at Austerlitz where he was mentioned in the report drawn up by Davout about the serious wound to his thigh and the loss of several horses.

De Montesquiou-Fezensac, Anatole. Mentioned in several books as having this job, he only occupied it in 1808. it was his brother Charles-Eugene who had the post, appointed on 21 December 1805 and attached to Berthier's Headquarters for Austerlitz. He died at Ciudad-Rodrigo in 1810.

The Chief of Staff was **Daultane** (Marquis d'Aultane), Gentleman-Cadet in 1776, Captain in 1792, he was a General in 1799 at Hohenlinden. At Austerlitz, he was considered to be brilliant during the battle by Davout. He became Major-General. In 1806, He was at Auerstaedt and replaced Gudin at Putulsk. Baron, Governor of Warsaw, he served in Spain and at Toulouse in 1814. Chief of Staff to the Duke of Angoulême, he was decorated with GdOLh in April 1815. Struck off and destituted by Napoleon (CrSL) he got his pension in October 1815.

Marès was born at Marseillan in the Hérault and was Battalion Commander, director of the Engineers' Pool in Italy in 1794, Brigade Commander in 1799. He commanded the Engineers at Genoa in 1800. He was Adjudant-Commandant in 1803 at the Camp at Bruges. He was Chief of Staff for the Friant Division and died as a result of his wounds at Austerlitz in January 1806.

The Chief Ordonnateur was **Chambon** (OLH in 1807), Chief Ordonnateur in 1800. CtLH. He continued in 1813 and 1814, he was in the Ministry of War during the Hundred Days. Retired in 1816.

Daultane's aide de camps were the Squadron Commander **Lefebvre** who had come from the 8th Hussars; He was Major in the 11th Dragoons and he was killed at Austerlitz.

A number of Adjudant-Commandants and deputies were mentioned, among whom:

Larcilly was battalion Commander of the 108th in 1800. He was on the General Staff in 1804 (LH). He was wounded just before Austerlitz on 20 November then at Wagram. Major in the 9th of the Line (OLH in 1810), he was killed at Lutzen.

THE INFANTRY OF THE LINE

Grenadier of the Regiment. The Grenadiers formed one of the two Elite companies of the regiment since the creation of the Voltigeurs, on 20 September 1804. They were distinguishable by the red fringed epaulettes and the fur hat, sometimes replaced by the hat with a red pompon.

Fusilier in marching dress.

In principle they were armed with the Dragoons rifle which was shorter, or even a shortened infantry rifle.

Voltigeur.

Grenadier wearing a greatcoat.

Grenadier Corporal wearing marching dress.

Grenadier Drummer.

Fusilier.

André Jouineau © Histoire & Collections 2003

Sorbier was commander of the artillery, a former pupil of the artillery school in 1782, he was made a General on the battlefield by Hoche in 1797. Appointed Major-General in 1800, he occupied this position in 1805. He was at Austerlitz, in Italy, at Raab. Made Gd Cordon of the Couronne de Fer in 1809, he commanded the Artillery of the Guard in 1811, then that of the Grande Armée in 1813 and 1814. (CrSL and GdCxLH in 1814) Deputy during the Hundred Days, exiled to Cognac, he was retired in 1815.

His aide de camps were **Sautereau du Part** from the School at Chalons and who became aide de camp to Sorbier in 1802. He was with the Guard in 1812 and was Chief of Staff of the Artillery of the Guard in 1813. He defended Besançon during the Hundred Days. As a Colonel, he was in Spain in 1823, CrLH; retired in 1829, he was Honorary Maréchal de camp in 1830…

Gering went to the School at Chalons, Sorbier's Aide de camp in 1802. He was on the Island of Oleron in 1811, at Toulon then Lyons in 1814. Colonel, OLH, he was in Spain in 1823, CrLH.

The Artillery's Chief of Staff was **Charbonnel**. Born at Dijon, a pupil at the School in Chamons, he served in Lyons and Toulon, in Italy, in Egypt. Sent back because of eye-trouble, he was captured, was cured and became a Colonel in 1804. He was in this post from 1805. He served at Austerlitz, Auerstaedt, Eylau, Eckmuhl, Essling and Wagram. Appointed General in 1809, he was in Spain and in Portugal at Busaco and Fuentes de Onoro. He was with Ney in 1813 for Lutzen and Bautzen but was wounded at Leipzig. He was present during the French Campaign, made a Count in 1814. He was with Suchet in the Alps and was President of Grouchy's Court Martial in 1817. GdCxLH in 1824, Peer of France in 1841, he died in 1846.

The Engineers were commanded by **Colonel Tousard** from the School of Mézières; he was in Malta and Egypt where he was wounded. He was a Colonel and OLH in 1805. He served at Austerlitz, Auerstaedt and Eylau. Appointed General in 1807, then Baron, he replaced Bertrand for three months in 1810. He was at Hamburg in 1813, where he died on 15 September.

Bouviers went to Mézières too and was wounded twice in 1793. he was mentioned in despatches at the Fort du Bard in 1800, then appointed Chief of Staff of the Engineers of the 3rd Corps. LH and Major in 1809, he became Colonel in 1810. He was killed at Krasnoy.

The following were mentioned by Headquarters:

Lacoste, Surgeon: *"Exposed himself like an ordinary soldier to succour the wounded. His conduct is above all praise."*

Girardin was Maréchal des logis in the 1st Battalion artillery train. At Austerlitz his wrist was sliced by a sabre when the Russian cavalry charged the 1st Division's artillery.

Curély was Adjudant-NCO with the 7th Hussars and became a famous General. *"At the head of ten men, he got two companies of enemy infantry to surrender."*

Frech, a Gendarme got himself noticed by his bravery. He had his shoulder shattered by a biscayen bullet.

Arnould, a Gendarme Maréchal des logis, served with Maréchal Davout with *"a lot of zeal and intelligence."*

Guilbeau a Chasseur with the 1st Regiment: *"Being on duty with General Daultane, rushed several times in the middle of the enemy battalions which he sabred, and took many prisoners."*

Saradin, a Sergeant in the 2nd Regiment of the Chasseurs à Cheval, **"In the presence of General Frial, he charged the Russians several times, killed several men and captured an officer."**

General **Caffarelli** 1st division of the 3rd Corps was taken away from the column and sent to the left wing, under Lannes. Only the Friant and Gudin Divisions were left. As they had come up from Vienna, fighting brilliantly, Napoleon's order to reach Raygern as quickly as possible could only apply to Friant's Division, who was 36 leagues away. Gudin was even further away and could only start to come up towards the battlefield. Friant's march was an example of courage. The soldiers had been well schooled with Davout, these soldiers were the most solid and reliable of the Grande Armée and they proved it at each battle. In 1806 they were rewarded by having the privilege of entering Berlin first as the victors of Auerstaedt.

FRIANT'S DIVISION

Urgently called up from the neighbourhood of Vienna, they made a remarkable forced march in a single stretch. They were billeted in Raygern. This remarkable march of 36 leagues done in 40 hours brought the elite regiments up at the right moment. Bedded down for the night of 1 December with Bourcier's Dragoons and the 1st Dragoons attached to Heudelet's Brigade, they tried to recover their strength after such an exhausting march. Stragglers continued to arrive as best they could, but the division was not up to strength and Gudin had just started his march towards Brünn, so he could not be counted on.

Friant entered the French Guards in 1781. Lieutenant-Colonel of the 9th Battalion of Paris cal-

Bourke, Davout's Aide de Camp. (RR)

led the 'Arsenal', he was wounded in 1793. Appointed General in 1794, he was in Italy, then in Egypt with Desaix and went up the Nile with Davout. Major-General in 1800, he had four horses killed under him at Austerlitz, where his division covered itself with glory at Telnitz and Sokolnitz. Friant was made Gd Aigle LH on 27 December 1827; he was as brilliant at Auerstaedt. Wounded at Eylau, entrusted with the vital outflanking movement at Wagram, his action was decisive for victory. In Russia, he was wounded twice at the Moskova, he was appointed Colonel Commandant of the Grenadiers à Pied of the Guard to replace Dorsenne. Napoleon's Chamberlain, he commanded the Division of the Old Guard in 1813 and 1814. Peer of France, First Colonel of the Grenadiers of the Old Guard at Waterloo, where he was wounded. He had married Louise Leclerc, the General's sister and Madame Davout, so he was the Marshal's brother-in-law.

His Chief of Staff was **Marès** who has already been mentioned above.

His aide de camps were the following. **Petit** was Mireur's aide de camp in Italy then was seconded to Friant in Egypt. Major in the 15th Light in 1806, he was in Portugal. Colonel of the 67th with Molitor, he was at Aspern and was wounded at Wagram. Baron and General in 1811 in Spain, First Major of the Grenadiers of the Guard in 1813, he was then Major-Colonel of the 1st Regiment of the Grenadiers at Waterloo where he covered the retreat. He retired as Honorary Lieutenant-General in 1825, his appointment was confirmed in 1831. Peer of France in 1837, GdCxLH in 1847, he was elected Senator in 1852. He died in 1852 and was buried at the Invalides.

Hols, Navy Lieutenant, transported the Army to Egypt, Lieutenant with the Légion Nautique, he was wounded three times. Aide camp to Friant in 1801, Captain and aide de camp at Austerlitz, LH and OLH in 1807. Battalion Commander of the Flankers of the Guard in 1811, he was made Colonel of the 111th of the Line in 1813. He died in Hamburg from his wounds in January 1814.

Binot was a volunteer with the Arsenal Battalion with Friant and became his aide de camp in 1797. He was in Egypt then in India with Decaen. Chief of Staff to Saint-Hilaire at Austerlitz, CtLH in 1805, he became a General in 1806 and was killed at Eylau.

Friant particularly mentioned (according to the report drawn up by Davout) **Bonnaire** who was born at Prouvais in the Aisne. He was wounded at Austerlitz. Colonel at Wagram in 1809, he was still with the 3rd Corps. OLH, Baron and Colonel of the 103rd in Spain where he was wounded. General in 1813, he commanded Condé in 1815 and shot at a negotiator. Arrested, reduced to the ranks and deported, whereas his aide de camp, Mietton was shot; he died of grief on 16 November 1816.

— THE 1st BRIGADE

Heudelet de Brière was born at Dijon and was with the Army of the Rhine in 1793. He crossed the Rhine in the lead in 1797, appointed General in 1799, he beat General Meerfeldt at Maria-Zeller where he captured three flags, 16 cannon and made 4 000 prisoners. At Austerlitz he had four horses killed under him and was made a Major-General. He was at Jena-Auerstaedt and was wounded at Eylau; he was made a Count in 1808, was with Soult in Spain, then in Portugal at Bussaco. He was at Danzig in 1812 (GdOLH in 1813). He was with the Army of the Rhine in 1815. Retired in 1824, Lieutenant-General in 1831, Peer of France in 1832, he retired in 1835.

His aide de camp was **Liégeard**, born at Dijon, was in Vendée where he captured Stofflet. Captain with the 14th Chasseurs, aide de camp to Heudelet at Austerlitz, he was wounded at Eylau. Squadron Commander with the 7th Hussars in 1807, he became Colonel of the 11th Hussars in 1812 in Russia. He was a Baron in 1813, wounded; he took part in the French Campaign. He took part also at Waterloo and retired in 1816.

● The 108th of the Line

Colonel Higonet, an Egypt veteran, Battalion Commander in Italy, was mentioned at Maria-zeller. He was at Austerlitz (CtLH) and killed at Auerstaedt.

Schmitz was present at Zurich, wounded, Captain in the 108th in 1805, OLH. He defended Sokolnitz. Present at Auerstaedt, was Battalion Commander in 1806. He was at Eylau and was wounded in 1809. Major with the 32nd, Colonel of the 2nd de Marche in Spain, he served with Ney in Russia and was wounded at Krasnoï. General in 1813, he served in Italy and then at Waterloo. Retired in 1815.

Baudoz, Lieutenant, Sabre of Honour, OLH, was killed at Eylau.

Also mentioned were **Gonichon**, Lieutenant: *"Behaved with the utmost courage, was one of the first to rush upon the enemy, killed several of them and took others prisoner."*

Pidolle, Adjudant-NCO; *"Did not stop moving up and down the ranks to incite the soldiers to do their duty, following his example."*

Humbert, Grenadier Sergeant: *"Was one of the first to charge, killed several of the enemy and took a good number of prisoners."*

Dupont, Sergeant: *"Rushed a gun which he captured after having killed with his own hands the gunners who were defending it."*

THE LIGHT INFANTRY

The Light Infantry was organised like the Infantry of the Line, even though it was considered to be an Elite regiment. The Chasseurs were the equivalent of the fusiliers for the Line; whereas the Elite companies were made up of Carabiniers, the equivalent of the Grenadiers and the Voltigeurs. The distinctions were identical to those of the Line, except for the plateless bearskin cap. On the other hand, the other companies were already wearing the shako, since 1801. This was a cylinder-shaped hat with a leather visor.

Chasseur.

Carabinier.

Voltigeur in marching dress.

Carabinier NCO in General Oudinot's Reserve.

NCO In the Corsican Tirailleurs.

Chasseur.

General Oudinot's reserve included companies taken from the different regiments of the Line and the Light Infantry.

André Jouineau © Histoire & Collections 2003

Drum-Major and Drummers of an infantry regiment of the Line before getting the order to lead the charge to the beat of the drums. (RR)

Burais, Sergeant: *"Held off four cavalrymen, killed some of them was himself wounded and made prisoner."*

Loisy, Corporal: *"Distinguished himself by capturing a flag at Marianzell."*

Mauzy, Grenadier: *"After having killed several Russians, he rushed a group of the enemy in the middle of which was a flag which he seized."*

Bardoux, Fusilier: *"Captured a canon, killed the gunner about to fire it and took three prisoners."*

Pront, Grenadier: *"Took a flag off the enemy."*

— **KISTER'S BRIGADE**

Kister was born at Sarreguemines and served with his father in 1764. General in 1799, he received several wounds and several horses killed under him, especially in Italy. He was in command of the 15th Light in 1795 and was in the Army of the Alps. He made the crossing of the Saint-Bernard easier and contributed to the success at Marengo through his use of diversions. CtLH, he joined Davout and served at Austerlitz. He was at Danzig in 1811 and became Commandant of the Seine-Inférieure. He retired in 1812.

● **The 15th Light**

Desailly was already a Brigade Commander in 1800. He was at Wertingen, Hollabrunn and Austerlitz. CtLH on 25 December 1805. General in 1809, wounded at Wagram then at Valoutina, retired in 1813. In his report on the battle Davout congratulated the Major who should have led the attack. This was Major Geither, born in Germany and joined up in 1784. He was a Captain in Italy and Egypt where he was wounded. Commanded the 5th Battalion of Oudinot's Grenadiers and was made a Major in 1804. Wounded twice at Austerlitz whilst leading the regiment, he was replaced by Dulong de Rosnay. OLH in and General in 1811, he was with Oudinot in Russia. He lost his right arm at the Beresina and was with Rapp in 1815 at Landau. Given leave of absence after the Hundred Days, he was appointed Maréchal decamp in 1817. Naturalised in 1818, he was retired in 1820 then in 1837.

Dulong de Rosnay was wounded in 1799, wounded three times at Montegaleazzo. Battalion Commander in 1803 with the 15th Light, he crossed the Alps over the Saint-Bernard Pass; his right shoulder was shattered at Austerlitz, served at Eylau and was made Colonel of the 63rd in Portugal; he joined the 12th Light. Couronne de Fer and General in 1813. He joined the Young Guard and was made a Baron. Wounded at Dresden, GdOLH in 1814, he was Lieutenant in the Havré Gardes du Corps then Lieutenant-General in 1815. Gd Cx SL in 1825, Count in 1827, he died in 1828. He was probably replaced by Licasse after his wound.

Hulot was already in the regiment in 1794, wounded twice at Gradisca, then twice at La Trebia, he received a Sabre of Honour in 1803. Promoted to Lieutenant in 1809, he retired in 1811.

Five companies from the regiment made up the 2nd Grenadier Battalion of the 5th Regiment of the reserve.

Also mentioned at Austerlitz were **Licasse**, Captain-Adjudant-Major who probably replaced the wounded Dulong in the village of Sokolnitz, and drove back vastly superior forces with a little unit.

Vignier was a Lieutenant whose extremely brave conduct got him praise by Colonel Bourke, first aide de camp to Maréchal Davout, in whose command he served.

Garay, Adjudant-NCO: *"One of the first to rush into the village of Sokolnitz and rallied the Chasseurs several times."*

Dorbeau, Sergeant: *"Seriously wounded by a shot and beaten down by several Russians he managed to wound several of them."*

Surdun, Sergeant-Major: *"Rushed a Russian platoon single-handed, grappled with three of them, killed one, wounded another and was wounded himself by the third with several bayonet thrusts."*

Brondès, Sergeant-Major: *"Carried the flag of the 2nd Battalion which he defended with great courage against two Russians who were intent on taking it off him."*

Aubouer, Corporal-Fourrier: *"One of the first to enter Sokolnitz and rushed furiously against the Russians Grenadiers. He received two bayonet wounds and continued to defend himself with courage until he dropped and had to be carried off."*

Dumont, Corporal: *"Contributed to defending the flag, killed a Russian and saved his captain's life."*

The companies of Voltigeurs of the 15th Light marched with Heudelet, completing his brigade with the support of the 1st Dragoons.

● **The 33rd of the Line**

Saint-Raymond was Colonel since 1794, OLH. He died on 1st December 1805.

Thoulouze replaced him after he died, was wounded at Eylau, and then at Wagram; he was killed at Valoutina in 1812.

Peigne was in Italy where he received a Sabre of Honour at la Trebia. Second-Lieutenant in 1806, he was a Captain and mentioned at the Beresina in 1812. Battalion Commander in 1814, he was dismissed in 1815.

Lieutaud took two flags near Verona and received a Sabre of Honour. OLH. He was a Captain at Austerlitz, he retired in 1810.

Thierry was a Captain in Italy in 1795, was wounded while capturing a canon in 1797. He received a Sabre of Honour in 1802. Battalion Commander in 1809, he was killed in front of Regensburg trying to get the enemy out of the houses where they were hiding.

Also mentioned were: **Belin**, Captain: *"Led the Voltigeurs with intrepidity in the village of Sokolnitz, where he killed 7 Russians, being put out of action by two shots."*

Tondut, Lieutenant. Replaced on the battlefield the aide de camp to General Kister, killed at the battle of Austerlitz, was particularly calm-headed, brave and intelligent. Had a horse killed under him by two shots. He was awarded the LH and was battalion Commander in 1809. Wounded at the Moskova, OLH in 1813, he was put on half pay in 1814.

Calliez, Second-Lieutenant: *"Distinguished himself and although hit by three bullets, he did not leave the battlefield."*

Barbanègre, the Colonel of the 48th of the Line. (RR)

Marc, Fusilier: *"Distinguished himself. Found himself to be surrounded by several Russians, he killed three and was saved."*

Villain took a flag from Butyrsk.

— **LOCHET'S BRIGADE**

Lochet joined up in 1784, served in Vendée. Commanded Friant's 1st Brigade, had two horses killed under him at Austerlitz. CtLH. Present at Auerstaedt, he was killed by a bullet in the forehead at Eylau. Friant said of him *"that nobody was more beautiful than him in combat."*

His aide de camps were **Jaeger** who was killed at the Moskova; and Galichet, a Captain with the 94th in 1803. LH in 1806, Battalion Commander with the 108th in 1808. He became Adjudant-Commandant and Baron in 1809. He was with Friant as Chief of Staff in Russia, OLH, captured and returned in 1814. He resigned and returned to Poland, his wife's Country.

● **The 48th of the Line,** the most deserving Regiment.

It was commanded by **Barbanègre** who came to the job on 29 August 1805. He was at Austerlitz, CtLH for this battle. Present at Auerstaedt and Eylau; he was made a Baron and General in 1809. He served at Eckmuhl and at Wagram with Morand. In Russia, he commanded at Smolensk and surrendered at Stettin in 1813. He was with Lecourbe in 1815. He was a hero of the defence of Huningue, he died in 1830.

The following were mentioned in this regiment. **Lacombe**, Battalion Commander: *"Ordered to attack the village of Sokolnitz with his battalion from the left, he did this with the greatest determination, got through vastly superior forces and was then wounded in the middle of the action."*

Pleindoux, Voltigeur Lieutenant: *"His Company being ordered to push back the enemy*

Tirailleurs at the beginning of the engagement, he rushed them leading his company with him by his leadership and his voice. He was one of the first to enter the village and conducted himself during the whole day with great distinction."

Lamaguet, Grenadier Second-Lieutenant: *"Particularly contributed to the capture of Sokolnitz by opening a way through a wall which was preventing the grenadiers from reaching the enemy."*

Mathieu, second-Lieutenant: *"During a charge, he reached two artillery pieces first; he captured the two gunners and the guns."*

Paul, Grenadier Sergeant-Major: *"He reached two cannon first and took them."*

Guilloteau, Sergeant-Major; *"With the first charge, he forced his way into a house defended by three Russians whom he disarmed."*

Sallé, Sergeant-Major: *"His Captain, the only officer present, having been wounded, he showed great presence of mind and keenness in taking over the command he was entrusted with; in particular he got a Russian platoon to put down its weapons."*

Ramoun, Grenadier Sergeant: *"In one charge he took four prisoners and killed four Russians."*

Dauvergne, Grenadier Sergeant: *"Helped by his Second-Lieutenant, he managed to knock over part of a wall which was holding up the Grenadiers' advance, saying 'When he is fighting, a Grenadier has to overcome all obstacles.' Once through, he face the fire of fourteen or fifteen Russians and without fear, he charged them with his bayonet, killed six of them and brought the others back prisoner."*

Bruxeau, Grenadier: *"Got through the enemy column, killing a lot of them. He was forced to fall back, covered in wounds, went into a barn where he found several of the enemy which he killed or made prisoner."*

Hubert, Voltigeur: *"Was one of the first to walk with three Chasseurs à Cheval from the 2nd Regiment, captured a canon with them and then single-handedly captured a Russian flag."*

Parent, Voltigeur: *"Captured a Standard-Bearer who had thrown away the shaft, but who hung onto the cloth which he had hidden among his neckerchief, but which Parent took off him."*

Osmont, Voltigeur: *"Went to the right of the village where a gun was firing grapeshot at the oncoming French troops, killed a gunner with his bayonet and taken the gun which the General ordered him to leave where it was and move forward."*

Alluin or **Halluin**, Voltigeur: *"Got hold of a canon and a Flag'* which was Austrian according to Andolenko.

● **The 111th Regiment** (made up of mainly Piedmontese troops).

Colonel **Gay** was born in Lyons and served in Italy, and Egypt. OLH, Baron, captured two cannon at Sokolnitz, retired in 1825, then in 1832.

Guigues de Revel, called Guigue, born at Chambéry, Captain on the Sardinian General Staff, naturalised French as Battalion Commander in the regiment in 1795, he was appointed Adjudant-Commandant in 1806. He was killed in Poland in 1807, mentioned and wounded at Austerlitz.

Also mentioned were:

Ojeda, Captain: *"When charging the Russians, the Standard-bearer of the 2nd Battalion was killed; it was Ojeda who saved the flag, because he rushed out of the ranks to take it."*

Busca, Lieutenant: *"When the Grenadiers of the 1st Battalion took a fortified position in the village of Sokolnitz, he was the first to rush the bridge which was still being protected by two Russian guns firing grapeshot."*

Nardin, Second-Lieutenant: *"Threw himself first, sabre in hand, upon a fortified position at Sokolnitz, took three Russian prisoners after the position was taken by our Grenadiers; received a bullet wound."*

Combet, Sergeant-Major: *"The 1st Battalion charging the enemy out beyond Sokolnitz and being pushed back by superior numbers, they started hesitating. The Sergeant-Major noticed this and moving further forward, flag in hand, he shouted 'Soldiers, rally on me!' This action broke the spell and they rushed upon the enemy and made him fall back leaving a large number of dead and two artillery pieces."*

Barison, Sergeant: *"Wounded by a biscayen bullet, he did not want to retire in spite of his wound before the end of the action."*

Sallio, Sergeant: *"wounded in the morning, he fought all day, in spite of his wound, at the head of his company."*

The Light Infantry of the 3rd Corps moving off into the attack. (Drawings by J. Girbal, RR)

Stuardi and **Roggio**, Corporals: *"These two corporals were wounded during the attack on Sokolnitz, but continued to fight with intrepidity and did not want to go back and have their wounds dressed."*

Chiapella, Grenadier: *"when the 1st Company of Grenadiers attacked and took Sokolnitz, he was one of the first to rush into the fortified positions occupied by the Russians."*

Baghi, Voltigeur: *"Being a Tirailleur, he jumped on four Russians all by himself to kill an officer who was the fifth of the group and, happily, succeeded."*

Grandeau was born at Metz, General in 1803, Major-General in 1812, he was in Russia. Captured when Stettin surrendered in 1813, he obtained the GdOLH in 1814. He commanded Besançon in 1815, retired in 1825. In fact, this General, who was ill from exhaustion after the campaign, did not take part in the battle. So the 108th was commanded by General Heudelet.

The dividing up of the regiments into brigades varies according to he sources. General Grandeau's illness changed the structure of the formation from the start and during the course of the battle the regiments found themselves all mixed up in the various complicated actions, especially in Sokolnitz. It was Friant who directed these operations depending on the needs of the moment. Davout was everywhere in the middle of the battle.

Legrand's battalions which were attacking were all mixed up as well, falling back and rallying outside the village in order to attack again. It really was a terrible struggle against superior forces.

Lochet and the 48th were the heroes of the day and at Tilsitt, during the banquet uniting the two Guards, Grand-Duke Konstantin congratulated an officer of the 48th, this regiment which had *'caused them a lot of trouble at Sokolnitz'.*

The citations which have been mentioned above were precise proposals, intended to obtain the Legions d'Honneur for each regiment. The list for the 48th was the longest. These citations were listed out in the book 'Centenaire d'Austerlitz' by Commandant Martin, published in 1905.

— THE CAVALRY OF THE 3rd CORPS UNDER VIALANNES *(Some elements)*

Vialannes was born at Riom, mentioned at Marengo, General in 1803, CtLH; he was judged unfavourably by Davout at Auerstaedt because he did not stay with headquarters to wait for the orders to arrive on the night before the battle, which meant he was late the following morning. He joined the

Dragoons of Beker's Division. He was at Putulsk and was made a Baron. He was invalided out in 1809. He was used in the commands of the Departments. Retired in 1815.

Only a little part of his brigade was on duty escorting Davout at Austerlitz. The marshal had Friant accompanied by detachments of his cavalry, taken from the 1st and 2nd Chasseurs and 7th Hussars.

It is precise for the **2nd Chasseurs:** three officers and 58 troopers were detached and fought at Austerlitz. Squadron Commander Vigée and Brigadier Gérard were killed. Maréchal des Logis chef Gaillot and Chasseur Boitelle were wounded. Brigadier Saladin was on the list of those mentioned. Colonel Bousson was made CtLH. He was listed as wounded at Auerstaedt with 5 officers. With Gudin, Captain Demaille was in command of 59 men from the 2nd Chasseurs with Lieutenant Goubet. Where the **7th Hussars** were concerned, it is must be noted only that Curély, then an Adjudant was mentioned at Austerlitz by Davout, thus starting his very successful career. For Montbrun's 1st Chasseurs, only Guilbeau was mentioned at Austerlitz. No cavalryman from the 12th Chasseurs appears on the lists.

The Chief of Staff was **Hervo**, born at Quimperlé, Adjudant-Commandant in 1800 at the camp at Bruges. He was mentioned by Davout who presented him rather as his personal Deputy Chief of Staff, which was subsequently true. Wounded at Auerstaedt, General in 1807, CtLH, Baron, he was killed near Eckmuhl in April 1809.

Already mentioned were: **Curély**, Adjudnat-NCO with the 7th Hussars: *"At the head of ten men, he got two companies of enemy infantry to surrender."*

Guilbeau, Chasseur in the 1st Regiment: *"Being on duty with General Daultanne, he rushed several times into the middle of the enemy battalions which he cut up with his sabre, taking several prisoners."*

Saladin, Brigadier with the 2nd Chasseurs: *"In the presence of General Friant, he charged several times against the Russians, killing several and taking an officer prisoner."*

Soult was born at Saint-Amand in the Tarn in 1769. A soldier in 1785, general in 1794, Major-General in 1799 after Stockash; he was with Masséna at Zurich, then at Genoa. A brilliant general, Colonel-General of the Consular Guard, the, of the Camp at Boulogne, he was also Maréchal and Gd Cordon LH. With his corps, he took the Pratzen Heights, commanded at Jena, Lübeck, and Kœnigsberg. He was made Duke of Dalmatia in 1808, served also in Spain, at Gamonal, la Coruna Fezrol, Oporto Arzobispo, and Badajoz. In Andalusia he took Seville. He was called back to the Grande Armée in 1813, he replaced Bessières who had been killed. He went back to Spain to bring back the debris of the Army beaten at Vittoria. On 10 April 1814, he fought at Toulouse where he could have done with Suchet's help. During the Hundred Days, he was appointed Major-General but did not do a good job replacing Berthier in his job. He was banished on 12 January 1816, he retired to Düsseldorf. Reinstated in 1820, Peer of France in 1827, he was Minister of War from 1830 until 1834. President of the Council of Ministers and GdCx of Leopold in 1834, he was appointed Ambassador to the Court of St James for Victoria's coronation. President of the Council again in 1839 until 1847, he died in 1851.

His aide de camps were: **Ricard**, born at Castres. This aide de camp to Suchet in 1799 became Soult's in 1805. Mentioned at Jena, General in 1806, Baron in Spain, dismissed for his intriguing in 1810, he was called back in 1811. In Russia, he replaced Friant who was wounded. He served at Lutzen and Hanau and was with Marmont for the French Campaign. He followed the King to Gand and was made a Peer of France in 1815, then a Count, GdCxLH and GdCx of St Ferdinand in 1823, retired in 1831.

Hulot was already Soult's aide de camp in 1803; he commanded the Pô Tirailleurs in Legrand's division and was wounded at Austerlitz. Present at Lübeck, he was wounded at Eylau. He was a Colonel with Soult in Spain, then General in 1812, Made baron, he was wounded again twice in 1813.; he fought at Leipzig and was wounded at Hanau; served at Ligny and Wavre. He was put on the non-active list in 1815, retired as Honorary Lieutenant-General in 1825.

Lameth, Soult's aide de camp in 1803 was Captain after Austerlitz, wounded at Heilsberg. Promoted to Squadron Commander in 1807, he was Murat's aide de camp in 1808. He was killed in an ambush in Spain.

Comte de Saint-Chamans was Soult's aide de camp in 1804 and was made a Captain after Austerlitz. LH and promoted to Colonel in 1806, he was Colonel of the 7th Chasseurs in 1812 in Russia where he was wounded. Wounded again at Leipzig, he was put on the non-active list during the Hundred Days. Maréchal de camp at the end of 1815, he served in Spain in 1823. GdOLH, discharged and retired in 1830 and 1831. He was the author of memoirs.

Petiet was born at Rennes was with the 10th Hussars in Italy and with Soult in 1803. He was promoted to Lieutenant and aide de camp in 1804. By charging with the Dragoons, he contributed to the capture of 4 cannon at Austerlitz. Made Squadron Commander in 1811, he was with the 2nd Chevau-Légers of the Guard in 1813. Piré's Chief of Staff during the French Campaign, he was mentioned at Brienne and at Nangis where he took 14 guns having being wounded twice. Baron, he was at Waterloo; made a General by the Emperor, he was reduced to Colonel. Recalled in 1823, he was Chief of Staff for the expedition to Alger, and Maréchal de camp in 1830. GdOLH in 1846, Deputy in 1852, re-elected in 1857, retired in 1848.

Delachau was born in the Drome, a soldier in 1779, Second-Lieutenant in Guadeloupe in the 84th. He became Soult's aide de camp in 1802. Squadron Commander, OLH, mentioned at Lübeck; he was made a Chevalier in 1809, he was with Berthier in 1810, retired in 1811.

The Chief of Staff was **De Saligny**, Duke of San Germano. General in 1799, he served at Hohenlinden, CtLH, Major-General in February 1805, he went to Naples. Made a Duke by King Joseph, he followed him to Spain and commanded the Royal Guard. He died in Madrid in 1809; he was the nephew of Julie Clary, Joseph's wife.

His aide de camps were **Compère** who began his career as Saligny's aide de camp in 1799. He went to Naples in 1806, became Garde du Roi, then a Major in the Grenadiers. Cr of the Two Sicilies, promoted to General in 1808, he returned to France as a General in the 3rd Corps for Russia. OLH, he was killed at the Moskova; mentioned by Soult at Austerlitz.

Schmitt was born at Thionville, served in 1790. Lieutenant, he was wounded in the West in 1794. He became aide de camp to Pelletier, then to Saligny. LH. Mentioned by Soult in his report, he was a

Colonel in 1815, retired and pensioned in 1833. He died in 1848.

The Deputy Chief of Staff was **Mériage**, who was born in the Manche. Adjudant-Commandant in 1801 he was with Soult in 1805. He was appointed a General in Moscow, wounded and taken at Krasnoï and returned in 1814. He served during the Hundred Days. He was till active in 1823. Baron, GdOLH in 1826, he was mentioned by Soult at Austerlitz.

Cambacérès was born at Montpelier and served in the 23rd Dragoons. Appointed Squadron Commander in 1801, he was wounded twice and had two horses killed under him. Wounded and mentioned at Hohenlinden, he was made an Adjudant-Commandant in 1803 and attached to the 4th Corps in St-Omer camp. He was mentioned by Soult at Austerlitz. General in 1806, then Baron he was in command at Mainz. He was at the General Headquarters in 1813 and commanded the Indre et Loire Department, then the Aveyron in 1814.

Cosson was born at Lansac in the Gironde; he was Second-Lieutenant in 1784, Brigade Commander in 1794, Chief of Staff of the St-Omer camp and Adjudant-Commandant in 1804. CtLH in 1807. He was made Baron and General in 1808; He was wounded at Wagram, served in Russia, retired in 1813. Appointed Commandant of Belfort in 1815 during the Hundred Days, he retired to Paris and died in 1839; mentioned by Soult.

Lemarois, brother of the General was Battalion Commander and was made Colonel of the 43rd after Austerlitz. He was killed at Eylau; mentioned in the report.

Dufay was subsequently mentioned by Soult as being a Squadron Commander. The author has only found a Captain from the Carabiniers, LH, who had a horse killed under him at Wagram and who retired in 1811.

Arcambal was born in the Puy, former Guard of the Porte du Roi from 1778 to 1787. He became Commissioner forward in 1791, Deputy to Petiet, then Scherer in the Ministry of War. He was Review Inspector in 1800. He was Chief Ordonnateur of the 4th Corps at St-Omer was mentioned by Soult. In 1806, he went to Naples where he became Comissioner-General of the Armies, Grand Préfet of the Palace, Councillor of State and Intendant-General of the King's Household in 1809. From 1813 to 1814, he was Director-General for War. When Murat defected, he went back to France where he was retired as Honorary Chief Review Inspector. He died in 1843.

Above, from left to right: Maréchal Soult and Lariboisière who commanded the 4th Corps' artillery. (RR)

THE 4th CORPS' ARTILLERY

Basto, Comte de Lariboisière was a General in 1803, he commanded the corps' artillery in 1805. Major-General in 1807, he commanded the artillery of the Guard (GdOLH) in 1807. He became Commanding Officer of the Grande Armée's Artillery in 1809 and GdCx of the Couronne de Fer. He died of exhaustion after the retreat, at Kœnigsberg, 21 December 1812.

His Chief of Staff was **Demarçay**. A Pupil of the School at Chalons, he was in the Army of the Rhine, then Egypt and at Marengo. CtLH, he went into Dutch service (Cr.Union) and returned as a Colonel to France in 1808. Retired as a Maréchal decamp in January 1815, he served during the Hundred Days at Poitiers. Imprisoned, elected Deputy for the far left in 1819 in the Vienne, he took part in the 1830 revolution. Re-elected Deputy in 1831, 1834, 1837 and 1839, the year of his death, he was mentioned by Soult.

The director of the reserve pool was **Cabeau**, LH. Made a Colonel in 1806, OLH and Baron he served in 1809 and was retired in 1810. Mentioned by Soult, he was proposed for a Colonelcy.

Cuny, born at Baulay was a gunner in 1769, he took part in the American Campaign from 1780 to 1783. He went to St Domingo. He came back in 1803, appointed Major, commanding Legrand's artillery. Promoted to Colonel in 1806, he retired in 1809. He died in 1827. He was proposed by Soult for the rank of Colonel after 36 years' service.

Degennes was born at Vitré was at the Chalons school. He returned from St Domingo in 1803. Mentioned by Soult, he was made Battalion Commander in 1806. OLH in 1807, promoted to Chevalier and Colonel in 1809, he was killed at the siege of Cadiz at the same time at General Hureau de Sénarmont.

THE 4th CORPS' ENGINEERS

Poitevin was born at Montpelier, came from the School at Mézières and took part in very many sieges and the crossing of the Rhine. He was in Egypt with Caffarelli, then went to the West Indies. Appointed General in 1805, he served in Dalmatia. He was made Baron of Maureillan in 1808 and

THE INFANTRY OF THE LINE

Sapper.

Drum major
of the 18th
of the Line.

Drummer from
a company of Fusiliers.

Subaltern
from
a Fusilier
company.

Sergeant-Major
Standard-Bearer from
the 4th of the Line.
At the beginning
of the Empire,
the flags were still
borne by NCOs except
in the Guard.
This disappeared
during the Empire.

Flag and Eagle, 1804-model.
The reverse was identical
and bore the motto
VALEUR ET DISCIPLINE
Xe BATAILLON
In order to get to know
the history of the Flag of the 4th
of the Line, consult the plate
in *le Plumet* N° 78.

André Jouineau © Histoire & Collections 2003

replaced Marmont in Illyria in 1809.he was with the 4th Corps in Italy and Russia. He served with Ney at the Moskova, surrendered at Thorn and became Lieutenant-General in 1814. He was with Rapp at Strasbourg. Viscount in 1822, GdOLH and Cr du Mérite in 1825, he died at Metz in 1829. Proposed for the rank of General by Soult in his report.

The Engineers' Chief of Staff was **Gerbié**. He served in the army of Italy, took part in the crossing ot the Pô, was at Mantua, in Egypt. He became Battalion Commander in September 1805. He served at Hollabrunn and Austerlitz and was made a Colonel after the battle. He fought at Jena, Lübeck, Hoff and Eylau and was a General in Spain in 1809. He was at Cadiz. Baron. He fought again at Bayonne and at Waterloo. Viscount in 1822, GdOLH in 1823, St-Ferdinand of Spain, Deputy in 1830, re-elected, he died in 1831. He was mentioned by Soult in his report asking for the rank of Colonel for him.

Tholosé. His father died of yellow fever in 1802 at St Domingo, where he was in command of the Engineers. He went to the Ecole Polytechnique, then was a pupil of the School at Metz, he was made a Captain in the 1st Sappers. Mentioned by Soult, he became his aide de camp in 1807 and followed him to Spain. He was promoted to Colonel but remained an aide de camp in 1814. He followed Soult to Waterloo. Put on the Non-active list in 1815, he was called back for the expedition to Spain. Maréchal de camp in 1825, St-Ferdinand of Spain, CrLH, GdOLH in 1833, he died in 1853.

Marie, commanded the Engineers at Perpignan in 1794. He was at Metz. He became Battalion Commander after Austerlitz where he was mentioned by Soult. Aide de camp to Jerome at Naples, he followed him to Spain where he was appointed Maréchal de camp. He returned to France as a General in 1813. OLH, he was with Joseph during the Hundred Days, retired in 1825, Viscount of Fréhaut in 1827, he died in 1835.

Constantin was born at Châteauroux went to the Ecole Polytechnique and was a pupil of the *Ecole d'Application*. Napoleon's Ordnance Officer in 1808, Colonel in 1813 he served at Mainz. In 1815, he was Chief of Staff of the Engineers. He retired as Maréchal de camp in 1831. He was a Chevalier of the Empire in 1810, OLH, Chevalier of the Two Sicilies.

Above from left to right. **Captain Vivien of the 10th Light and the famous General Thiébault commanding the 2nd Brigade.** *(RR)*

SAINT-HILAIRE'S 1st DIVISION

Saint-Hilaire was a cadet in 1777, served in India, at Toulon in 1793, in Italy. He was promoted to General in 1795; he lost two fingers at Logano, was wounded in both legs at Saint-Georges. He became a Major-General in 1799. He was wounded at Austerlitz on the Pratzen Heights. Gd Aigle LH, he served at Jena, Eylau and Heilsberg. Cr of the Couronne de Fer, Count in 1808. Wounded at Essling, he died from his wounds in Vienna. He had a very promising career as a Marshal in front of him and was regretted by all.

The Aide de camps mentioned by Soult were **Roederer** and **Lafontaine**.

The Chief of Staff was **Binot**, a former volunteer of the Arsenal section, aide de camp to Friant in Italy and Egypt. He served in the Indies, returned in 1804. He joined Saint-Hilaire on 24 September 1805. Mentioned by Soult, CtLH after the battle, he was killed at Eylau.

THE ARTILLERY
Cadet de Fontenay, Artillery Captain in 1793. He was at Austerlitz and was mentioned by Soult, becoming a Major in 1806. OLH and Chevalier in 1811, he served in Spain and was wounded at Toulouse. He retired in October 1815 for health reasons.

— MORAND'S 1st BRIGADE
Morand was born at Pontarlier. He was in Italy and Egypt. He was a General in 1800, wounded at Austerlitz; he was promoted Major-General after the battle. He was wounded at Auerstaedt, and Eylau. He was made a Count in 1808. He served at Eckmuhl and was wounded at Wagram. He was wounded at the Moskova, GdCx of the Reunion, he defended Mainz and became aide de camp to Napoleon in 1815. Colonel in the Chasseurs à Pied of the Guard, Peer of France, he recaptured Plancenoit, was sentenced to death in absentia, and went into exile in Poland. He was acquitted in 1819. Retired in 1825, GdCxLH in 1830, Peer of France, he died in 1835. He had the right qualities to be a future Marshal.

His aide de camps were **Morand**, his brother who became a Lieutenant in 1801. LH. He was wounded at Auerstaedt; he was a Colonel Second-in-command with Oudinot in 1809. Made a Baron, he was wounded and discharged because of his wounds. Recommended by Soult for promotion.

Lagarde was born at Lodève. He served in Italy and Egypt. Morand's aide de camp, Squadron

Commander, wounded at Austerlitz, he was recommended for a promotion by Soult in his report. Colonel of the 21st Light in 1807, he was in Spain with Gazan. Promoted to General in 1813, he was CrLH in January 1815. Wounded at Namur on 20 June 1815, he was put on the non-active list then given leave of absence in 1818. He died in 1822.

● The 10th Light
Colonel Pouzet de Saint-Charles was born at Poitiers, commanded the regiment in 1803, OLH. He was wounded at Austerlitz, at Jena and at Eylau. Promoted to General in 1807, he was made a Baron in Spain and was killed at Essling. Mentioned by Soult under the name of Pouret.

Battalion Commander Simonin was killed in combat, encouraged his men before dying.

Captain Vivien, mentioned by Soult as he commanded a battalion during the battle.

The following were mentioned: **Géant**, Commissioner for War: *"Thanks to his good offices, all the wounded were succoured and dressed."* Appeared with **Chappe**, Surgeon Commander of the Corps in Soult's report.

Adam, Captain: *"During the battle he lived up his reputation for bravery."*

Jacot, Captain: *"Commanded the battalion with distinction after the death of Mr Seignoli."*

Thivolle, Captain: *"Displayed intrepidity at Austerlitz."*

Piet and **Dubois**, Second Lieutenants: *"Rushed an artillery piece which they took after cutting to pieces and put to flight the Russian gunners."*

Colet, Sergeant: *"Got hold of an artillery piece, killed the gunner and put the others to flight."*

Jacot, Corporal: *"Captured a flag at Austerlitz."*

Charpentier, Carabinier: *"Captured a flag at Austerlitz."*

Boisson, Sergeant-Major: *"Distinguished himself, was wounded and did not go to the ambulance until after the action."*

Varennes, Chasseur: *"Got hold of a cannon and killed two gunners."*

Phillipon, Chasseur: *"On the third shot which he received, he asked his Captain if he could leave his rank to get care."*

Besançon, Chasseur: *"Got hold of a hitched up gun with four horses and then returned to his place in the ranks."*

Pintard, Voltigeur: *"Took all by himself on his second charge a canon, after killing two gunners; he helped his mate Couturier to capture a second one which these two Voltigeurs turned on a big enemy after having taken five prisoners."*

Pague, Chasseur: *"During the second charge he got hold of a canon and although wounded, forgot his pain and rushed the enemy."*

Lecoq, Chasseur: *"He cut a gun carriage up with his sabre to put it out of action after having helped to capture it."*

Guéroux, Chasseur: *"served a gun which he had just taken after having recovered a lever to load it which was between the gun and the enemy."*

Lebas, Chasseur: *"Having lost his arm near the shoulder, he said very cold-headedly to one of his mates 'Take off my haversack for me, will you?' before going to the ambulance.*

— THIÉBAULT'S 2nd BRIGADE
Thiébault was born in Berlin, volunteered for the Battalion of the Butte des Moulins was imprisoned for being Dumouriez' accomplice and became Solignac's deputy in Italy. Mentioned at Naples, General at Genoa with Masséna in 1800, he was wounded in the shoulder at Austerlitz. Chief of Staff to Junot in Portugal, he was made a Major-General and Baron in 1808. He commanded Burgos in 1809. He disagreed with his boss, Caffarelli and went to Hamburg. Retired in 1825 and then again 1834, he was GdOLH in 1843. He was the author of famous memoirs and was thought of as a butcher, and knew how to be very unpleasant in his memoirs. He was always accompanied by his faithful valet **Jacques Dewint** who was very useful to him during his time spent in hospital. He was also helped a great deal by the Governor who was none other than the defeated strategist, Weyrother, who was a victim of his devotion to the wounded, of whom he saved a great number by improving hospital conditions: he caught hospital fever and died of it.

Thiébault's aide de camp was **Richebourg**, killed at Austerlitz by a bullet through the neck, cutting the air pipes and the big arteries. It was only after the battle that Thiebault found two other aide de camps one of whom, **Parguez**, was sent to him by Morand; the other was a cavalry captain, **Thomassin de la Portelle**.

Parguez was a Second-Lieutenant in the 7th Hussars in 1803, Lieutenant aide de camp to Thiébault at the end of 1805 and joined Morand in 1806. He was a Colonel at Moscow, Adjutant-Commandant, wounded at Leipzig, he was made a Baron and OLH. He served in 1815, retired in 1826 as Honorary Maréchal de camp.

● The 14th of the Line

Colonel **Mazas** was born at Marseilles, became Colonel in 1795. In Italy, he took four cannon in 1800. He joined the 14th of the Line in 1804, but was killed at Austerlitz. He was part of the project of erecting statues to the heroes on the Pont de la the Concorde with Morland and Valhubert. He had not seen an ambush prepared by a Russian battalion who had lain down in front of Pratzen, and was the victim of their first volley.

Fifteen officers were wounded at Austerlitz among whom the two Battalion Commanders Blanc and Rouvelle, together with six captains.

Peugnet was a Captain in the 14th from 1793; he was wounded seven times and was awarded a Sabre of Honour in 1803. Battalion Commander of the 61st after Austerlitz; he was wounded at Auerstaedt. He commanded a temporary half-Brigade from the Pachtod Division at Wagram where he was wounded in the right arm. This wound caused him to be made Commandant in various garrison towns. Baron, he was at La Rochelle in 1814 and served in 1815. Retired and CtLH in 1832.

Reverdeau, drummer, LH. retired in 1811.

Also mentioned were: **Courtois**, Surgeon-Major: *"distinguished himself by dressing the wounded right in the fire of the enemy and by obliging the lightly wounded soldiers to regain their places in the ranks."*

Chauroux, Captain: *"Although seriously wounded he did not leave the battlefield before having taken part in the day's victory."*

Stahl, Captain: *"Distinguished himself by continuing to lead his company against although he was wounded."* He was wounded again at Heilsberg as Battalion Commander; he was killed at the siege of Saragossa.

Montauban, Corporal: *"This soldier having been wounded in the arm by a bullet, took his Sabre and did not want leave the battlefield until he dropped exhausted from his wound."*

Cadet, Voltigeur: *"Distinguished himself."*

Vaillet and **Longuet**, Drummers. *"They distinguished themselves and were always the first beat the charge."*

● The 36th of the Line

Colonel **Houdar de Lamotte** was aide de camp to Baraguey d'Hilliers in Egypt, was at Marengo. LH. Colonel of the regiment in 1805, he served at Ulm and Austerlitz where he was lightly wounded and had a horse killed under him. OLH. Killed at Jena. Mentioned by Soult.

Périer was born in the Orne. He was Captain in the regiment in 1796, Battalion Commander in 1800. LH. Wounded at Austerlitz, he was mentioned by Soult. Major with the 18th in 1806, Colonel of the 55th in 1807, he was killed at Heilsberg.

Also mentioned were **Mother 'Lajoie'** the regiment's famous camp-follower who gave a glass of alcohol to Thiébault before he was carried away.

Labadie who was mentioned by Soult as *"having got the men back into line by using the flag in spite of heavy firing from the enemy."*

Servaud-Guetre, Fusilier: *"Rushed at a gun and forced the enemy to abandon it."*

Chanot, Sergeant-major and Lecachet, Sergeant: *"Charged a canon served by five men at the moment they were about to fire. They killed one and put the others to flight and captured the gun."*

Captain Guilon captured a Flag.

— WARÉ'S 2nd BRIGADE

Waré was born at Versailles, dragoon in 1782, he commanded the 43rd of the Line in 1794. He was at Hohenlinden. CtLH, wounded at Eylau on 8 February 1807, he died of complications on 14 March.

● The 43rd of the Line

Two officers were killed and 24 wounded at Austerlitz.

Colonel **Raymond-Viviès** was born in the Aude, served in the armies of the Pyrenees and Italy. He commanded the regiment in 1800. OLH Mentioned at Austerlitz, he was made a General on 24 December 1805. He was at Jena and captured the cemetery at Eylau. Baron de la Prade in 1808, he was with Molitor at Essling and in Russia with Loison. He died of fever at Vilna in January 1813. Deserved to be a General according to Soult.

Above, from left to right. **General Vandamme and Bigarré, Colonel of the 4th of the Line at Austerlitz.** *(RR)*

Gruyer, Battalion Commander, seriously wounded at Austerlitz, he was mentioned by Soult and became a General in 1813. CtLH Rallied to Napoleon during the Hundred Days; he was with Ney; Baron then deputy, he was outlawed and condemned to death, a sentence which was commuted to 20 years' imprisonment. Pardoned in 1818 he was given leave of absence. He died in 1822.

Also mentioned were: **Freyne**, the 43rd's Drummer: *"Received three wounds but did not stop beating the charge".* He was mentioned by Davout who supervised the elements of Legrand's Division operating with him.

Robet, Assistant-Surgeon-Major: *"This Health Officer went onto the battlefield on the morrow of the battle to dress and recover our wounded. During the battle he followed the regiment's movements and cared for the wounded under enemy fire."*

Vaguener, Voltigeur: *"Captured a flag."*

Mathelin, Grenadier Corporal: *"After getting shot through the arm, he used up all his cartridges before being ordered back to the ambulance by his Second-Lieutenant."*

The regiment lost three officers killed and 11 wounded at Austerlitz.

● The 55th of the Line

Colonel **Ledru des Essarts** was born at Chantenay in the Sarthe. This notary's son went to Italy with Bernadotte and crossed the Tagliamento; then he was Hollabrunn and Austerlitz on the Pratzen Heights. He was promoted to General on 24 December 1805; he was at Lübeck; seriously wounded, he was left for dead at Eylau. Baron des Essarts. He was at Aspern in 1809, wounded in the neck in July, he was replaced by Stabenrath at Wagram. Major-General in 1811, he was in Russia with Ney. He was one of the last to cross the Beresina. Wounded at Leipzig, he fought at Hanau, protested against Marmont's defection (he was under his command in front of Paris) and served with Suchet in the Alps in 1815. He became Inspector-General for the Infantry in 1816, 1820 and 1827. GdCxLH in 1827, Peer of France in 1835, he died in 1844. Already in 1805, he deserved to be a General, according to Soult.

Soult also mentions **Rabié** or **Rabiés**, Battalion Commander. Born at Pauillac, he was wounded three times at Austerlitz, then twice at Saragossa. LH. Commandant d'Armes until his retirement in 1815. OLH in 1836, Mayor of Pauillac.

Oury, Adjutant-Major: *"set an example of courage at the battle of Austerlitz. He was concussed but continued to direct the movements of the 2nd Battalion with just as much calm as if he were on a peacetime exercise."*

Rabion, Captain: *"Although wounded very seriously by a shot to his head while advancing on an enemy battery at Austerlitz, he did not want anybody to leave his place to help him to the*

Maybe a picture of Mother Victory the famous 4th Corps camp-follower. (RR)

ambulance."

Vivien, Captain: *"He drew attention to himself at the head of his company, was wounded and by keeping his chin up and giving a good example of courage to his soldiers."* His memoirs were published in La Sabretache.

Allais, Sergeant-Major: *"Everywhere he went he set an example of a high standard. He killed a Russian at the very moment he was going to plunge his bayonet into the body of one of our Voltigeurs."*

Guilbert, Grenadier: *"Although the oldest in the company, this brave grenadier reached the artillery pieces first, killed the Russian gunner just as he was about fire the gun."*

The regiment had one officer killed and 12 wounded at Austerlitz.

VANDAMME'S 2nd DIVISION

Vandamme was Comte Unseburg and was born at Kassel, joined up in 1788 in the Regiment of the Martinique. Deserted and came back, struck off in 1790, he nevertheless was a General in 1793. Discharged for exactions in 1795, he was recalled and promoted to Major-General in 1799. He was charged with depredation and embezzlement. He took command of the division in 1805 and fought on the Pratzen at Austerlitz. Gd Aigle LH, he fell out with Soult. Count in 1808, he served at Eckmuhl and Wagram where he was wounded; He commanded the Westphalians in Russia under Jerome. Captured at Ulm, he replied to Alexander, who took it badly: "I have never been accused of murdering my father." He fought at Wavre and Ligny with Grouchy. Exiled to Gand, he retired in 1825.

His aided de camps were: **Gobrecht** was also born at Kassel. He was Vandamme's aide de camp from 1794, became Squadron Commander with in 1803 with the 4th Dragoons then Major with the 24th Dragoons in 1806, after Austerlitz; he served at Wagram, was Colonel of the 9th Chevau-Légers Lancers — the former 20th Chasseurs — in 1811. He fought in Russia, found Vandamme again in 1813. Captured at Dresden, he fought at Waterloo and was retired in 1825 with the rank of Honorary Lieutenant-General. CrLH.

Féron was Vandamme's aide de camp in 1796, Squadron Commander in 1799 and received a Sabre of Honour. He was with Vandamme again in 1803, Colonel of the 7th Dragoons in 1806, he was made a Baron and General in 1811. He died during the retreat from Russia. His younger brother was assistant to the division at Austerlitz. The two aide de camps were mentioned by Soult.

The Chief of Staff was **Dubois**, born at Arras, Adjudant-Commandant in 1803, he died in 1808 in Paris.

— SCHIRNER'S 1ST BRIGADE

Schirner was born in Switzerland. He joined up in 1788 and became a General in 1794. He served in the Pyrenees, the Armies of the West and Italy in 1801. He fought at Marengo, CtLH. Mentioned by Soult at Austerlitz, he became a Baron. He was beside Carra St-Cyr in 1809. Retired as a Honorary Lieutenant-General in 1818, then again in 1832.

● The 24th Light

Colonel **Pourailly** was in the Army of the Pyrenees, his brother was killed at Castiglione, and he was wounded twice. He resigned in 1796 and came back in 1799 as a Captain in the 4th of the Line, then as Battalion Commander in the Guard. He was appointed Colonel of the regiment in August 1805. He served at Austerlitz, was wounded at Eylau, made a Baron, and wounded again at Wagram where he lost his left arm. General in 1811, he was CtLH in 1813 and permitted to return home because of his infirmity. He defended Saint-Denis in 1814, served in 1815 and retired definitively in 1825; he was mentioned by Soult.

Kuhn was born at Strasbourg, served at Mainz, then in the Vendée with Kléber where he was wounded twice. He took part in the Irish expedition then fought at Marengo. LH. Major of the Isemburg Regiment in Naples, he died of illness in 1808.

Pépin was born in Switzerland, was a Guide with Kellermann then a Guide in Italy. He fought in Egypt and was awarded a Rifle of Honour for St John of Acre. He was with the Chasseurs of the Guard at Marengo and Lieutenant with the 24th Light at Austerlitz. He returned in 1811. He was wounded 6 times and lived through 14 campaigns.

Also mentioned were: **Belbeze**, Lieutenant: *"He was the first to reach an artillery piece which the enemy was still defending and go it hold of it."*

Pierson, Second-Lieutenant: *"Commanding the Tirailleurs, he got hold of the first two cannon which were aimed and the division's columns."*

Legendre, Sergeant: *"Being used as a Tirailleur, he was charged by three troopers and despite three serious wounds to the head, he killed one of them, wounded the two others and drove them off."*

Barjent, Sergeant-Major: *"He was a standard-bearer on the day and was wounded seriously five times without abandoning the flag."*

Pariaux, Sergeant: *"Being out as a Tirailleur and his officer having been wounded, he took over the command and marched with great intrepidity to the positions occupied by the enemy."*

Labrousque, Chasseur: *"Being a Tirailleur, he had slipped in among the enemy's ranks, wounded and captured a senior officer."*

Dieuzède, Chasseur: *"Being charged down by several enemy troopers, he killed one despite*

several serious wounds, defended himself with his bayonet and threw another trooper off his horse."*

Flamin and **Quitté**, Chasseurs: *"These two soldiers were set out as Tirailleurs, ran to the enemy very intrepidly and brought back twenty prisoners including an officer."*

Maladry, Sapper: *"He was taken prisoner on the eve and freed by the Cavalry of the Guard. The enemy was retiring in disorder, with the help of a Chasseur à Cheval he ran towards a gun and together they brought it back to HM's Headquarters."*

— FEREY'S 2nd BRIGADE

Ferey was the son of a General, joined up in 1788; he was at Mainz then in the Vendée. He commanded the 24th Light in 1796, fought at Marengo. He was a General in 1803, CtLH; he was at Austerlitz and was wounded at Heilsberg.

● The 4th of the Line

The Colonel-in-Chief was theoretically **Joseph Bonaparte**. But for practical reasons, it was Bigarré who directed things at Austerlitz.

Bigarré was born at Bell-Isle-en-Mer; he was a gunner in the Navy in 1791, was wounded twice at Hohenlinden. Major with the 4th in 1805, he was at Austerlitz. He went to Naples as aide de camp to Joseph Bonaparte, he was decorated with the Cross of the Two Sicilies. Promoted to General in 1808, he followed Joseph to Spain. General of France in 1813, he was with the Young Guard. Wounded at Craonne in 1814, he was made a Count in 1815 and Lieutenant-General during the Hundred Days. He was in turn elected Deputy, given leave of absence, and retired in 1825. He was GdOLH in 1833 and Inspector-General of Infantry until 1838, the year of his death.

Guye was born at Lons-le-Saulnier, wounded at Austerlitz, served with Joseph in Naples and became Colonel of the Corsican Legion. Aide de camp to Joseph, he followed him to Spain. Maréchal de camp in 1810, he returned to service in France in 1814. OLH, he was wounded in front of Paris, wounded again at Waterloo; he was put on the non-active list and retired in 1825. Recalled in 1830, he commanded La Flèche.

Calès was born at Caraman, was a Captain at Toulon, joined the 4th in 1796. Mentioned in despatches at Castiglione, he became Battalion Commander 20 March 1805 and Colonel of the 96th in 1807. OLH. In Spain he was wounded at Somo Sierra then at Talavera. He was invalided out in 1810 and made a Baron. He was elected Deputy during the Hundred Days, he died in 1853. Mentioned by Soult.

Duval was present in the Army of Vendee and of Italy; he won a Sabre of Honour for Arcola. At Marengo, he commanded the Tirailleurs. He went over to the Fusiliers-Grenadiers of the Guard and died at Essling.

Vivenot, barrister, was Battalion Commander in 1799, mentioned as being against Dumouriez, mentioned at the Grand St-Bernard Pass, he obtained a Sabre of Honour for Marengo. OLH. Retired in 1807 because of the infirmity caused his wounds.

Lanusse was born at Pau was in the Army of the Pyrenees then in Italy. He became a Second-Lieutenant; he was at Austerlitz, then Lieutenant at Eylau where he was wounded. He served at Essling and Wagram. Retired in 1812, nothing is known about him afterwards.

Gourrat was a hero of Saint-Laurent de la Monga in 1792 where he was seriously wounded. He was wounded again in 1800 at Engen; he won a sabre of Honour. Mentioned in 1809, he was made a Captain. Infirm after Russia, he retired in 1813.

Héricey served at Arcola where he won a Sabre of Honour. Promoted to Second-Lieutenant in 1808 he was killed at Essling.

Twelve officers of the regiment were wounded at Austerlitz.

● The 28th of the Line

Colonel **Edighoffen** was born at Colmar. He was a soldier in 1777, he took part in the siege of Gibraltar. OLH. CtLH for Austerlitz, he was promoted to General in 1806. He served in Spain where he was made a Baron in 1809. He fought at Ciudad-Rodrigo and Bussaco; he became Major-General in 1810, served at Fuentès de Onoro and was killed at Los Arapiles on 22 July 1812.

Bourotte was born in the Meuse, wounded in 1800, became Battalion Commander attached to the General Staff at Austerlitz. He was mentioned by Soult. OLH in 1807, he retired.

Boy was born at Lunéville, wounded and mentioned at Montebello, mentioned at Marengo, mentioned at Mincio, became Battalion Commander. LH. Mentioned by Soult at Austerlitz, he kept him afterwards. He went to Naples, he was a Colonel in the Tyrol in 1809, and commanding Maréchal de camp at Capri in 1811. He came back to France as Colonel on the General Staff in 1816. retired in 1823 with the rank of Honorary Maréchal de camp. He died in 1842.

Also mentioned was Captain **Clunet**: *"with his company he evacuated the village of Aujezd which was dominated by the chapel, took prisoners and captured thirty artillery pieces and just as many caissons."* One officer was killed and one wounded at Austerlitz in this Regiment

— CANDRAS' 3rd BRIGADE

Candras came from burgundy, served in Italy and commanded the 4th of the Line in 1800. General in 1804, CtLH, he joined Saint-Hilaire's division in 1806. He fought at Jena, Eylau and Heilsberg. He was made a Baron, he commanded in Swedish Pomerania. He was in Russia with Oudinot, fought at Polotsk and was killed at the Beresina on 28 November 1812.

ARTILLERY AND ENGINEERS

Senior Officer
in an Artillery
Regiment.

Junior
Officer.

Gunner.

Gunner wearing
trousers.

Drummer.

Soldier
in the Engineers.

Artillery
server.

André Jouineau © Histoire & Collections 2003

● The 46th of the Line

Colonel **Latrille** (Baron, then Count of Lorencez) was born at Pau; He was a volunteer of the Basses-Pyrénées and became Colonel of the regiment in 1805. He was at Ulm and Austerlitz where he was mentioned by Soult. He became a General in 1807 and married Oudinot's daughter in 1811. Wounded in Catalonia, he followed the Marshal into Russia where he was wounded three times. Major-General in 1813, he was wounded twice at Bautzen. GdOLH in 1814, Inspector-General of the Infantry in 1818, CrSL in 1822, he was put on the non-active list in 1837 and was put on the reserve list in 1839.

Legros was born in the Aisne at Anizy-le-Chateau, was captured at Rivoli then returned. He went to Egypt with the 85th. When he returned he joined the Consular Guard then was made Battalion Commander with the 46th. LH. He was at Ulm and Austerlitz where he was mentioned by Soult. OLH. He was made a Major in 1807, he served at Friedland and Wagram. Commandant of Montargis in 1814, he was appointed Colonel in January 1815 but did not serve during the Hundred Days; CrLH in 1825, retired with the rank of Honorary Maréchal des Logis in 1827; he commanded Dunkirk in 1831 and died in 1832.

Menu de Menil was born at Douai, he became Battalion Commander in 1796 in the regiment. Mentioned by Soult at Austerlitz he was wounded at Eylau. Made a Major with the 93rd in 1811 then Colonel in Russia with the 2nd of the Mediterranean which became the 133rd; he was wounded and captured in 1813. OLH. Returned to the 37th in 1814 which was the 39th during the Hundred Days; he was with the Army of the Rhine. He retired in 1816.

Mieu won a Sabre of Honour and was mentioned at Austerlitz, Lieutenant in 1806.

Also mentioned were: **Legagneur**, Sergeant-Major: *"He charged at the head of his soldiers very intrepidly and brought back a howitzer."*

Falaise, Sergeant: *"Charged at the head of the grenadiers and captured a flag."*

Lepoivre, Grenadier: *"This young soldier fought with great courage and although wounded by a bullet in the left arm, did not want to leave his line."*

Vitz, Fusilier; *"wounded in the head by a bullet, he refused to leave his place, saying that he wanted to get his revenge."*

Forgues, Captain: *"remained at his post, even though he had been hit by several bullets."*

Pidoux, Captain: *"Although he had been hit by several bullets, he remained at his post and did not stop exhorting his men to charge."*

Londault, Lieutenant; *"put himself between the shooting of the battalion and that of the enemy to get the Tirailleurs who were exposed back into the ranks."*

Richard, Sergeant-Major: *"after the three officers were out of action, he took command of the company which was out as Tirailleurs and conducted himself with valour."*

The regiment had four officers killed and 9 wounded at Austerlitz.

● The 57th of the Line

Colonel **Rey** was a soldier in 1786 in Italy and served at Mantua, Bassano, Arcola and then at Hohenlinden. Colonel of the regiment in 1803, he was mentioned by Soult at Austerlitz. OLH. Couronne de Fer. He fought at Heilsberg, in Spain where he was made a Baron in 1809. Governor of Burgos in 1812, he served at Toulouse, then during the Hundred Days. Put on the non-active list in 1815, retired in 1825. Recalled in 1830, then retired again in 1832.

Lebondidier was in the regiment in 1796, and became Battalion Commander in 1801. He was at Austerlitz, Jena, Golymin and Eylau (OLH), then Spain and Portugal where he was wounded three times in 1810. Wounded at Bidassoa, he was promoted to General in 1814. On sick leave, he left the Army in 1815.

Also mentioned were the following: **Arnaud**, Lieutenant: *"distinguished himself by acts of bravery, especially by being the first to fall upon artillery pieces which were taken."*

Defrançais, Second-Lieutenant: *"distinguished himself at the head of the Tirailleurs he was in command of; he was always in the middle of the enemy. He made two Russian officers surrender their swords and then took them away with twelve soldiers."*

Guimé, Adjutant-NCO: *"distinguished himself by rare courage and reached artillery pieces first; they were taken by the division."*

Richard, Sergeant: *"reached a gun first and took it, was wounded by a bayonet."*

Above, from left to right: General Legrand commanding the 3rd Division and General Merle, his First Brigadier. (RR)

Colonel Rey of the 57th of the Line. (RR)

Chance, Corporal: *"distinguished himself. In the charge that the 1st Battalion made, he killed five gunners who were serving the guns, which were taken."*

Coulon, Corporal: *"distinguished himself by capturing two officers and eight Russian soldiers."*

The regiment lost six officers at Austerlitz

LEGRAND'S 3rd DIVISION

Legrand was a trooper in 1777, General in 1793 and Major-General in 1799. He served at Hohenlinden, Wertingen, Hollabrunn, Austerlitz and was made Gd Aigle LH in January 1806. He fought at Jena, Lübeck, Eylau and Heilsberg. He was made a Count in 1808, he received a lot of endowments before being wounded at Aspern; he was brilliant at Wagram, was with Oudinot in Russia, fought at Polotsk and was seriously wounded at the Beresina. Senator in 1813, Peer of France in 1814, he died from the wound he got at the Beresina in 1815.

His aide de camp were: his brother **Legrand** and **Lemarois**, himself a general's brother. Volunteer of the Manche, Adjutant-General attached to headquarters, he was at Austerlitz and became Colonel of the 43rd in December 1805; he was killed at Eylau.

The Chief of Staff was **Cosson** born in Gironde. He was an Adjudant-Commandant in 1803, fought at Austerlitz and Lübeck. CtLH, Baron and General in 1808, he was with Carra St-Cyr in 1809; wounded at Wagram, joined Augereau with the 11th Corps in 1812, he retired in 1813.

Also mentioned were: **Rey**, Capitaine-Adjoint to headquarters: *"after having had his horse killed from under him, he charged at the head of a company of the 26th Light, was wounded by a bullet in the chest whilst fighting hand to hand with a senior Russian officer, whom he disarmed."*

— MERLE'S 1st BRIGADE

Merle served in 1781 and became a General in 1794, and Major-General after Austerlitz. Chief of Staff of the 4th Corps in 1806, made Baron. He was in Spain with Masséna and at Medina del Rio Seco with Bessières. GdOLH in 1808. In Portugal, he was wounded at Oporto in 1809 then wounded at Busaco and Fuentes de Onoro. He was with Oudinot, in Russia and fought at Polotsk. He served in the Var in 1815, retired in 1816. He died in 1830.

● The 26th Light

Colonel **Pouget** was the son of a surgeon to King Stanislas at Nancy. He became the Colonel of the regiment in 1805. Mentioned at Austerlitz, he served at Lübeck, Hoff and Eylau. He had half his left foot shot off by a cannonball at Aspern. He was promoted to General in May 1809. He served in Russia with Oudinot and was wounded at Polotsk, twice. Captured by the Russians he was returned in 1814. He was at Marseilles during the Hundred Days, retired in 1816, GdOLH in 1831, retired again in 1832.

Brillat-Savarin was born at Belley in the Ain; he fought in the Alps, in Italy and in Egypt. He was Battalion Commander with the regiment in 1803. He was mentioned at Austerlitz and wounded at Hoff. Chevalier and OLH in 1807, he was wounded in 1813; during the Hundred Days he commanded a regiment of National Guardsmen; he retired in 1816.

François was born in the Meuse and join the regiment in 1796. Wounded in Italy, LH, he served Austerlitz and Jena. He was wounded twice at Eylau. He was mentioned at Ebensberg in 1809, OLH. He served in Russia, Saxony and in France. He defended Strasbourg in 1815. He retired in 1816.

Were also mentioned: **Arnaud**, Second-Lieutenant: *"distinguished himself by his courage. He was the victim of his own bravery for he received five bayonet wounds to his thigh and was left for dead on the battlefield".*

Lemaire, Sergeant-Major: *"he distinguished himself by carrying the flag with the utmost courage in the most dangerous places as much to rally as to encourage the soldiers."*

Lepreux, Sergeant-Major: *"distinguished himself and contributed to the capture of several artillery pieces."*

Baglin, Sergeant: *"took a flag at the battle of Austerlitz."*

Leboue, Corporal: *"he took a flag at the battle of Austerlitz."*

Sainte, Voltigeur: *"distinguished himself by rushing a Russian battery which was shooting;"*

● The 3rd of the Line

Colonel **Schobert** was appointed in 1805, born at Sarrelouis, child of the regiment in the 96th, he was a Captain in the Directoire Guard and then the Consular Guard; he was at Marengo and defended Telnitz at Austerlitz; wounded and captured at Heilsberg, wounded at Wagram, General in 1811. In Germany he was with Augereau in 1812 (11th Corps); he commanded at Stettin, but surrendered in December 1813. He served in April 1815 in the Army of the Rhine and was put on the non-active list in August 1815.

Heidet was a captain, mentioned in 1796 and 1800, LH, wounded by a shot at Austerlitz and retired in 1816.

THE 4th CORPS LIGHT CAVALRY

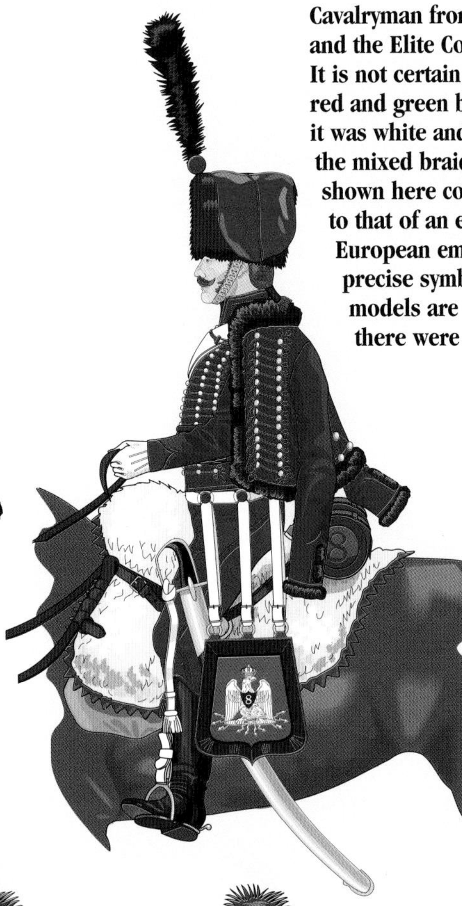

Cavalryman from the ordinary company and the Elite Company of the 8th Hussars. It is not certain whether the 8th Hussars wore red and green braiding. During the Consulate, it was white and it is not known when the mixed braiding was adopted. The sabretache shown here corresponds more to that of an established European empire with precise symbols; no other models are known though there were a lot of variants.

Brigadier in the 11th Chasseurs à Cheval. At the beginning of the Empire, a lot of regiments had abandoned the dolman for the less fragile and especially cheaper 'à la Chasseur' coat .

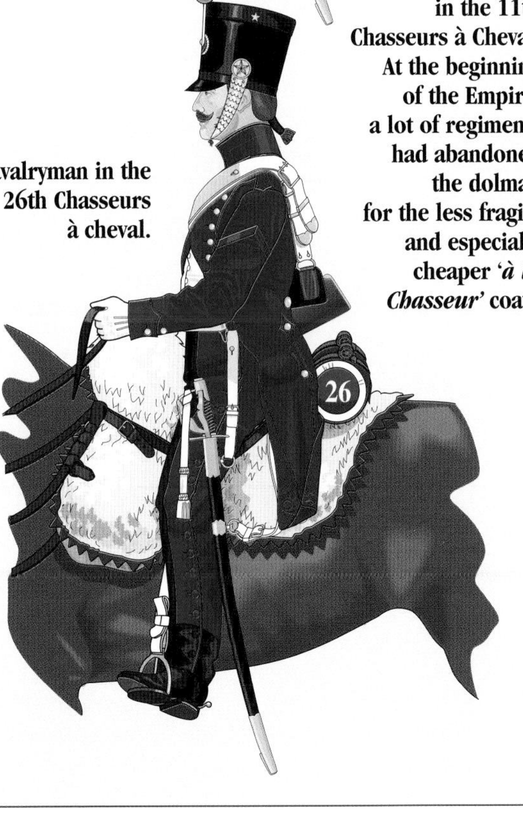

Cavalryman in the 26th Chasseurs à cheval.

Cavalrymen from the ordinary company of the 11th Chasseurs and from the Elite Company of the 26th Chasseurs à Cheval. The Elite Company can be distinguished by their wearing the colback and fringed epaulettes.

André Jouineau © Histoire & Collections 2003

Also mentioned were: **Rist**, Surgeon-Major: *"exposed himself to enemy fire in order to give succour to the wounded."*

Baurain, Second-Lieutenant: *"distinguished himself and got wounded."*

Chagniot, Sergeant-Major: *"distinguished himself and got wounded in the arm by a dangerous shot whilst pushing the Russians off."*

Leroux, Sergeant-Major: *"distinguished himself and was wounded by a biscayen bullet in the shoulder."*

Fournioux, Sergeant-Major: *"received seven bayonet wounds, the last of which went through his right hand; he was disarmed but continued to fight gallantly with his sabre. He fell and was left for dead on the battlefield."*

Decalongne, Sergeant: *"seeing that a Russian was about to fire, this soldier jumped on him, killed him and did the same thing to a few others. Seeing the advancing enemy column, he made his comrades follow him which they did successfully since they got through the column and dispersed it. A great number of Russians fell victim of his valorous bravery."*

● **The Pô Tirailleurs**

They were commanded by their **Battalion Commander Hulot** who was a former Chasseur from Reims; this ordnance officer of Soult's in 1799 was wounded at Austerlitz. He became aide de camp to the Marshal in 1806 and became Colonel in 1808, then General in 1812 in Spain. Baron, he was wounded three times in 1813, at Leipzig and Hanau. He fought at Ligny and Wavre in 1815. He commanded the division after Bourmont deserted. Retired in 1825, Honorary Lieutenant-General, he was recalled in 1831 confirmed in that rank. GdOLH in 1831, Inspector-General, he retired in 1818.

Also mentioned were **Falguière**s, Adjudant-Major and **Pezza**, Carabinier Captain: *"these two officers were in the first charge that the battalion made against the Russian infantry which was emerging from the castle at Sokolnitz; on their own initiative they rushed ahead of the battalion very audaciously and with a lot of intrepidity, cutting down a lot of Russians and taking prisoners. The example they set their soldiers went a long way to inciting their courage; they continued to distinguish themselves and were eventually both wounded."*

Ritta, Sergeant: *"although wounded, he distinguished himself by staying in the fighting until the end."*

Caloris, Sergeant: *"rushed forward and got himself noticed by his conspicuous bravery."*

Fabaro, Corporal: *"was always a close as possible to the enemy in order to better aim at them, taking pleasure in showing the ones he had downed; he remained admiringly calm. He was wounded at the end of the fight."*

Viberti, Carabinier: *"was always the first when they charged; he incited his comrades to follow him and was wounded in the middle of the fighting."*

The Tirailleurs lost two officers killed and eight wounded at Austerlitz.

● **The Corsican Tirailleurs**

Commanded by **d'Ornano**, a cousin of Bonaparte, he fought in Italy, St-Domingo and became aide de camp to Berthier in 1804 then Battalion Commander, commanding this battalion in March 1805. Mentioned at Austerlitz, he became the Colonel of the 25th Dragoons in 1807 and was at Jena and Lübeck. Count in 1808, he served in Spain where he was promoted General in 1811. He was in Russia where he charged at the head of the 4th Corps Cavalry at the Moskova. Seriously wounded at Krasnoï, he was then Major-Colonel of the Dragoons of the Guard in 1813 and replaced Bessières. He was at Dresden, Kulm and Leipzig, Hanau and at the defence of Paris. Arrested and exiled in April 1815 to Liège where he married Count Walewski's widow, he returned in 1818, unemployed. CrSL in 1829. He was in the Vendée in 1832 and became Peer of France. Retired in 1814, Deputy in 1849, he was GdCxLh in 1850.elected Senator in 1852 and Gd Chancelier of LH in the same year. Governor of the Invalides he was made Maréchal de France in 1861. The battalion lost three officers wounded at Austerlitz.

— **LEVASSEUR'S 2nd BRIGADE**

Féry replaced **Levasseur** was born at Chalons-sur-Marne. Dragoon in 1774, he was in the Vendée in 1792 and became General in 1800 in Italy. CtLH. He replaced Levasseur in this job because he was ill. Fery was given leave of absence and sent to Spandau on 29 October, so he was not at Austerlitz. He died at Mainz in 1809. It was thus Levasseur who commanded this brigade at Austerlitz.

Levasseur was born at Caen, served at Mainz and in the Vendée with Kléber. Promoted to General in 1800 in Legrand's Division (CtLH), he was therefore at Austerlitz and was wounded at Eylau. Baron, he died in 1811.

● **The 18th of the Line**

Colonel Ravier was a Captain in 1792. In Egypt he commanded the regiment. He was the Duke of Enghien's judge (CtLH), he received the Couronne de Fer and became a General in 1807. He captured Stettin in 1813. He was out on the non-active list in 1814. He served at Waterloo however. Retired in 1815.

Combelle, Captain. He served at Toulon, in Italy and Egypt and won a Sabre of Honour for St John of Acre. Made Colonel of the 94th in 1807 (OLH), he was made a Baron and General in 1813. Seriously wounded at Dresden, he died as a result of his wounds.

● **The 75th of the Line**

Margaron was at the head of the 4th Corps' Cavalry. (RR)

Colonel **Lhuilier de Hoff** was wounded at Austerlitz and recommended by Soult for General. He was awarded a Couronne de fer, was wounded at Hoff before becoming a General then Baron in 1807. He was at Eckmuhl and Wagram. He was Major-General in 1811, retired in 1814, GdOLH and retired again in 1815.

Eméry was born at Grignon. He volunteered for the 2nd Regiment of the Côte d'Or; he was at Toulon where he was wounded twice. He served in Italy, was mentioned at Dego and Arcola. He was wounded twice in Egypt and received a Sabre of Honour. Promoted to Battalion Commander, OLH, he was mentioned by Soult at Austerlitz and was wounded at Eylau then at Talavera where he lost an eye; he retired in 1811.

Hermann was at Arcola, Rivoli and in Egypt. LH, made a Lieutenant in 1806, he served at Lübeck and Eylau, and was wounded in Spain, then at Dresden; he retired in 1814 and OLH in 1831. The regiment lost one officer killed and three wounded at Austerlitz.

— **THE 4th CORPS' LIGHT CAVALRY BRIGADE**

Margaron was born at Lyons, wounded twice in Italy and became General in 1803. CtLH, he was wounded twice at Austerlitz. In Spain he was made a Baron in 1809. He was on the Staff, General in July 1812, then promoted Major-General in 1813, and Inspector of Depots in 1815. Put on the non-active list, he was recalled in 1821. He died in 1824. Milhaud replaced Margaron in January 1806 at the head of this cavalry.

His Chief of Staff was **Cambacérès**, the brother of the Arch-Chancellor. He was a trooper in the 14th Chasseurs in 1793, served at Lyons and Toulon, wounded at Zurich; he was also wounded at Hohenlinden and Mœsskirch. He was Adjudant-Commandant with Margaron at Austerlitz, was promoted to General in 1806. He served in Spain and was made a Baron there. He was with the 1st Corps of cavalry in 1813 and fought at Lutzen, Bautzen and Dresden. He joined General Headquarters then was put on the non-active list in 1814. Retired in 1824.

● **The 8th Hussars**

Colonel Francheschi-Delonne was born at Lyons. He was first a sculptor then became Second-Lieutenant in the Compagnie des Arts in 1792 and served in the Mounted Cavalry. He was aide de camp to Soult in 1799, then Squadron Commander. He carried out a dangerous mission to Genoa and was made Colonel with Soult in 1802 in the 8th Hussars. He went to Naples and then after Austerlitz he joined to Soult in Spain. Captured and imprisoned in the Alhambra at Grenada, he caught an infectious disease, from which he died. He had married the daughter of Mathieu-Dumas.

Rebillot served in 1785 and then became aide de camp to Klein in 1803 and Squadron Commander in the regiment 31 March 1805. Wounded at Austerlitz, he was mentioned by Soult. He was wounded at Eylau. He became a Major with the 16th Chasseurs in 1807. He was appointed OLH and Chevalier in 1801. His title was hereditary in 1814. He ended as Mayor of Faverney (Haute-Saône) in 1824 and died in 1834.

Also mentioned by Soult were: **Vatar**, Captain: *"Distinguished himself and had his horse killed under him but continued to command his men."* He was one of the 60 'Intrepids' who got 3 000 Russians to surrender.

Materre was born at Limoges, a volunteer from the Corrèze, he served in Italy and in Egypt. Captain in 1805, wounded at Austerlitz, he was Battalion Commander at Wagram and OLH in 1811. Major of the 4th of the Line in Russia, he was wounded in 1812. He had his left leg frozen during the retreat. He was appointed Colonel after the campaign. In 1814, he was a General. Left for dead at La Rethière, he was saved by his men. He served in 1815 and was put on the non-active list, retired in 1825, recalled in 1843, he died in 1843.

Francheschi, Second-Lieutenant: *"he fought extravagantly and when the regiment got 3 000 Russians to lay down their weapons, accompanied by the Adjudant-Major and 10 Hussars, he charged the five guns which were firing grapeshot at us to try to force us away and give the initiative back to the surrendering Russians; the guns were captured."*

Michy, Brigadier: *"by charging an artillery piece which was taken by those who were following him, he was knocked under his dead horse and only left the battlefield when he passed out. He was one of the 'Intrepids' who got 3 000 Russians to lay down their weapons."*

Lété, Hussar: *"distinguished himself by his courage. Pursuing Russians the day after the battle, he took a lot of prisoners in the village where the enemy had shut themselves in protection. He dismounted twenty times and entered the houses which were full of men, whom he took prisoner or killed. He was also one of the 'Intrepids' who got 3 000 Russians to lay down their arms."*

Graff, Captain-Adjudant-Major: *"accompanied by Lieutenant Francheschi of the 10th Hussars, they captured five guns which were firing grapeshot. He was wounded by a bullet in the right hand."*

● **The 11th Chasseurs**

Colonel **Bessières** was Marshal's brother. He was born at Preyssac in the Lot. He served in Italy and became Captain in Bonaparte's Guides. He fought in Egypt. Commanding Officer of the 11th Chasseurs, he was wounded at Austerlitz. Promoted to General on 24 December 1805, he was made Baron in 1810. Appointed Major-General in 1811, he refused the promotion. In Russia, he commanded the 1st Brigade of Saint-Germain's Division with Nansouty's 1st Corps. He was wounded at the Moskova and Leipzig, OLH, he was put on the non-active list in 1814. Commandant of the Military Divisions in 1821, retired in 1824, he was reinstated on the Reserve Béssières was born in the Ardennes at Sévigny, he was a trooper in 1779 and was in the regiment in 1791. Captain in 1793, Squadron Commander in 1803, he was wounded twice; retired in 1806, OLH, he was mentioned by Soult.

Also mentioned were **Pegueux** and Aubertin, Chasseurs: *"At Austerlitz they reached a canon first which they captured with its caissons and ten gunners."*

Bonnet, Chasseur: *"This soldier, himself fourth, took 200 prisoners together with 4 cannon."*

● **The 26th Chasseurs**

Colonel **Digeon**, the son of a Farmer-General was a Captain in the 19th Dragoons. He commanded the regiment which came from the Piedmont Dragoons. He took two standards at Austerlitz and was wounded on his collarbone by a bullet. General in 1807, Major-General in 1813, he served in Andalusia. He commanded the cavalry at Lyons in 1814. Aide de camp to the Comte d'Artois, Viscount in 1818, Peer of France in 1819, CrSL, GdCxLH in 1821, he was Minister of War and Minister of State in 1823. Aide de camp to the King, he commanded the 2nd Division of the Royal Guard in 1825, he died in 1826. He was mentioned by Soult.

Bourbel de Montpoinçon was born at Dieppe. Knight of Malta, he volunteered for the Maltese Legion; he was Captain of the Légion Nautique in Egypt. Made a Captain AM in the regiment in 1803,

LH, he was at Austerlitz, Jena and Eylau. Squadron Commander in the 7th Chasseurs in 1811, OLH and Russia in 1812, he was killed at Leipzig

Zucchino was in the Piedmont Hussars in 1800 and took part in the regiment's campaigns. He won a Sabre of Honour in 1803, was made a Lieutenant in the 5th Hussars in 1814; he was at Waterloo and retired to Saumur in 1816.

In his publication on the official reports about Austerlitz, Jacques Garnier used Soult's report which was very detailed and mentioned all those worthy of consideration. I found service record for the majority of them, with the exception of some like Surgeon-Commander Chappe, War Commisaries **Géant** and **Lenoble**. Battalion Commander **Mouton** caused a problem because of his special reputation. In Soult's report he appears in the 43rd of the Line; but in the 3rd of the Line, there was a Battalion Commander Mouton-Duvernet who was a General in the Guard in 1811, CtLH, Major-General in 1813, captured at Dresden and returned in 1814, Deputy for the Puy during the Hundred Days and who tried to have Napoleon proclaimed before being outlawed; he hid then returned to be judged, sentenced to death and shot on 27 July 1816, a victim of the 'White Terror'.

In his report, Soult supports his 'children' well. When he mentioned the Generals he said nothing about Thiébault except that his Grenadiers replaced the prisoners who were supposed to carry the stretcher, saying: "You are not worthy to carry a French General." Thiébault no doubt expected to be covered in praise and that is no doubt why, in his own memoirs he insinuated so much about Soult.

LANNES' 5th CORPS

Lannes' aide de camps were: **Delage**, Baron of St-Cyr; opposed Dumouriez at the camp of Maulde, at Lyons, saved his cannon in Vendée in 1795, took 20 guns at Le Mans, congratulated by Hoche; hero of the Vendée and Marengo; Adjudant-Commandant in 1803, OLH, sent by Lannes to Napoleon at Austerlitz; Baron, mentioned at Saragossa, Chief of staff to Ney in Russia, General at Moscow, CrLH in 1815, retired in 1826, then again in 1832.

Guéhéneuc, the Marshal's brother in law; his father was noble, Equerry and Senator, he was a soldier in 1803 in the 10th Light, aide de camp to his brother in law in 1805. Captain after Austerlitz, wounded at Friedland, Battalion Commander in Spain, wounded at Tudela; Baron, Colonel of the 26th Light; he went to Russia with Oudinot, wounded at the Beresina, General aide de camp to the Emperor in 1812, on half pay in 1814, was appointed to the Army of Africa in 1830 but did not go. He was at Morée in 1831, Lieutenant-General in 1836, and commanding Oran Province in 1838. Count on the death of his father, retired in 1848.

Quiot du Passage, aide de camp to Lannes in 1805 until 1807, colonel of the 100th with Gazan, wounded at Jena, went to Spain, made Baron, wounded at Badajoz, taken wounded at Kulm, served at Waterloo. GdOLH in 1822 and Lieutenant-General in 1823, retired in 1831.

Subervie was born at Lectoure, aide de camp to Lannes in 1797; Italy, Egypt, remained on Malta, Squadron Commander in 1803, Colonel of the 10th Chasseurs after Austerlitz; at Jena with Colbert and Ney; in Spain with Lasalle at Medellin. General in 1811; went to Russia with Montbrun's 2nd Corps, wounded twice at the Moskova, went to Vilna to recover. With Pajol in 1813; Couronne de Fer, French Campaign in 1814, wounded in front of Paris, Lieutenant-General in 1814, Waterloo, inactive and retired in 1825. Took part in 1830, deputy in 1831, re-elected in 1834, Inspector-General of cavalry. Re-elected in 1839 and 1846, GdCxLH in 1848 and Grand Chamberlain of LH, re-elected in 1849, then on the Reserve List, died in 1856.

The chief of Staff was **Compans**. Born at Salies-du-Salat, a volunteer from the Haute-Garonne; Pyrenees then Italy with Grenier, he was a General in 1799. Here in August 1805, wounded at Austerlitz; Chief of Staff to Soult in 1806, Jena, Major-General in 1806; with Davout in Germany then in Russia where he took the Schwardino redoubt on 5 September before the Moskova where he was wounded. Lutzen, Bautzen and wounded at Mockern. GdcXLH in 1815; refused the job offered by Napoleon in 1815, Peer of France in August 1815, voted for the death of Ney, he swore an oath to Louis-Philippe.

Above, from left to right and top to bottom. **Quiot du Passage aide de camp to Lannes; Compans , the Chief of Staff; Foucher de Careil commanding the Artillery and Oudinot at the head of the 1st Division.** *(RR)*

Decouz was Deputy Chief of Staff. He was born at Annecy. Egypt, Captain-Adjoint with Lannes in 1798, here in 1805; Austerlitz, Baron, General CtLH and Couronne de Fer in 1809, Naples Major of the 1st Chasseurs of the Guard in 1813, Major-General in 1813 with the Young Guard instead of Delaborde, he was mortally wounded at Brienne on 29 January 1814.

Favereau was his assistant: Rivoli, Sabre of Honour for Mantua, OLH, Ulm and Austerlitz, retired in 1808.

THE ARTILLERY

Foucher de Careil. School at Metz, Vendée, mentioned at Hohenlinden, General in 1803, here in 1805, Ulm, wounded, Austerlitz, Jena, Pulutsk, Major-General in 1807, Baron. He followed Lannes to Saragossa, with Ney in Russia, GdOLH in 1813, Lille in 1815, he retired in 1818.

THE ENGINEERS

Colonel **Kirgener**, Marengo, General after Austerlitz, present at Ulm and Hollabrunn; Jena, CtLH, Baron, Colonel commanding the Engineers of the Guard in 1810, siege of Danzig; Spain, the Isle of Walcheren where he directed the works. Russia, Major-general in 1813, he was killed by the same cannonball as Duroc.

OUDINOT'S 1st DIVISION

Oudinot was a soldier in 1784, General in 1794, was very often wounded: six in 1795, five in 1796; Major-General in 1799; Gd Aigle LH, Couronne de Fer, ordered to form and organise the combined Grenadier and Voltigeurs Division, the quality reserve unit of the Guard. After being wounded at Hollabrunn, Napoleon asked him to share the command of his Grenadiers with Duroc. Maréchal after Wagram where he commanded the 2nd Corps towards the Russbach, took Wagram. In Russia, at Polotsk; 1813 in Saxony, beaten by Bernadotte, wounded at Brienne, victor at Bar-sur-Aube (a bullet hit his LH insignia), Peer of France in 1814, GdCxSL in 1816, Duke in 1817. In Spain in 1823, Grand Chancellor of LH, Governor of the Invalides, he died in 1847.

At the request of the Emperor, he shared the command of the reserve division with Duroc because of his recent wound which he had received at Hollabrunn.

His aide de camps were **Hutin**, killed by a cannonball at Friedland.

Demengeot, Squadron Commander in 1801, Marengo, also wounded at Marengo, Baron, Colonel of the 13th Chasseurs in 1806, wounded at Golymin and at Eylau, one horse killed under him, OLH, two horses killed under him at Wagram, he retired in 1809.

Lamotte, Captain Aide de camp in 1801, wounded at Hollabrunn, Colonel of the 4th Dragoons in 1806, wounded at Deppen and at Friedland. Baron, General in 1809; in Portugal in 1810, sent back by Marmont for negligence, retired in 1812. Recalled in 1813 for the French Campaign, CtLH, Lieutenant-General in 1814, dismissed by Napoleon in April 1815 for having wanted to cede Bayonne to the Spanish. Reservist in 1831, he died in 1836.

The recently created reserve of the Grenadiers and the Voltigeurs was made up of three brigades, each brigade having two battalions united together in a regiment.

— LAPLANCHES-MORTIÈRE'S 1st BRIGADE

General de **Laplanche-Mortière** was born at Aulnay (Aude), page to the King in 1785, School at Brienne. In the Indies from 1791 to 1793; in the Vendée with Hoche, Ireland, commanded the 14th Light in 1797, Adjudant-General of the Consular Palace, General here in 1803, CtLH, Hollabrunn and Naples where he died of smallpox in October 1806.

● **The 1st Regiment** consisted of a battalion originating in the 13th of the Line and a second battalion coming from the 58th.

● **The 2nd Regiment** had a 1st Battalion from the 9th of the Line and a 2nd Battalion from the 81st.

In the Six there was Brayer, commanding the 2nd Regiment formed from the 58th and 81st.

Brayer was born at Douai, captured 4 cannon at Hohenlinden; Sabre of Honour in 1803, appointed here on 5 February 1805; Hollabrunn, Austerlitz and Colonel of the 2nd Light after the battle. Danzig, seriously wounded at Friedland; Spain, Baron, leg shattered at Albuhera. Major-General in 1813, wounded at the Katzbach and at Leipzig, French Campaign, rallied to Napoleon in 1815, Chamberlain and Governor of Versailles Palace, went to Lyon and Angers. Sentenced to death in absentia, exiled to America, served in Chile, returned in 1821. Peer of France in 1832, and GdCxLH in 1836, in the Reserve section in 1839. Espert de Latour succeeded him at the head of this 2nd regiment in 1806.

— DUPAS' 2nd BRIGADE

Dupas was born at Evian, served in 1773, victor of the Bastille, joined the Allobroges in 1792, Toulon, Mantua, Egypt; commanded the Mamelukes in 1802, General in 1803, on the Staff of the Palace, Major-General after Austerlitz, Friedland. Count in 1809, Wagram, replaced Frère in 1810, retired in 1813. He had married the daughter of General Hulin.

● **The 3rd regiment** (with one battalion from the 2nd Light and one from the 3rd Light).

It was commanded by **Schramm**, 2nd Light in 1794, Italy, Egypt; General on 24 December 1805, CTLH in 1807, Danzig; Couronne de Fer, wounded and captured at Baylen, Spain, Baron, Swedish Pomerania in 1812. Strasbourg and Kehl in 1814; wanting to negotiate the surrender to

Below and following pages. **This sequence of drawings (after the archives and contemporary observations and in particular the witnesses to a series of camp reviews at Saint-Omer) which we owe to Henri Boissellier shows us the silhouettes of the infantrymen of the Line (p. 100, 102 and 103) or the Light (p. 104) from the summer of 1805 to the beginning of 1806. A better idea of Oudinot's and Dupas' Grenadiers will be had by looking at these tough chaps as the pages are turned.**
(Author's collection)

leads thecommande le 2nd regiment
from the 1st brigade. *(RR)*

Louis XVIII, he was ill-treated by his soldiers. Retired in 1815, Lieutenant-General in June 1815, retired again as Honorary Maréchal de camp in 1816. with him was his son, Schramm, 2nd Light with his father, captured a canon at Wertingen and another at Hollabrunn; aide de camp to his father in 1806; Danzig, wounded at Heilsberg; mentioned at Madrid, Wagram; he was with the Fusiliers-Chasseurs of the Guard. Major commanding the 2nd Voltigeurs of the Guard in Russia, in Saxony; served at Dresden, wounded and captured. Returned in 1814, served during the Hundred Days, Viscount in 1827, Lieutenant-general in 1832; in command of the reserve at the siege of Antwerp, at Lyons against the insurrection of 1833. Deputy re-elected several times. He was Commandant of Alger in 1840 and GdCxLH. Director of the Ministry of War, Minister in 1850, Senator in 1852 and Military Medal. On the active list in 1864, he died in 1884.

● **The 4th Regiment.** The battalions came from the 28th and 31st Light.

It was commanded by **Cabanes de Puymisson**, Major of the 28th Light; here in 1805; Wertingen, wounded at Hollabrunn, Austerlitz; Colonel of the 17th after the battle. OLH, Baron, Spain, wounded at Oporto, General in 1810; served during the Hundred Days, retired in 1815. He was Campredon's Brother in law.

● **The 3rd and 4th Regiments** seem to have been the only ones engaged, in order to crush once and for all the Allied left wing towards the lakes and towards Aujezd.

— DUPIN'S 3rd BRIGADE

General **Ruffin** was born at Bolbec, a former aide de camp to Jourdan; Hohenlinden, General 1805. Austerlitz, CtLH after the battle. Ostrolenka, Friedland; he was made a Major-General in 1807, replaced Dupont in Spain with Victor. Count in 1808, he was mortally wounded at Chiclana.

● **The 5th Regiment** had two battalions coming from the 12th and the 15th Light.

It was with the order dated 13 March 1804 that the creation of the Voltigeurs was decided; in these terms: *"In each Light Infantry Battalion, there will be a company of Voltigeurs… This company will include a Captain, a Lieutenant, a Second-Lieutenant, a Sergeant-Major, four Sergeants, one furrier, eight Corporals, 120 Voltigeurs and two cornets. They will be equipped with an infantry sabre and a very light rifle, like that of the Dragoons. The officers and the NCOs will have a rifled carbine; their uniform will be the same as the Light Infantry."*

CAFFARELLI'S 2nd DIVISION

Caffarelli, the Emperor's aide de camp, replaced Bisson, wounded at Lambach crossing the Traun on 1 November 1805. It was the first from Davout's 3rd Corps and was placed under Lannes' command for the duration of the battle. Thus Napoleon tried to balance his forces, giving two divisions to Lannes who marched with all the cavalry available – entrusted to Murat, including that of the 1st Corps - despite all the complaining from Bernadotte.

The Chief of Staff was **Coehorn**, a Dragoon in 1783, aide de camp to Decaen; Lambach and Austerlitz, wounded at Auerstaedt; General in 1807, commanded the 3rd Brigade of the Grenadiers of the Reserve in 1807, after Jarry. Present at Danzig, he was wounded at Friedland; Baron,

THE LIGNE

| Fusilier | Voltigeur | Grenadier | Grenadier | Sappur | Grenadier | Officiredofficier | Voltigeur | Copporalfourrier |

THE LIGHT INFANTRY

Corporal and
Drummer from the
Pô Tirailleurs.

Flag and Eagle, 1804-model.
The reverse was identical and
bore the motto
VALEUR ET DISCIPLINE
Xᵉ BATAILLON.

L'EMPEREUR
DES FRANCAIS
AU 10ᴹᴱ RÉGIMENT
D'INFANTERIE LÉGERE

Voltigeur
Cornet from
the 17th Light.

Sapper.

Musician from
the 17th Light.

Subaltern from
a Carabinier company.

André Jouineau © Histoire & Collections 2003

Ebersberg, CtLH, Essling with Frère under Oudinot. Wounded at Wagram, Lutzen, Bautzen, had his thigh shattered, died after being amputated in October 1813.

— DEMONT'S 1st BRIGADE

Demont was the son of a Swiss Guard who joined up in 1764, Captain in 1795, wounded at the crossing of the Rhine. General in 1799. His left arm was shattered by a bullet at Austerlitz; Major-General on 22 December 1805, Senator in 1806, with Davout in 1809; Eckmuhl, Essling, defended Strasbourg in 1814; Peer of France, voted for the death of Ney. Died in 1823.

His aide de camp was **Lafitte**, here in 1804, Ulm and Austerlitz, joined Durosnel in 1806, Eylau and Heilsberg, had a horse killed under him at Friedland; Spain, three horses killed, OLH, broke into an English square, wounded, Colonel of the 20th Dragoons in 1811, called into the Chasseurs à Cheval of the Guard, Squadron Commander in Russia, Saxony and in France. Baron, charged at Waterloo, wounded, thrown from his horse. He retired in 1821.

● **The 13th Light.**

Colonel **Castex** was in Italy, here in 1804, killed at Austerlitz attacking Blasowitz. Three officers killed and three wounded

— THE 2nd BRIGADE

De Billy was born at Dreux, a National Guardsman in Paris, teacher of mathematics, commanded the gunners, wounded at Zurich, General in 1799, Hohenlinden, CtLH, Austerlitz with Morand at Auerstaedt where he was killed.

● **The 17th of the Line**

Colonel **Conroux** was the son of an artillery officer, aide de camp to Bernadotte in 1795, followed him to Italy, Colonel of the 43rd then of the 17th in 1802. General after the battle of Austerlitz, he commanded the 2nd Brigade of Oudinot's Grenadiers at Danzig; CtLh, Wagram with Oudinot. He was in Portugal, Fuèntes de Onoro, then Spain and died from wounds received at Ascain in 1813.

Were also mentioned: **Croizet**, captain *"distinguished himself at the battle of Austerlitz by his cool-headedness and zeal which he used to electrify the soldiers in the ranks, in the presence of the enemy cavalry."*

Cronier, Captain; *"This officer was with the four companies of the 2nd Battalion which freed two regiments surrounded by the enemy, upon whom he rushed and with that example which was followed by the soldiers, determined the success of the operation."*

Codère, Adjudant: *"Distinguished himself by his activity and his courage which got him the capture of a canon where there were still three enemy soldiers."*

● **The 30th of the Line**

Colonel **Valterre** was Battalion Commander in 1796, Italy, wounded at Gadisca, Rome in 1798, Marengo with the 30th. He received CtLH after Austerlitz. General in 1808, Baron St-Ange in 1809, Commanded Metz in 1815, retired in 1819.

Also mentioned were: **Colon**, Sergeant: *"Got himself noticed in particular by advancing towards two guns which were not yet abandoned; he was wounded and in spite of his wound,*

Claparède leads the 1st Brigade from
Suchet's division.
(RR)

encouraged those who were following to capture them."

Blanpain, Captain: *"from the first charge which begun the action, he advanced with a few men from his company to rush a group of Hussars who were cutting our gunners to pieces, forced them to flee and returned to his place in the ranks."*

Lassègue, Captain; *"From the first charge, since the standard-bearer was wounded, he seized the flag and marched until and NCO was sent to recover the Eagle of the battalion."*

Gautron, Captain: *"he charged a gun with his company, which he captured after having killed all the servers. He continued to incite his soldiers during the whole of the battle."*

Vernère, Captain: *"during the enemy infantry's first charge which managed to overwhelm the 2nd Battalion's left flank, he got his company to change direction and set themselves up as Tirailleurs and rushed upon the enemy with such zeal that he made them flee, leaving a howitzer hitched to its caisson behind them."*

Aulard, Sergeant-Major: *"Moved forward from his company, rushed a canon with some of his men and captured it."*

Bulot, Sergeant-Major: *"on the first charge, he carried the flag forward telling the soldiers to imitate his example; he was wounded and had to abandon the flag and recommended it to the bravery of his soldiers."*

Judin, Grenadier: *"he moved forward from the road and fell upon a gun which had been abandoned still hitched up; as the regiment had had its orders to leave its position, he gave it over to the 34th of the Line."*

Forment, Corporal: *"seeing his Captain in the middle of several Russians who were holding him by the neck, he rushed into the middle of them and using his bayonet, he wounded or killed several of them; the Captain could thus use his sword and with the brave Corporal, they killed off the remainder."*

— THE 3rd BRIGADE

Eppler was born at Strasbourg; soldier in 1774, Italy, Rome, Egypt, wounded twice, General in 1801, OLH, Austerlitz, died from the exhaustion of war.

● **The 51st of the Line**

Colonel **Bonnet d'Honnières** was a Gentleman-Cadet in 1774, Port-Mahon and Gibraltar, wounded crossing the Rhine in 1795, Ireland, captured, exchanged then commanded the 51st in 1800, Hohenlinden, OLH General in 1805, after Austerlitz, killed at Eylau.

Baile was born in the Var, the Alps then Italy, Egypt, wounded twice; Major in the regiment in 1803 Austerlitz, replaced Bonnet d'Honnières, appointed general at the head of the regiment; wounded at Golynin, Baron, General in Spain. He was wounded in 1813, Toulouse, commanded in the Lozère, kept during the Hundred Days, went to Belgium and commanded at Montmartre, CrLH, on the active list in 1818, died in 1821.

Bony was from Burgundy, a volunteer from the Côte d'Or, Italy, Arcola, captured two canon at Hohenlinden, took 300 prisoners at Austerlitz; wounded at Auerstadt, Chevalier of the Empire, General in 1813, Lutzen, wounded and captured at Leipzig, Waterloo. CrLH in 1820, retired in 1825. Recalled and retired again in 1833.

Paradis was born at Bourg, won a Sabre of Honour for Hohenlinden, joined the Chasseurs à

THE LIGNE

| Musician from 64th line | Sapper | Surgeon's orderly | Sapper | Officer | Grenadier drummer | Drum Master | Drummer | Voltigeur |

Cheval of the Guard in 1808, Captain with the 2nd Voltigeurs of the Guard in Russia; mortally wounded at Lutzen.

Gallo was from Sardinia, joined the Army of Italy, Battalion Commander in the 51st in 1804, LH, Austerlitz, shattered his left shoulder at Jena, Colonel of the regiment in 1806, retired in 1807, Garrison Commandant in Italy, served in the Army of the Alps in 1815 at Suchet's headquarters. Resigned and went home in 1816.

● **The 61st of the Line**

Colonel **Nicolas** was a colonel in 1805, CtLH for Austerlitz where he was wounded three times. General in 1806, Pyrénées Orientales, Commandant at Barcelona, served in 1815 and retired in 1825.

No officers were lost

SUCHET'S 3rd DIVISION

Suchet was born at Lyons in 1770, volunteered in 1791, captured the English General O'Hara at the siege of Toulon, 18th at Dego, Lodi, Arcola and Rivoli, with Brune in Switzerland, General in 1798. He did not go to Egypt as planned as he had to go to Paris instead to defend himself against accusations of mismanagement in Switzerland. Italy, Chief of Staff. Married the daughter of the Mayor of Marseilles whose own mother, née Clary was Joseph Bonaparte's sister-in-law. Major-General with Joubert in 1799, defended the Var bridgehead, with Masséna; commanded the 4th division of Soult's Corps which was given to Lannes for Austerlitz; Saalfeld, Jena, Pulutsk and Ostrolenka; Couronne de Fer, Count; he was in Spain where he covered the siege of Saragossa, captured Lerida and Tarragona; wounded taking Sagonte; Maréchal de France in 1811, Duke of Albufera in 1812. Evacuated Catalonia in 1814, served at Lyons during the Hundred Days. Peer of France, struck off in 1815, reinstated in 1819, he died in 1826.

His aide de camps were: **Gaudin** was from Charente. Alps, then Toulon, Italy captured with several wounds in 1796, exchanged in 1798, Suchet's aide de camp in 1800; subsequently Squadron Commander in the 10th Hussars, LH, Major in the 22nd after Austerlitz; with Oudinot at Wagram, wounded; Spain, Colonel of the 27th in 1811, he retired in 1823.

Meyer was a Lieutenant who came from the 9th Dragoons, wounded beside his General at Austerlitz.

Mesclop, Captain AM, Staff assistant had a horse killed under him by a cannonball at Austerlitz near his General and despite the concussion, he did not leave the battlefield.

Travaux was a captain of engineers, was noticed for his precision in carrying out orders and by the accuracy of his judgement.

CLAPARÈDE'S 1st DIVISION

Claparède was born at Gignac (Hérault), volunteered in the 4th battalion, Captain with the 23rd Light in 1796, assistant to the staff of the Army of the Rhine, in charge of intelligence gathering; Hohenlinden, General at St Domingo in 1802. Rochambeau sent him back to France in 1802; he commanded the vanguard of the division with the 17th Light. At Austerlitz, napoleon entrusted him with the Santon set up with 18 Austrian cannon and fortified. Took part before at Ulm, Wertingen, Hollabrunn. Mentioned at Saalfeld, Jena, Prenzlow and wounded at Pulutsk, Ostrolenka; Count in 1808, Major-General; Spain with Oudinot, wounded at Ebersberg and at Essling, Wagram, wounded at Znaïm. Organised and commanded the 'Légion' at the Vistula with his Poles, his unit being attached to the Guard in Russia. Wounded at the Beresina, captured at Dresden, returned

This rather naïve engraving shows the role of the canteen girl (vivandière) within the regiment quite well. Even in the heart of the fray, old Mother Hulotte or Mother-Victory did not hesitate to bring a tonic to the wounded. (RR)

in 1814, GdCxLH in 1815; he did not serve during the Hundred Days; one of Ney's Judges; Inspector-General, Peer of France rallied in 1830, kept inactivity with no age limit.

His aide de camp was Captain **Peyrard** who conducted himself very correctly at Austerlitz and was mentioned.

● **The 17th Light**

Colonel **Vedel** was born in Monaco, the son of a noble officer. He was a soldier in 1784, Battalion Commander at the Army of Italy's Headquarters, wounded twice at Ulm where he was taken, then freed; Austerlitz, General in 1805; Saalfeld, Jena; wounded at Pulutsk and at Heilsberg, wounded again at Friedland. CtLH. Then Baylen, tried, imprisoned and dismissed upon his return in March 1812. He was recalled in 1813, sent to Lyons with Augereau. On the active list in 1818, he was on the Reserve List in 1831.

Also mentioned were **Marin**, Master-Drummer: *"while the enemy had made themselves masters of the village of Kausnitz, he marched at the head of his drummers, threw himself into the fray, beating the charge to such an extent that it caused panic among the Russians who fell back."*

Rode, Sergeant: *"on the IX Frimaire, Year XIV, being set out as Tirailleurs out in front of the Santon,, he was charged by two Cossacks. He held firm and only fired his rifle only when they were in range of his bayonet."*

— **BEKER'S 2ND BRIGADE**

Beker was born in Obernai, joined up in 1786; Vendée, Le Mans, negotiated the surrender of Stofflet, in the Army of the North, then St-Domingo. returned to Italy, General in 1801; Austerlitz, Major-General after the battle. He was with Grouchy' 2nd Division of dragoons at Zehdenick in

THE LINE

Drummer — Fife player — Drum-Major — Sapper — Grenadier drummer — Drum-major — Colonel — Voltigeur cornet — Musician

1806. With Masséna, Count de Mons, Chief of Staff; Essling, denounced for his untoward remarks? He was replaced by Fririon at Wagram. Couronne de Fer, elected Deputy during the Hundred Days; escorted Napoleon onto the *Bellerophon*, re-elected in 1816, Peer of France in 1819, CrSL in 1825, GdCxLH in 1831, he died in his castle at Mons near Clermont-Ferrand in 1840.

His aide de camp was **Guérinat** who conducted himself very well and was mentioned at Austerlitz.

● The 34th of the Line

Colonel **Dumoustier** was born at St-Quentin was in the Directoire Guard in 1797, with Bonaparte on 18 Brumaire, Marengo; Colonel of the 34th in 1804; Ulm, Austerlitz, Saalfeld and Jena where he was wounded, and at Pulutsk. He replaced Reille in command of the Brigade in 1806. Spain, Saragossa, Baron, second in command of the Chasseurs à Pied of the Guard under Curial. Wagram, went with the Young Guard in Spain; Major-General in 1811; Lutzen and Bautzen; Couronne De Fer, wounded at Dresden, Count in 1813, retired in 1814. GdOLH in 1831. He broke his thigh in a riding accident an died after the amputation in 1831.

Also mentioned were **Robert**, Second-Lieutenant: *"Charged a Russian battery with 30 Voltigeurs from his company, and when surrounded he made himself some space by taking two hundred prisoners."*

Lebrument, Furrier: *"having seen all who were near the standard-bearer, himself knocked over, he seized the flag and only gave it back at the end of the battle to the Battalion Commander."*

Lafargue, Grenadier Captain: *"Even though wounded, he did not want to leave his post to go and get himself dressed in the ambulance."*

● The 40th of the Line

Colonel **Legendre d'Harvesse** was a General after Austerlitz, Baron, Chief of Staff to Dupont, signed the surrender at Baylen, Baron and insulted by Napoleon right in the middle of a review in 1809. Imprisoned in March 1812, Dupont's Chief of staff at the Restoration; CrLH, retired in 1824.

Also mentioned were **Piché**, Second-Lieutenant: *"distinguished himself by his bravery. He rushed an artillery piece, took it and killed the gunner and made a few prisoners."*

Berry, Adjutant-NCO: *"distinguished himself by his bravery. Learning that the battalion had run out of cartridges, he rushed into the middle of the enemy firing in order to bring some up himself and when wounded he refused to leave his post before the battle finished."*

Loutrel, adjutant-NCO: *"distinguished himself by his bravery when he spurred on some young conscripts who were frightened by the enemy fire."*

Legrain, Sergeant: *"distinguished himself by his bravery. He rushed forward with Captain Duval and seized two cannon, at the moment when the enemy was about to fire them."*

Lemmonier, Sergeant: *"distinguished himself and was wounded but he did not leave his company until the end of the battle."*

Surceaux, Sergeant: *"distinguished himself when he saw two files of Grenadiers mown down by enemy cannonballs and shouted: 'in a moment we will make them pay for the death of our brave comrades. Keep cool, take aim well, victory will be ours. Our Emperor promised us. Long Live the Emperor!' This shout was repeated by all the companies and the regiment charged the enemy."*

Valhubert was born at Avranches, commanded the 1st Battalion of Manche Volunteers. Wounded at Marengo, Sabre of Honour, General in 1803, CtLH, killed at Austerlitz. He was one of the planned statues Concorde Bridge, like Morland.

● The 64th of the Line

Colonel **Nerin** was not at Austerlitz since he was appointed Commandant at Ulm and remained there until 1806. After the battle he was replaced by Chauvel who was a Major in the regiment at Austerlitz. Jena, Baron, General in 1809, Saragossa, CtLH, on health leave in 1813, retired in 1815, then in 1832.

Also mentioned were **Nory-Dupart**, Captain: *"Two of his sons had been killed; the third a Sergeant was killed before his eyes. He said 'Forward' and continued his action in spite of this tragic loss; he replaced his wounded Battalion Commander Joubert."*

Querquetone, **Petit**, **Baudoin**, **Baudry**, all Grenadiers; **Marchand Héraut**, Fusiliers: *"They distinguished themselves for, although wounded they remained in their places in their ranks."*

● The 88th of the Line.

Colonel **Curial** was a Savoyard with the Allobroges in 1792, Italy and Switzerland; Egypt, wounded, Regiment's Colonel in 1803, Austerlitz, Major in the Chasseurs à Pied of the Guard in 1806,. Jena, Eylau, wounded at Heilsberg. Couronne de Fer, General in 1807, Colonel of the 2nd Chasseurs. Baron, commanded the 1st Division of the Young Guard under Mouton at Essling, Major-General in 1809, commanded the 1st division of the Guard, then the 3rd (the Old Guard) in Russia. Commanded the 1st Division of the Young Guard in 1813 in Saxony, Hanau and the French Campaign, GdCxLH in February 1815, Peer of France, Commandant of the Chateau at Rambouillet; he was with Suchet in the Alps, voted for Ney's deportation. Gentleman of the King's Bed-Chamber, commanded a Division in 1823 in Spain. CrSL, GdCx St Ferdinand. First Chamberlain to the King, he died when he fell from his horse during Charles X's Coronation.

Cambronne was born in Nantes, Battalion Commander in the regiment in 1805, Austerlitz, mentioned at Jena, OLH, in the Guard in 1809. He commanded the 3rd Voltigeurs of the Guard in Russia. Saxony, CtLH in 1813 with the 2nd Chasseurs of the Guard; wounded several times during the French Campaign. He was with Friant with the Grenadiers of the Guard; General commanding the Island of Elba Battalion. Count and Lieutenant-General, GdOLH and Peer of France,

commanded the square of the 2nd Battalion of the 1st Chasseur at Waterloo, wounded and vulgar to the English, struck off and sentenced to death in absentia, returned to France, arrested, acquitted in 1816, on half pay, Viscount in 1822, retired in 1823, died in 1842.

Hurel was born in the Eure; Italy; Egypt, wounded, LH, Austerlitz, Captain in 1806, joined the Chasseurs of the Guard, endowed in 1810; Russia, wounded in 1813, Baron, Reunion Island, commanded the 3rd Voltigeurs at Waterloo, on the non-active list in 1815, Maréchal de camp in Spain in 1823, GdOLH in 1831, Lieutenant-General in Belgium in 1836. GdCx Order of Leopold.

Also mentioned were **Authier** and **Henning**, Captains: *"they particularly distinguished themselves when their battalion moved forward to push the enemy into a ravine"*

Marguet, Captain and **Fromont**, Lieutenant: *"in the bayonet char-*

Centre. **Colonel Curial.** *(RR)*

THE LIGHT

| Officer | Carabinier | Sapper | Chasseur | Voltigeur | Carabinier | Carabinier | Voltigeur | Carabinier Officer |

HORSE ARTILLERY AND ARTILLERY TRAIN

Artilleur à Cheval.

Artillerie à cheval
officer.

Artillery
train driver.

Trumpeter.

NCO wearing the *'à la chasseur'* coat.

ge which the regiment against the enemy, they reached a gun first with only three Voltigeurs, when they killed the gunners and seized the gun. The captain had three bullets in his clothes and one slightly scratched his thigh."

Moreau, Lieutenant: *"with six Voltigeurs captured six caissons of the enemy and was seriously wounded."*

Couturier, Second-Lieutenant: *"distinguished himself when he did not want to quit the battlefield although he was ill."*

Henin, Lieutenant: *"seeing that two artillery pieces on his right were being taken away as the gunners had all been killed or wounded, he made them come back, got his men to man them and directed their fire for some time."*

Dautrement, Second-Lieutenant: *"all alone in front of his platoon, he took three prisoners and received a bullet in his clothes."*

Museau, Baillargeau, Sergeants; *"they rushed into the enemy ranks and killed several Russians as much with axes as with bayonets."*

Michant, Richer, Sergeants: *"were wounded and refused to leave their ranks before the end of the Battle."*

Perrier, Sergeant: *"took several prisoners and was wounded.*

Jeannes, Sergeant: *"took several prisoners."*

Meneut, Grenadier: *"seriously wounded in the thigh during the battle of Austerlitz, he refused to be carried to the ambulance by his comrades. 'Stay where you are at your posts, I don't want to deprive the corps of such brave men as you.'"*

Vatrain, Sergeant: *"was seriously wounded when he charged an artillery piece which had been taken by the Voltigeurs who were with him."*

Roussel, Fusilier: *"although he was wounded, he continued to charge the Russians with his bayonet and only left his post when he was wounded a second time by a dangerous shot."*

KELLERMANN'S VANGUARD

It normally marched with Bernadotte's Corps, but in order to reinforce his left wing which was going to have to face a zone which was very suitable for cavalry movements and massed cavalry, the cavalry of the 1st Corps had been given over to Murat's reserve.

Kellermann was born in Metz in 1770; at five he was a pupil with the Hussars of the regiment of the Colonel-General. He went to America protected by his uncle Barbé-Marois and came back in 1793, called back by his father, entrusted with the command of the Army of the Alps.

He became his first aide de camp, the second being Lasalle. They left together to join the Army of Italy commanded by Bonaparte. Kellermann was Adjudant-General Brigade-Commander, Lassale was only his deputy. Hero of the crossing of the Tagliamento where he took five cannon off the Austrian General Schulz, he was made a General in 1797 and carried the captured flags back to the Directoire. He was not chosen for Egypt and stayed in Italy, under the command of Forrest. He was sent to Rome commanding a vanguard comprising three squadrons of Chasseurs, two light artillery pieces and two battalions of infantry; He routed Damas' Neapolitans. He took part in the attack on Naples very brilliantly. In 1800, he was in command of a cavalry brigade with the 2nd; 6th and 20th Regiments of heavy cavalry. It was at Marengo that he was at his most glorious. Thinking that they had won, Mélas' Austrians were surprised by Desaix' arrival. Kellermann was given the 1st and 8th Dragoons; the young General made his charges coincide with a salvo from a battery of 18 cannon shooting grapeshot at the disbanding enemy; the vigour and the appropriateness of this famous charge was supported by Bessières with the Cavalry of the Guard. General Zach was captured and 6 000 men were taken prisoner. The rank of Major-General rewarded this exploit, but he showed off a bit too much about it, and Napoleon disapproved. He fell head over heels in love with a beautiful Italian girl and got divorced, marrying her in France. But the divorce was opposed. In 1804, he was appointed Commanding Officer of the Cavalry of Bernadotte's 1st Corps in Hanover. He was appointed GdOLH. At Austerlitz, Kellermann drew Konstantin's lancers who were decimated when they passed through Caffarelli's battalions then were attacked by the French cavalry, in an action in which their commanding officer Essen II was killed. Kellermann went to Portugal with Junot and helped him obtain the convention of Cintra, bringing the troops back on English boats. At Valladolid, the General was accused of prevarication and misappropriation of public funds which caused his disgrace. He should have gone to Russia with Grouchy's 3rd Corps, but he retired with his father and was replaced by Chastel. He was with Ney in 1813, leading two Polish Divisions. He was ill and was replaced by Letort. Peer of France in 1814, he distinguished himself during the French Campaign, especially at St-Didier. During the Hundred Days he charged at Quatre Bras, and was brought back post haste by two troopers, hanging from the manes of their horses!. He served at Waterloo. Duke of Valmy and Peer of France at the death of his father in 1820, he died in 1835.

An aide de camp of the General was killed and the Chief of Staff of the Engineers, **Dufriche**

Kellermann at the head of the vanguard. (RR)

de Valazé was wounded. Out of Polytechnique, he was a General and CtLH in 1813. He served in 1815 and was Inspector-General of Engineers in 1819. He commanded the army in Algeria and was Lieutenant-General in 1830, Deputy in 1832.

Jacquenard, assistant to the Staff, was in this post at Marengo; Austerlitz, Jena, wounded at Eylau, mentioned at Danzig, OLH, Colonel of the 43rd in 1813, Colonel-Major of the 5th Voltigeurs of the Guard, Antwerp, CtLH and Baron, French Campaign, appointed General in 1814. Commandant of the Puy de Dome during the Hundred Days, retired in 1824, then again in 1832.

— VAN-MARISY'S BRIGADE

Van-Marisy (called **Vagnair**) was a cadet with the 4th Hussars in 1791, noticed by Bourcier who said: *"a quite distinguished leader whichever way you look at him, he has a good lifestyle, he is brave, and a good soldier but he has no knowledge of administration and does not let that worry him."* General in 1803; CtLH, brigade with the 4th and 5th Chasseurs, wounded at Austerlitz, Spain, wounded at the Arzobispo Bridge in 1809, murdered at Talavero in February 1811.

● **The 4th Hussars**

Colonel **Burthe**: Zurich, two wounds at Genoa, carried the flags taken in 1800, Colonel of the regiment in 1805, Austerlitz where he was captured for a moment then released by the next charge by Kellermann, Baron, Spain, General in 1810, 2nd Division of Light Cavalry in Russia with Pajol at the Moskowa. Captured, returned in 1814, at Ligny in 1815, retired in 1825, he died in 1830.

Labiffe was born at Strasbourg; 4th Hussars, Captain AM in the 7th Hussars on 2.12.1805, Ordnance Officer to Napoleon in 1807, Chasseur à Cheval of the Guard in 1811, Squadron Commander in Russia. Colonel of the 17th Dragoons at Waterloo, retired in 1822.

● **The 5th Chasseurs**

Lieutenant-Adjudant-Major **Corbineau**, Jean-Baptiste, was born in 1776,,with his brother the Captain in 1802, Major in the Hanoverian Legion in 1804, Major with the 10th Hussars in 1806, Colonel of the 20th Dragoons in 1807, General in 1811. In Spain, with Oudinot in Russia, Polotsk; he found the passage across the Beresina which enabled the bridges to be built. Major-General and Napoleon's aide de camp in 1813, wounded at Kulm, saved Napoleon at Brienne; wounded in 1814. At Waterloo, Count, retired in 1824, Peer of France in 1835, GdCxLH in 1838 Had Louis Napoleon Bonaparte arrested in 1840. Retired in 1848. He was not with his brother at Austerlitz. There was a third brother born in 1780.

Corbineau, Hubert, Lieutenant in the 5th Chasseurs in 1800. He was probably at Austerlitz as Captain-Adjoint to the staff of the Guard, wounded twice in 1806, wounded at Eylau, Baron, OLH 1808; His right knee was blown apart by a cannonball at Wagram, he was amputated from the thigh down, invalided out of the army in 1810, he died in 1823.

— PICARD'S BRIGADE

Picard was a Dragoon in 1780; Italy in 1796, Colonel of the 1st Hussars in the same year, General in 1803, Austerlitz, Jena, Eylau where he was seriously wounded, discharged in 1809, was employed with the remounts in 1812; retired in 1815, Honorary Lieutenant-General in 1820.

● **The 2nd Hussars**

Colonel **Barbier** commanded the regiment in 1793, CtLH, General Commandant d'Armes in 1806. Baron, served in the Tyrol, then in Russia. On the non-active list in 1814, he retired in 1818.

Becker was wounded at Austerlitz, Squadron Commander in the 9th Hussars in 1807, OLH in 1809, Major in 1812, was wounded six times at Grossbeeren, 12th Hussars, 6th Lancers, retired in 1814.

Braun was a Captain who lost a horse and was wounded while removing a standard at Austerlitz; Jena, Lübeck, Eylau, Squadron Commander in Spain, 9th Hussars in 1812, OLH, he was on the non-active list in 1815.

● **The 5th Hussars**

Colonel **Schwarz** was born in the duchy of Baden; he was a Baron of the Holy Empire and Bavarian General, Cadet in the 2nd Hussars in 1776, captured in Ireland, returned in 1799, appointed to the regiment at that date, CtLH after Austerlitz with Lasalle in 1806 and 1807, Baron, commanding a Neapolitan brigade under Duhesne, captured by the English, returned in 1814, half-pay, retired in 1815, SL in 1818.

A group of 8 cavalrymen distinguished themselves by taking 4 cannon and a number of their servers. They were commanded by Adjutant Ferrier, who was appointed Second-Lieutenant and awarded LH.

Trumpeter **Pincemaille** wounded the Russian General Incomelski, commanding the Uhlans of Baron Meyer, with his sabre and took him prisoner.

Squadron Commander **Hirn** contributed to the capture of several artillery pieces.

Two officers and 4 men were killed, 4 officers and 15 hussars were killed.

CAVALRY RESERVE

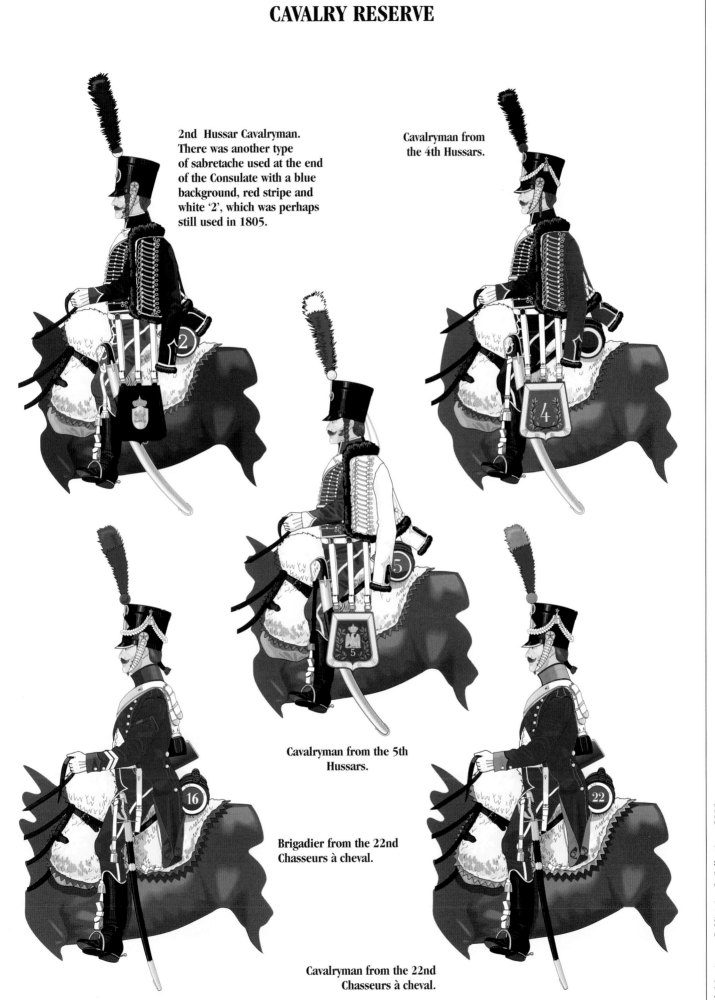

2nd Hussar Cavalryman. There was another type of sabretache used at the end of the Consulate with a blue background, red stripe and white '2', which was perhaps still used in 1805.

Cavalryman from the 4th Hussars.

Cavalryman from the 5th Hussars.

Brigadier from the 22nd Chasseurs à cheval.

Cavalryman from the 22nd Chasseurs à cheval.

André Jouineau © Histoire & Collections 2003

Brigadier from
the 9th Hussars.

Brigadier from the 9th
Hussars in full riding dress.

Trooper from
the 10th Hussars
in marching dress.

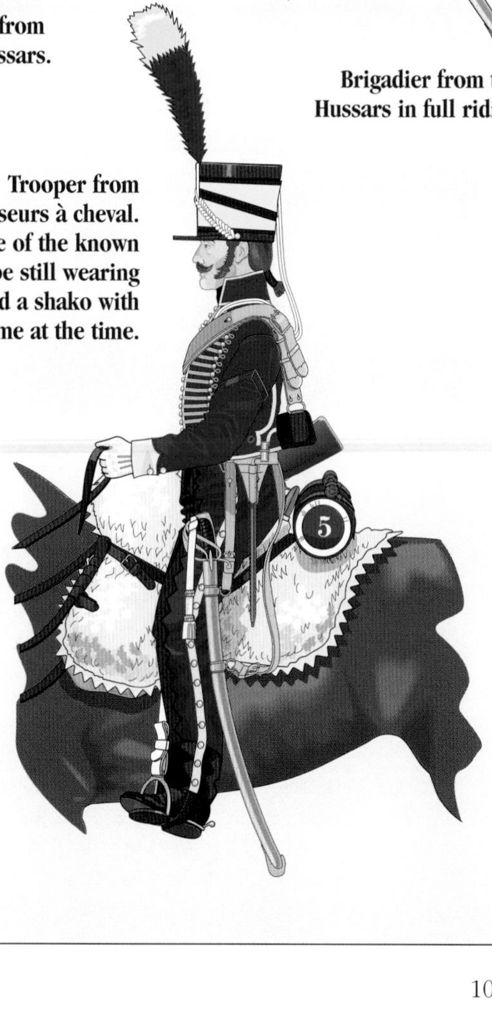

Trooper from
the 5th Chasseurs à cheval.
This is one of the known
regiments to be still wearing
a dolman and a shako with
a flame at the time.

Trumpeter from the 5th
Chasseurs à cheval.

Murat's aides de camp were.

Beaumont was a Dragoon in 1791. He served in the Vendée, Italy and Egypt as Dumas' aide de camp. He was Squadron Commander and aide de camp to Murat in 1799. At Marengo he was with Lannes' corps and became the Colonel of the 10th Hussars. He was at Ulm and Austerlitz. Made a General after the battle. First aide de camp to Murat in 1806. He was Eylau, Danzig and Friedland. CtLH. After Spain, he went into the 2nd Cavalry Corps in Russia. Major-General in 1812, he was at Lutzen, Leipzig, Hanau (Couronne de Fer), he died at Metz in 1813.

Exelmans was born at Bar-le-Duc, was aide de camp to d'Eblé in 1798 in Naples. He was then Captain of the 16th Dragoons then aide de camp to Broussier in 1799. He joined the 15th Chasseurs and became aide de camp to Murat

Above, from left to right.
Flahaut de la Billarderie, aide de camp to Murat and Belliard, the Cavalry Reserve's Chief of Staff.
(RR)

in 1801. He had two horses killed under him at Wertingen, present at Austerlitz, he was Colonel of the 1st Chasseurs after the battle. He was with Marulaz in 1806, was also present at Golymin and Eylau. General in 1807., he was still with Murat at Friedland and was made a baron. He was sent to Spain, captured, he escaped in 1811. Grand Maréchal of the Palace of the King of Naples, Grand Equerry, he became the Major of the Grenadiers à Cheval of the Guard in 1812, then Major-General. He was wounded at Vilna, Count in 1813, was arrested for having sent a letter to Murat, a letter seized on the bearer's person. Acquitted, he played an important role during the Hundred Days. Peer of France, he was with Grouchy and beat the Prussians at Roquencourt on 1st July. Exiled to Brussels, he was allowed to return in 1819. Still active in 1830, he was GdCxLH and Grand Chancellor of LH in 1849, Maréchal de France in 1851 and finally Senator in 1852, the year he died from a riding accident.

Flahaut de la Billarderie emigrated and returned in 1797, was with the 5th Dragoons at Marengo. He became aide de camp to Murat in 1802. The son of Talleyrand and Mme de Souza, his father was worried for him and recommended him to Murat. Wounded on 3 November 1805, he was probably absent on 2 December. Squadron Commander in the 13th Chasseurs, aide de camp to Berthier, Grand Equerry and Queen Hortense's lover with whom he had a son (the Future Duke of Morny), made a Baron in 1810. In Russian he became a General on 4 December 1812 and Count in 1813. Major-General and aide de camp to the Emperor, he followed him during the Hundred Days and fought at Quatre-Bras and at Waterloo. Outlawed he left for England. He was re-instated in 1830, GdCxLH in 1838, Ambassador to Vienna, then London, he was elected Senator in 1852. Grand Chevalier in 1864, Military Medal in 1866, he died in 1870.

Lanusse Was born at Habas in the Landes was captured in the Pyrenees and escaped. Aide de camp to his brother in Egypt (he was killed at Canope on 21 March 1801), he was recruited by Murat as aide

Below.
Exelmans, another of Murat's intrepid and dashing aide de camps abandoning his horse,
shot by the enemy, and climbing onto the mount of an Officer of Dragoons – orders couldn't wait.
(RR)

de camp in 1802. Colonel of the 17th with Morand after Austerlitz, he was at Auerstaedt, was at Eylau. His right shoulder was shattered at Heilsberg. Couronne de Fer and General in 1808, he followed Murat to Naples where became Grand Maréchal of the Palace and Major-General commanding the Neapolitan Guard. He married Perignon's daughter and was made a Baron in 1810. he returned as a General of the Guard in 1811 in Dumoustier's Division and served at Lutzen. CtLH and Major-General in 1813, was put on the non-active list in 1814, then in 1815 after the Hundred Days. He was retired in 1833.

Brunet-Denon, Second-Lieutenant aide de camp to Murat in 1800, wounded at Austerlitz, he became Captain in 1806 and Colonel of the 24th Chasseurs in 1807. Lost his right arm at Essling, Baron, he was appointed Director of Studies at the Ecole St Germain. Honorary Maréchal de camp, confirmed during the Hundred Days, he retired with a pension in 1816. CRLH in 1845, he retired definitively in 1848.

Belliard was Chief of Staff. He was born at Fontenay le Comte, was promoted General on the battlefield of Arcola. In Egypt, he beat Murad-Bey and was wounded at Cairo. Major-general in 1800, he was appointed to Murat's staff on 30 August 1805. He took part in the capture of the bridges in Vienna. Her served at Austerlitz, Jena, Lubeck, Eylau and Heilsberg and Friedland; went to Spain. Chief of Staff to Jourdain, then Governor of Madrid. He was with Murat in Russia, Wounded he was appointed Colonel-General of the Cuirassiers on 5 December 1812. Wounded at Leipzig, he was at Hanau and commanded the cavalry in Champagne in 1814. GdCxLH on 23 August 1814. He served during the Hundred Days was then sent to Murat by Napoleon. Peer of France, he was struck off after Waterloo then re-appointed in 1819. Ambassador to Brussels in 1831, he died of a massive stroke leaving the King's Palace.

Deputy Chief of Staff was **Girard**. He was with Monnier at Marengo in 1800. He took his job up in 1805 and fought at Austerlitz and Jena. Appointed General in 1806, he was made a Baron then left for Spain. Major-General in 1809, he organised a Polish Division in Victor's 9th Corps in Russia. Wounded at Lutzen, he was at Magdeburg. GdCx Reunion in 1813. He was in the vanguard during the Hundred Days and was killed attacking St-Amand on 16 June 1815.

His deputies were **Berthollet** – used by Murat on his left wing – and **Forgeot** who was a former volunteer from the Cote d'Or. He was appointed to these headquarters in 1805. LII in 1806, OLII in 1809, he became a Major in the 48th in 1811. Wounded at Bautzen, he was promoted to Colonel in 1813. He had his left thigh shattered and was amputated. Chevalier, retired in 1814.

Donop was born at Kassel and served in the 3rd Hussars in 1789. He became Murat's assistant in 1801, he was promoted to Captain in the 9th Hussars after Austerlitz. Squadron Commander, mentioned in Spain in 1809, he was Chief of Staff of the Army of the Centre and commanded the general depot in 1813 and 1814. He was seriously wounded at Waterloo and disappeared, probably died from his wounds.

The Surveyor **Brousseaud**, Battalion Commander was attached to Murat because he was mentioned in the after-battle report as were Lemesle and Moysant, commanding the Chasseur escort.

The artillery was entrusted to **Mossel**, wounded in 1793, 1796 and in Italy. Promoted to General in 1805, he commanded the reserve artillery. He went to Naples, CtLH in 1806 then Baron. He behaved in an insolent manner and was retired in 1811.

THE 1st DIVISION OF THE HEAVY CAVALRY

Nansouty was born at Bordeaux, he was the son of Major Chateau-Trompette. Gentleman-Cadet in the Paris School in 1782, he became a General in 1799 then Major-General in 1803. First Chamberlain to the Empress in 1805, Gd Aigle LH in 1807, First Equerry to Napoleon in 1808, he was made a Count. He commanded the 1st Cavalry Reserve Corps in Russia, wounded at Hanau. Commanded the Cavalry of the Guard in 1814, he was wounded at Craonne. Aide de camp to the Comte d'Artois in 1814 he died at Paris in February 1815.

Nansouty's aide de camp was Thierry, born at Sedan, this Lieutenant with the 13th then the 11th Dragoons was appointed Captain in 1800 (wounded twice that year). Nansouty's aide de camp he was promoted to Squadron Commander after Austerlitz then chief of Staff for the division in 1809. OLH, wounded at Essling, lost the use of his right leg. Retired in 1813, Baron, recalled and became Maréchal de camp in 1815, retired again in 1825, he finished his career as Honorary Lieutenant-General.

The Heavy Cavalry General Nansouty in Full dress Uniform.
(Author's Collection)

— 1st BRIGADE CARABINIERS

Piston was born at Lyons joined up in 1772, was in the Army of the Alps with Berthier as Chief of Staff. CtLH. He was with Lannes, then took this job, and charged at Austerlitz, he was Major-General after the battle, Baron then retired in 1808.

● The 1st Carabiniers

Colonel was **Cochois** but he was wounded chasing Arch-Duke Ferdinand's Corps near Nuremberg. He obtained a Sabre of Honour for this action but was unable to join his regiment until the 3 December, the day following the battle of Austerlitz. Appointed General on 24 December 1805, he commanded in France and was retired in 1814.

He was replaced by **Chouard**, Squadron Commander, born at Strasbourg. Wounded several times in 1793; he was aide de camp to Moreau then to Delmas. He was wounded by a biscayen bullet and four sabre blows at Austerlitz. Appointed Colonel of the 2nd Cuirassiers on 27 December 1805 then General in 1811, he commanded the Carabiniers in Russia. Wounded at the Moskova, he was sent to recover in 1813. Commanded the 2nd Dragoon Division, he defended Langres in 1814. CrLH. He was at the head of two regiments of Lancers in the Haut-Rhin during the Hundred Days. Retired in 1815, recalled and retired again in 1833, he died at Nancy in 1843.

Lannelongue was in the regiment in 1774, knocked over by a horse in 1799, he was wounded and appointed Captain in 1805. LH. He fought at Austerlitz and retired in 1806.

Leroy was born at Landrecies, was present at Austerlitz, Lieutenant in 1809 and became an officer in the Grenadiers à Cheval in Russia. OLH in 1813, retired because of his wounds in 1813.

Plançon was wounded at Nancy in 1780 and three times in 1792, he captured a canon and a caisson and took a lot of prisoners, saved an officer who was caught under his horse as well as capturing forty men in 1796. He was wounded again taking lots of prisoners 1800, which got him a Sabre of Honour. He had a horse killed under him and was bruised a lot at Austerlitz. Captain in the 4th Cuirassiers in 1806, mentioned at Heilsberg, his horse was killed and he was wounded at Essling. Wounded again at Wagram, he was made Squadron Commander. OLH in Russia. He took 14 cannon at Polotsk and was mentioned at the Beresina where his fifth horse was killed. He charged at Waterloo and retired in 1815.

Labeille was wounded at Nordlingen then appointed Squadron Commander. LH He was wounded and his horse killed at Austerlitz. Seriously wounded at Wagram.

Etienne, Maréchal des Logis was wounded and had his horse killed under him at Austerlitz. Wounded again at Wagram he died of his wounds.

Lieutenant **Chevillet** was wounded at Austerlitz, his horse was killed.

Captain **Coiffier** was wounded at Austerlitz. LH, he was Squadron Commander in Russia and OLH in 1814.

Second-Lieutenant **Coiffier** was probably the brother of the above was wounded and mentioned at Austerlitz.

Also mentioned were Captain who led his charge very well, probably in place of Chouard who was wounded. Captains **Biendiné** and **Cardon**, Lieutenants **Habert** and **Albet**, Second-Lieutenants **Bréjat**, **Chantel** and **Juning**, Trumpeter **Reep**. Second-Lieutenant **Chambrotte** was wounded at Austerlitz and

A carabineer in full dress. The Uniform of this elite heavy cavalry corps is still very close to that of the Ancien Régime. It was only after 1810, that these cavalrymen wore the more brilliant uniform of the Grande Armée.
(Author's Collection, DR)

killed at Friedland. Brigadier **Silvestre** was dismounted but continued fighting on foot. Carabinier Cervin had his horse killed, but found a stray so he mounted it and charged again.

At the start, the regiment had 23 officers, 443 men and 478 horses before the battle. It lost 7 officers wounded, two troopers killed and 24 wounded. Another source gives only 195 men present on 2 December.

● The 2nd Carabiniers

Colonel **Morin** entered the regiment in 1782 and became its colonel in 1803. CtLH after Austerlitz, General in 1807, Inspector of Depots in 1809, Baron in 1812, he finished by retiring in 1813.

Ismert was with the 2nd Carabiniers in 1801. He was appointed Colonel subsequently, then Colonel of the 2nd Dragoons in 1807. He was at Medellin, OLH, Baron. Had a horse killed in Russia. Couronne de Fer and retired in 1814.

Borel was already a Carabinier in 1758, senior in the regiment in 1804, OLH, retired in 1806, being *"rather old and tired"*.

Duclos- Grenet was in the regiment in 1789, wounded in the Vendée, made Captain in 1793. Dismissed in 1806, called back he became assistant in 1807 to Oudinot's 2nd Corps. Squadron Commander in 1808, he was with Oudinot in 1809. He served in Russia, was at Wesel in 1813 and died in October 1813.

Priolet won a Rifle of Honour in 1803 and retired in 1808.

Benoit was born in Soissons was in the regiment in 1797, Sabre of Honour in 1803, appointed Second-Lieutenant in 1806, Squadron Commander in 1813, dismissed in 1815.

Normand was in the regiment in 1794 and received a Sabre of Honour in 1802. Promoted to Lieutenant in 1806, after Jena, he retired in 1810.

Vanroye was in the regiment in 1794, he freed his Squadron Commander in 1800, committed prodigious deeds of bravery and was riddled with wounds at Austerlitz; he died at Brunn.

The regiment only had 182 men at Austerlitz and only lost one officer and 16 Carabiniers wounded and two killed.

— GENERAL DE LA HOUSSAYE'S 2nd BRIGADE.

De la Houssaye commanded the 3rd Hussars, then the 16th Chasseurs. Promoted to General in 1804, CtLH and Major-General in 1807. He was in Grouchy' 3rd Cavalry Corps in Russia. Seriously wounded at the Moskova, he was captured at Vilna and returned in 1814. He served in 1815 and was put on the non-active list. Count in 1819, he became an Inspector of Gendarmerie and retired in 1833.

● The 2nd Cuirassiers

Colonel **Yvendorf** was born in Hamburg. He was at St Domingo and returned in 1790. Colonel in 1799, he served at Marengo. He was appointed General on 27 December after Austerlitz where he was

Brigadier and Trumpeter
in the Carabiniers.
The difference between
the 1st and the 2nd
Carabinier Regiment lay
in the facing flaps
and the number worn
on the grenade
on the button.

Trooper from
the 2nd Regiment
of Cuirassiers.
Originating in the cavalry
regiments of the Ancien
Régime, the Cuirassiers
were thought of as elite
regiments. Because
of this they wore
the fringed epaulettes
of the Grenadiers
and a red plume.

Trooper and Officer from
the 9th Cuirassier
Regiment.

André Jouineau © Histoire & Collections 2003

CAVALRY RESERVE

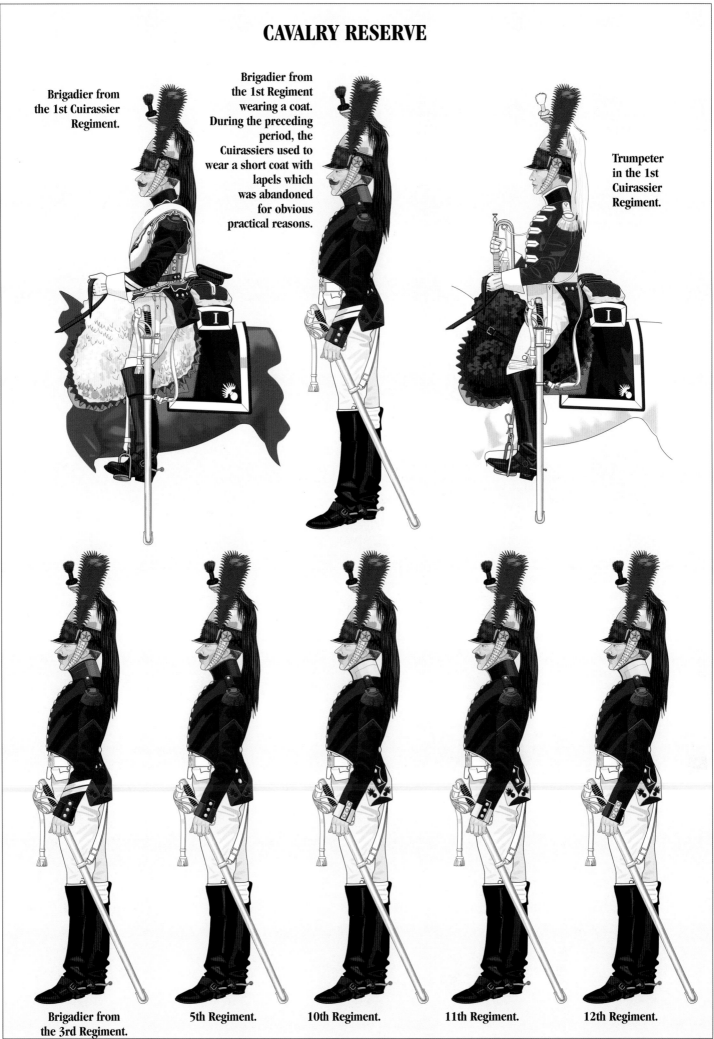

Brigadier from the 1st Cuirassier Regiment.

Brigadier from the 1st Regiment wearing a coat. During the preceding period, the Cuirassiers used to wear a short coat with lapels which was abandoned for obvious practical reasons.

Trumpeter in the 1st Cuirassier Regiment.

Brigadier from the 3rd Regiment.

5th Regiment.

10th Regiment.

11th Regiment.

12th Regiment.

André Jouineau © Histoire & Collections 2003

wounded. OLH, retired in 1811, he was recalled for the Hundred Days as Inspector. Retired in 1815.

Alix was in the Army of the North in 1792 and received a Sabre of Honour in 1800 for taking a canon and 200 Englishmen, then 53 Austrians in Italy. Squadron commander in the regiment, he was at Marengo where he seized a flag, received a second Sabre of Honour. OLH. At Austerlitz, retired in 1808, he was Mayor of Neuville-sur-Saone, in the Rhone; denounced by Royalists he was arrested but later freed.

Guépratte was in the regiment in 1791. He was a Lieutenant at Austerlitz and Jena; LH, Captain after Wagram, he was at Hamburg in 1813 and was retired in 1815.

Also mentioned were **Erard**, second-Lieutenant: *"having charged through the enemy lines, he was knocked over onto the shafts of horses which were pulling a canon. He cut up the gunners and owed his life to his own courage."*

Saissette, Brigadier: *"Carrying the Eagle of the 1st Squadron at Austerlitz, he hit the enemy with it, drew his sabre, fought and brought back the flag."*

● The 9th Cuirassiers

Colonel **Doumer** was born at Montauban. Only a Dragoon in 1783, he was a Colonel in 1800. He was at Austerlitz and was appointed a General in 1806. He replaced La Houssaye. He was at Friedland then with Oudinot in Russia, at Polotsk. Hero of the Beresina. He served in the French Campaign and in 1815. Was put on the non-active list, he was retired in 1825. GdCxLH in 1832. Permanently retired in 1833.

Squadron Commander **Leblanc**, LH, served at Ulm and at Austerlitz. Seriously wounded in 1800, he was discharged on health grounds. Garrison Commandant in 1812, Adjudant-Commandant in 1813, retired in 1814. Adjudant in 1815, retired in 1816.

Viel was mentioned in 1800, Sabre of Honour in 1803, he was at Austerlitz. Made Lieutenant he served at Jena, was wounded at Wagram, then fought in Russia and Saxony. OLH. He was at Dresden and was wounded three times at Leipzig. Squadron Commander in the 10th Cuirassiers, he was at Ligny and at Waterloo. Dismissed, he returned home.

Lefèvre, Captain, wounded, captured freed was appointed Squadron Commander in 1804, major then Colonel of the 11th in 1813. OLH in 1814, he served in the French Campaign and became Adjudant-Commandant in 1815. This promotion was cancelled. He died in 1835.

The regiment had two officers and 11 troopers wounded, and two killed at Austerlitz.

— SAINT-GERMAIN'S 3rd BRIGADE

Saint-Germain was a Gendarme in 1778, Brigade Commander in 1793, he was wounded twice in 1796.and 1797. He was with Ney at Hohenlinden and became a General in 1805, then Major-General in 1809. He was with Bordesoulle in 1813 at Lutzen. Count; he charged at Hanau, took part in the French Campaign, GdOLh in 1814 then retired in 1826, then again in 1832, he died in 1835.

● The 3rd Cuirassiers

Colonel **Preval** was born at Salins and became a Lieutenant in 1792. Colonel of the 3rd in 1801, he refused to Judge the Duke of Enghien. He was at Austerlitz and became a general in 1086. Couronne de Fer, Baron, Master of request on the Council of State, Inspector of Cavalry, he commanded the larger depots before becoming Lieutenant-General in 1814. He joined the Ministry of War as Director, Viscount in 1817, then Peer of France in 1837. He was promoted to President of the War Section of the Council of State; GdCxLH in 1843, Senator in 1852.

Below.
A clash of Titans between a carabineer of Piston's Brigade and an Austrian Cuirassier.
(Author's Collection, RR)

A Major-General in a Heavy Cavalry Regiment, perhaps D'Hautpoul also wearing full dress uniform, during a parade. (Author's collection)

Eberlin, Sabre of Honour in 1804, Captain in Spain in 1809, he was promoted to Squadron Commander in 1814 with the 14th cuirassiers. OLH. He served in 1815 and retired in the same year.

Land saved the regiment's standards in 1793 and was wounded several times. Lieutenant on the battlefield at La Trebia, he won a Sabre of Honour and was promoted to Captain. He lost a horse and was wounded at Austerlitz. He served at Jena and Eylau; lost a horse at Friedland and retired in 1808.

Gaignemaille was wounded at Famars in 1792, saved the regimental standard, wounded at Marengo, LH, he was a Lieutenant at Austerlitz then Captain in 1808. He died in 1811.

Also mentioned in the Century Memorial Book were **Gérardin**, Maréchal des logis: *"while defending his standard which he kept he received several sabre wounds."*

Bela, Cuirassier: *"was one of the fifty brave soldiers who rushed in front of the enemy to stop the artillery which they were still trying to cover; seven guns were captured and Cuirassier Bella who had contributed a great deal to this capture gave one to the artillery pool."*

Four officers from the regiment were killed and four wounded at Austerlitz.

● The 12th Cuirassiers

Colonel **Belfort** was a trooper in 1770, Brigade Commander of the 12th Cuirassiers in 1794, he served at Wertingen and at Austerlitz. General after the battle, CtLH, he was made a Baron then retired in 1815.

Ferley joined up in 1779, he was with the Army of the Rhine, LH. Served at Austerlitz, Jena, Eylau and Friedland, and retired in 1809.

Paquié, Captain; **Lecherpy**, Squadron Commander, Lieutenants **Chobriat**, wounded, **Rouyer**, **Rivat**, **Bernard** and Brigadier **Morelle** were decorated at Austerlitz.

The regiment had 4 officers and 12 troopers wounded and two killed including one officer.

D'HAUTPOUL'S 2nd HEAVY CAVALRY DIVISION

The division was placed behind Suchet's Division on the left wing.

D'Hautpoul was born at Sallettes in the Tarn and joined up in 1777, became Brigade Commander in 1794, then General in 1795. He was with Marceau and was wounded in 1796. He replaced Richepanse then became Major-General in 1796. Suspended by Jourdain then acquitted, he served at Hohenlinden.; he commanded that division in 1805, served at Austerlitz, became a Senator, fought at Jena, Lubeck and Hoff. Gd Aigle LH in 1806. His right thigh was shattered and he died of his wounds.

His aide de camps were Squadron Commander **Petit** and Captain **Desaignes** who obtained a Sabre of Honour in Italy. He was mentioned at Austerlitz and became Squadron Commander in 1811. Wounded at the Moskova, he served in 1813, 1814 and 1815. He retired in 1820.

The other aide de camps were Captains **Noirot** and **Lejeune** and Lieutenants **Ginsl** and **Rousisky**.

The Chief of Staff was Adjudant-Commandant **Fontaine**. He served in America from 1779 to 1782 and became a General before Ireland. Captured he was subsequently on Belliard's staff in 1802, then on d'Hautpoul's at Austerlitz. He was with Lasalle in Spain, then with Dorsenne; he died in 1812. Mentioned by

The Cavalrymen of the 1st Cuirassiers of Colonel Guiton advancing. The Grande Armée's 'Gros Talons' (Big Heels) were above all the arm used for breaking through the enemy.
They did not have a determining role to play during the battle.
(Drawings Jack Girbal, Author's Collection)

d'Hautpoul and congratulated by him for Austerlitz in the official report.

— SAINT-SULPICE'S BRIGADE

General **Saint-Sulpice** was Colonel of the 5th Chasseurs in 1797, General in 1803, Equerry to the Empress, then he served at Austerlitz. Major-General in 1807, he was with Bessières in 1809; with Davout at Eckmuhl and Essling. He commanded the Dragoons of the Guard in 1809 instead of Arrighi. He was with Nansouty in Russia in 1812. He then commanded the Dragoons of the Guard. Governor of Fontainebleau in 1813, Colonel of the 4th Regiment of the Guard of Honour in 1813, he fought in Saxony then at Lyons in 1814. He served at Tours in 1815, retired in the same year. Peer of France in 1831, he retired definitively in 1832.

● The 1st Regiment of Cuirassiers

Colonel **Guiton**, CtLH for Austerlitz, became a General in 1807 (he commanded the 10th and 11th Cuirassiers); Baron, he served at Wagram, at Hamburg in 1813 and 1814. Returned, he fought Waterloo, retired in 1815.

Daudies, Squadron Commander at Austerlitz, OLH he became Colonel and Chevalier in 1810. He had four horses killed at Dresden and at Leipzig. Maréchal de camp in 1815, his rank was cancelled. He was retired with the rank of Maréchal de camp in 1816.

Squadron Commander **Pierrot** was mentioned at Austerlitz, as was Demongin, who had that rank since 1799; he had two horses killed and he was wounded at Austerlitz.

Berckeim, (Baron de) was a Captain in the 2nd Carabiniers in 1802. He captured 5 cannon. Squadron Commander in 1805, he became the Colonel of the regiment in 1807. He served at Heilsberg, Friedland, Essling and Wagram. General in 1809, Baron; he was in Russia with Oudinot. Present at Polotsk and the Beresina. He was CtLH and Major-General in 1813. He defended Alsace, in command of the division of the Guards of Honour and served at Arcis d'Aube, Deputy from 1815 to 1817, he died in 1819.

Badey Captain in 1803, LH in 1806, died in 1809.

Dauphin was a Grenadier à Cheval of the Guard in 1796, LH in 1806, wounded at Hoff he had two horses killed at Essling, wounded again at Eckmuhl, he served at Eylau, Moscow and Chalons in 1814.

Petit captured a howitzer all by himself, killing all the gunners. LH in 1807, he was wounded the same year, Captain at Essling.

Pierredon was a child of the regiment, present at Austerlitz became Captain in 1807 (LH) then served at Essling and at Leipzig, being wounded in each battle.

Schlesser was appointed Lieutenant in 1806 after Austerlitz, killed at Eylau.

Thuon was a Lieutenant died from his wounds at Austerlitz.

Jarsaillon, killed at Eylau.

Pescheloche was Squadron Commander in 1808 then a Major in the 15th Dragoons.

Roize, aide de camp to Davout in 1801, Squadron Commander in 1806, wounded at Jena and Hoff.

Saint-Georges, LH in 1806, wounded at Austerlitz and at Eylau, captured in Russia.

Varrocaux, Rifle of Honour after Verona, Second-Lieutenant in 1807, Killed at Essling.

Parès wounded three times at Austerlitz, wounded and captured at Leipzig, returned, LH and retired in 1814.

Monteil, called **Duteil** was a sailor, wounded in 1793 joined the 1st Cuirassiers in 1794. Wounded at Austerlitz, became Squadron Commander in 1807 then Major in 1809. Wounded at Eckmuhl, LH and Chevalier. Colonel – Major in the 4th Regiment of the Guard if Honour in 1813, retired in 1818.

Guiton recommended Surgeon-Major Kaiser for the medical care he gave to the wounded during the campaign but also on the battlefield

Second-Lieutenant **Dessaignes** won a Weapon of Honour in 1803 and mentioned by the Colonel. The regiment lost one officer killed and four wounded at Austerlitz.

● The 5th Cuirassiers

Colonel **Noirot** was a Garde du Corps in 1788, aide de camp to his father in law, Jean du Tell, then served at Toulon. Colonel in 1802, he was mentioned at Austerlitz (CtLH). General in 1806, imprisoned for negligence, discharged and appointed Inspector of Gendarmerie By Louis XVIII, he retired in 1825.

Squadron Commander **Jacquemin** was at Marengo, took a flag at Austerlitz (OLH), was wounded at Heilsberg and killed at Eylau.

Berthenot was in Italy and won a Sabre of Honour. Lieutenant in 1806, killed at Eylau.

Bonvalet won a Rifle of Honour in 1801, Lieutenant was wounded twice at Hoff and retired as a Captain in 1813.

Rémy received a Sabre of Honour in 1802, became Adjudant-NCO was mentioned at Hoff and Eylau where he had three horses killed under him. Captain in Russia, made a Baron, served at Waterloo and retired in 1815.

Also mentioned were **Rondot**, Second-Lieutenant: *"This officer having already accomplished prodigious feats of courage, was dismounted in the middle of the enemy battalions; he grabbed the tail of one of his platoon's horses and told the cuirassier riding it to 'get a move on'. He was thus dragged out of the fray; he saw the horse of a dead Cuirassier, chased it, remounted and returned to the battle where he was able to distinguish himself by his courage and by the hold his presence had on the platoon he was in command of."*

Ouriet, Maréchal des logis: *"had his helmet broken by several bullets and found himself off his horse at the moment when the mass of enemy infantry was retreating. He ran to the guns that the infantry had abandoned, cut the shafts off one of them, freed the horse, rode it bare-back back into the fight."*

Jude, Cuirassier: *"this Cuirassier who had been conscripted a year ago, dismounted in the middle of the enemy infantry, managed to get out and not wanting to leave, he got hold of a Russian rifle and cartridge pouch, joined an infantry battalion and spent the rest of the day there."*

Veyssey, Captain: *"this captain was in command of the 2nd Squadron, he found himself at the head of the column in a charge carried out in serried ranks. He managed to extract his squadron in a most vigorous manner and although bit in the thigh by a bayonet and losing a lot of blood, he only left the fighting zone after the enemy had been defeated."*

Armand, Maréchal des Logis-chef: *"this NCO with three comrades saved his Colonel's life several times. He is the only one of the four who has not received his cross."*

Dégremont, Cuirassier: *"Dismounted, he took the horse of one of his dead comrades and returned to his place in the ranks."*

Three officers killed and four wounded at Austerlitz for this regiment.

● The 10th Cuirassiers

Colonel **La Taye** was a Colonel in 1797, took 9 cannon in 1800 and received a sabre of Honour. Served at Hohenlinden, Austerlitz, CtLH after the battle. Made a General in 1806 and retired for health reasons. Made a Baron in 1808.

Scherb was a Captain, wounded at Austerlitz, promoted to Squadron Commander in the 11 Cuirassiers before being killed at Eylau.

Scherb, brother of the above, served in Russia and retired in 1816.

Pierrot, Squadron Commander congratulated by Napoleon, LH in 1813.

The regiment had 32 officers, 551 troopers and 475 horses at Austerlitz. It lost 8 men killed, two officers and 74 troopers wounded; 16 horses were killed and two wounded.

● The 11th Cuirassiers

Colonel **Fouler** was Colonel in 1802, appointed General after Austerlitz. Equerry in charge of the Empress' stables; he was mentioned at Austerlitz. Count in 1808, he served in Spain and became Equerry to the Emperor in 1810. After the French Campaign he was promoted to Major-General in 1814 and GdCxLH in 1815. He was with Napoleon at Waterloo. Retired in 1815.

Rémy was mentioned at Naples, won a Sabre of honour in 1802. At Austerlitz he took a canon and had a horse killed, he was wounded and his horse killed at Essling. OLH. He lost a horse ay the Moskova, and was wounded twice in Russia where he was taken prisoner. He returned in 1814 and retired.

2nd DRAGOON DIVISION

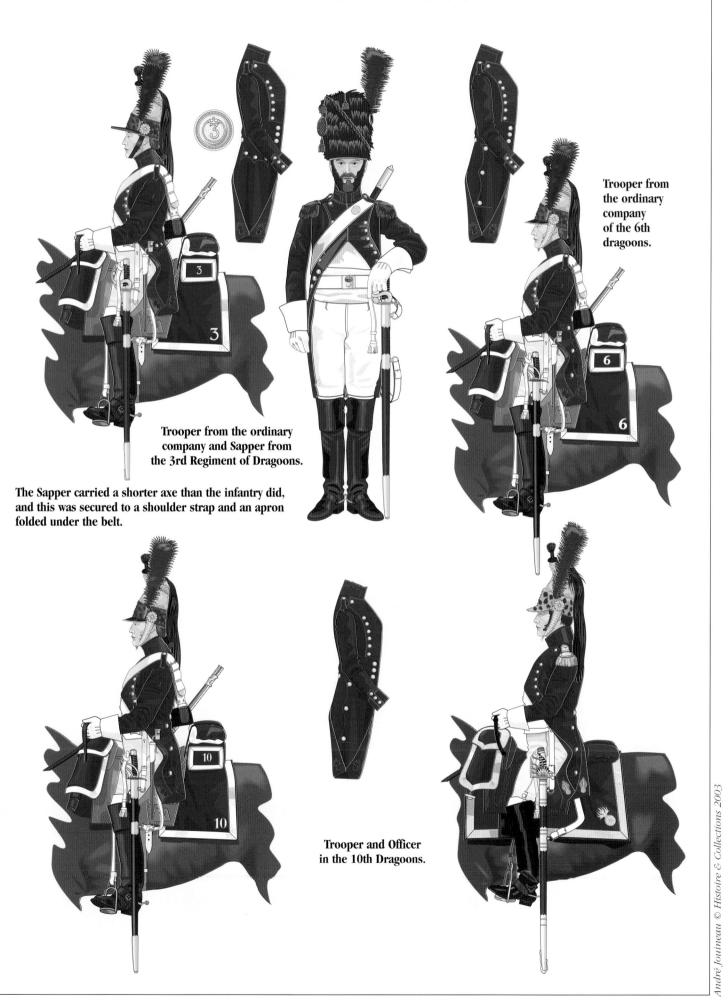

Trooper from the ordinary
company and Sapper from
the 3rd Regiment of Dragoons.

The Sapper carried a shorter axe than the infantry did,
and this was secured to a shoulder strap and an apron
folded under the belt.

Trooper from
the ordinary
company
of the 6th
dragoons.

Trooper and Officer
in the 10th Dragoons.

André Jouineau © Histoire & Collections 2003

The regiment lost four officers wounded at Austerlitz.

D'Hautpoul's division lost four officers and 46 troopers killed, 79 wounded; 93 horses were killed and 65 wounded.

KLEIN'S 1st DRAGOON DIVISION

General **Klein**, Senator General in 1795, he was made Major-General in 1799. Hero of Zurich (CtLH) he was mentioned at Eylau and became Count and Governor of the Palace in 1808. Retired, he was Peer in 1814 and GdCxLH in 1834.

His Chief of Staff was **Bertrand** in 1805. Wounded at Eylau, he became a General in 1808. He was with Bessières in 1809, then was made a Baron. He was with General Headquarters in Russia, served in 1815 and was wounded at Belfort. Retired in 1815.

Only the 1st Dragoons took part in the battle with Davout accompanying Heudelet's Division. The rest of the division reached Raygern at the end of the day.

— FORNIER (FÉNÉROLS)'S 1st BRIGADE

Fénérols was born in the Tarn, became a General in 1803 (CtLh) and commanded the 1st, 12th and 20th Dragoons. He was killed at Golymin in 1806.

Above, from left to right and top to bottom.
Major-General Klein, Arrighi de Casanova, Colonel of the 1st Dragoons; Major-General Walther who commanded the 2nd Dragoon Division and Sébastiani de la Porta who commanded the 1st Brigade of Walther's Division.
(RR)

● **The 1st Dragoons**

They were commanded by Colonel Arrighi. His father was Napoleon's cousin. He was aide de camp to Berthier in Syria, served at Marengo and became Colonel of the regiment in 1800. CtLH. Major-Colonel of the Dragoons of the Guard, he was also Aide de camp to Berthier at Wertingen. He was at Austerlitz. Promoted to General, he fought at Benavente, Essling and Wagram where he replaced Espagne killed at Essling. Duke of Padua in 1808, he commanded the 3rd Cavalry Corps in 1813. He served at Dennewitz, Mockern, Leipzig, Hanau, took part in the French Campaign and was wounded at Paris. Peer of France during the Hundred Days, he left for Lombardy; recalled in 1819, he was retired. Recalled in 1837, Deputy in 1849, Senator in 1852, he was Governor of the Invalides. He had married Anne de Montesquiou-Fezensac.

Sopransi was the son of Mme Sopransi, Berthier's mistress; he was wounded as a Second-Lieutenant at Marengo then was made a Lieutenant in the 1st Dragoons. He fought at Ulm, Wertingen and Austerlitz where he captured General Wimpfen. Captain with the 4th Cuirassiers, aide de camp to Berthier in 1807, he became Squadron Commander. He took 7 flags and 6 cannon at Uclès, served at Wagram and in Russia where he was wounded at the Moskova. General in 1813, wounded at Leipzig, OLH and Couronne de Fer. He died in Paris in 1814.

It seems that the regiment was in fact commanded at the end of the battle by Captain Ménard (according to Colin). There was a General Ménard who was Chief of Staff of the 2nd Reserve Corps of the Grande Armée

Six officers killed in this regiment.

● The 2nd Dragoons.

Colonel **Pryvé** was the commanding officer of the 5th Dragoons instead of the titular head, Louis Bonaparte, in 1803. He was in the 2nd Dragoons in September 1805, he fought at Wertingen and Austerlitz and was CtLH after the battle. Mentioned at Jena, he was at Golymin and was wounded at Eylau. General in 1807, taken at Baylen, returned from England in 1814. Retired in 1818.

Mimin, wounded in 1796, LH served at Wertingen and Austerlitz, Eylau, Medellin where his arm was blown off by a cannonball. He died from his wounds on 15 July 1810.

Hetru was born at Vincennes and distinguished himself in 1796, 1797 and 1800. He won a Sabre of Honour in 1802 and was made a Captain AM and OLH in 1804. He was wounded at Ulm, he charged at

Colonel Privé of the 2nd Dragoons. *(RR)*

Austerlitz and died in August 1807, at Glogau after Friedland.

— LASALLE'S 2nd BRIGADE

Lasalle was the hero of Rivoli, Italy and Egypt; General in 1805, he received a Sabre of Honour and two Pistols of Honour. CtLH. He served at Austerlitz and afterwards commanded the 5th and 7th Hussars which formed his 'Infernal Brigade' which became famous during the chase after Jena. Fauconnet took his place in Klein's Dragoons on 13 December 1805. For some – Benjamin Six — he commanded the 4th and 14th Dragoons. But the 4th was at Dürrenstein. On the other hand the 14th was truly at Austerlitz and one can quote Lasalle who was next to Davout during the chase after the battle.

His aide de camps were **Wathiez** served in Italy with the 25th Chasseurs, as assistant to Murat's staff, serving at Ulm and Austerlitz. First aide de camp to Lasalle in 1807, he was at Wagram with him. Marulaz' Chief of Staff, he served in Russia, and in Saxony, at Leipzig, and was wounded at Hanau. Made a baron in 1813, he was in France in 1814. Wounded at Waterloo, Viscount in 1824 and CrSL in 1825, Lieutenant-General in 1837, GdOLH in 1843, he was on the Reserve list in 1853.

Théron was wounded in the Pyrenees was wounded in the Army of the West twice then served in Italy. Lieutenant in the 10th Hussars, he was mentioned in 1800 and won a Sabre of Honour in 1803, OLH. Aide de camp to Lasalle at Austerlitz where he was mentioned, he was promoted on the battlefield to Squadron Commander at Jena. Mentioned at Friedland, he was wounded 16 times and lost 4 horses. Major in the 4th Dragoons, wounded and mentioned for Portugal by Junot, he died in 1812 at the depot of the 4th Dragoons. He had been wounded 29 times in all.

● **The 14th Dragoons**

Colonel Lafon-Blaniac was born at Villeneuve-sur-Lot. This assistant to the Adjutant-Generals was wounded in 1797 and made a Captain on the battlefield. He served in Egypt where he was wounded twice, once seriously at Canope. He joined the regiment in 1081; after Austerlitz he was Equerry to King Joseph in Spain as aide de camp and Major-General. Governor of Madrid, wounded at Vittoria, he returned to France with his rank in 1813. Put on the non-active list in August 1815, he retired in 1825. He was elected Deputy in 1831, GdOLH in 1833, the year of his death.

— GENERAL MILET'S BRIGADE.

Milet was born in Martinique and served at Marengo. He was appointed General in 1800, CtLH in 1804. He commanded the 3rd Brigade of Klein's Division in October 1805 and went over to the 2nd Division in place of Sébastiani on 24 December after the battle. He served in Spain and was retired in 1812.

His aide de camp was **Du Coetlosquet**. He was aide de camp and friend of Lasalle in 1806 and followed him. General in 1813, wounded at Leipzig, Lieutenant-General in 1821, CrSL became interim Minister of War in 1823. Councillor of State, he served against the uprisings in 1830, retired in 1831.

● **The 20th Dragoons**

Colonel Reynaud was in the 22nd Dragoons in 1793 then served in Egypt. CtLH after Austerlitz, General in 1806, he commanded the 4th and 6th Cuirassiers in Espagne's Division. Wounded at Wagram under Arrighi, he served in Russia with Valence. In 1813, served domestically and did not rally during the Hundred Days. He retired in 1821.

● **The 26th Dragoons**

Colonel **Delorme** was Squadron Commander in 1793, was mentioned in Italy. He was Colonel of the Regiment in 1800, at Hohenlinden, OLH, CtLH after Austerlitz; and served at Eylau before he was retired in 1807.

2nd DRAGOON DIVISION

Senior officer in the 11th Dragoons;
Like all officers of rank higher
than Squadron Commander,
he is wearing the *'Spinach seed'*
epaulettes, double stripes on the
saddle blanket and the *chaperons*.

Brigadier-Furrier in the ordinary
company of the 13th Dragoons.
The furrier wore a silver stripe
across his arm, as well
as his stripes of rank.

Trooper and Trumpeter
in the 22nd Dragoons.

Trooper in the 13th
Dragoons wearing
round-cloak
and overcoat.

André Jouineau © Histoire & Collections 2003

Laguerre was from the Ariège and was in the Army of the Rhine and Italy. LH, retired in 1807 after the Prussian and Polish Campaigns.

Crépin, LH. Did the Austerlitz campaign with the division; then served at Wagram and in Spain where he died at Seville in 1811.

Hacquart was wounded three times. LH He took part in the 1805 Austrian campaign, retired in 1806.

Lavalette was with the Army of the North and of Italy, fought at Rivoli, Hohenlinden, LH, Lieutenant wounded in 1813, he was caught near Maestricht, returned he was at Waterloo, retired in 1816.

Coulon had two horses killed at Marengo, LH, retired in 1806.

Vial was the brother of the General, born near Antibes, he served in Egypt and was in the regiment from 1803. He was its Colonel in 1807; made Baron, he was at Jena, in Spain at Toulouse in 1814. After Waterloo he was put on the non-active list, retired in 1824. GdOLH in 1850, he was on the Reserve List in 1852.

WALTHER'S 2nd DRAGOON DIVISION

Walther was in the 1st Hussars in 1781, he fought in the Alps, in Italy, commanded Augereau's cavalry. Commanded the 3rd and 14th Dragoons under Dumas, was mentioned at Hohenlinden under Richepance. Major-general in 1803, served at Hollabrunn wounded at Austerlitz, he was Gd Aigle LH and Chamberlain to Napoleon. Promoted to Major of the Grenadiers à Cheval of the Guard in 1806, he charged at Eylau, became a Count. He commanded the cavalry of the Guard at Wagram. Fought in Russia, Saxony and at Hanau, he died in 1813 in the Sarthe.

Lacroix was at Hohenlinden, his appointment by Moreau for General was refused, OLH. He was on Walther's Staff at Austerlitz then he became Chief of Staff of the 3rd Division of Cuirassiers after Jena. Captured in Russia, returned in 1814, he was Maréchal de camp during the Hundred Days. Honorary retired in 1818, he was recalled in 1831 and regularised; he died in 1838.

— SÉBASTIANI DE LA PORTA'S 1st BRIGADE

Sébastiani served in Corsica then in Italy where he took part at Dego and Arcola. Brigade Commander of the 9th Dragoons in 1799, he was at Marengo. General in 1803, lightly wounded at Austerlitz he was promoted to Major-General in 1805 and sent to Turkey on a mission where he helped the Turks drive way the English in 1807. Gd Aigle LH in 1807, served in Spain, made a Count in 1809, fought in Russia with Montbrun whom he replaced after his death at the Moskova. He commanded the surviving cavalry – reduced to the "Sacred Squadron" during the retreat. Elected deputy during the Hundred Days, he went over to England after the defeat. Elected deputy in 1819, beaten in 1824 but elected for the Aisne in 1826 and re-elected in 1830, he became Minister of the Navy. Re-elected in 1834, he was appointed Ambassador to London in 1835, Maréchal de France. Re-elected in 1840, then in 1846 in Corsica, he was hated by many. He died in 1851.

Above, from left to right. **Lefebvre-Desnoettes, Colonel of the 18th Dragoons and Auguste de Caulaincourt, Corps Commander of the 19th Dragoons.**
(RR)

● The 3rd Dragoons.

Colonel Fiteau was with the Army of the Rhine, served in Egypt and became Colonel of the 3rd Dragoons. CtLH for Austerlitz. Appointed General in 1809, he was wounded at Wagram and was made a Count. He went mad and committed suicide on 14 December 1810.

Dubois was commander of the squadrons in 1804, he became a Major in the 5th Dragoons after Austerlitz. He had a horse killed under him at Eylau; as Colonel of the 7th he was at Essling, Wagram (OLH) and in Russia. He was appointed General before the Beresina. Wounded at Waterloo, retired in 1815, CrLH in 1831.

Hacquin was with the 3rd Dragoons in Italy, in Egypt he became Second-Lieutenant then Adjutant-Major after Eylau; he served at Friedland, became Captain in the 2nd Chevau-Légers in 1811. he was in Russia as Squadron Commander where he received 17 wounds at Katzbach; left for dead, captured, returned in 1814. He retired in 1824.

Guyon served at Arcola and Rivoli and then Egypt. Wounded at Austerlitz (LH) he fought at Jena, Friedland and became Squadron Commander in Spain in the 12th Chasseurs. He served in 1814 and 1815, retired in 1822.

Danel was wounded in 1793, served in Egypt, wounded four times and was captured. He was freed by the Pasha. LH. He saved Becker in 1806.was mentioned in despatches, and appointed Squadron Commander. He was mentioned again at Guttstadt and Friedland. He was with Milet in Portugal. OLH and Chevalier in 1810. He retired in 1816 as Honorary Lieutenant-Colonel, he died at Lille in 1838.

Sellier had a horse killed and was wounded at Austerlitz, he retired in 1809.

Vaquié was wounded and had a horse killed under him at Austerlitz.

Also mentioned were Maréchal des Logis Vailly and Dupuy as well as Brigadier Genot and Dragoon Douvry who bravely helped an officer and two of their comrades surrounded by the enemy and about to succumb.

● The 6th Dragoons.

Colonel Lebaron was born at Brest, served at first in the navy then with Hoche in the West at Quiberon; promoted Squadron Commander in 1793 in the 15th Chasseurs then became Colonel of the regiment in 1796. He was killed at Hoff in 1807.

Rémy, Squadron Commander, the hero of the 6th Dragoons, was wounded six times at Marengo. OLH, Squadron Commander in 1815 then on the non-active list.

Three officers were wounded at Austerlitz.

— ROGET DE BELLOGUET'S 2nd BRIGADE

Roget served in 1791, he was with Kléber in the West and was mentioned at Savenay. Colonel of the 13th Dragoons, he was promoted to General in 1799, then accused of misappropriation with Leva. During the battle he replaced Walther who was wounded and charged with his 10th and 11th Dragoons, followed by d'Hautpoul, CtLH after Austerlitz, Major-General. In 1806, he was made a Baron in 1810. He was retired in February 1815.

● The 10th Dragoons.

Colonel Cavaignac was in Italy; promoted to Squadron Commander in the regiment, OLH for Austerlitz; he became a General and Equerry to Joseph. Neapolitan Lieutenant-General, he was also the first aide de camp to Murat. He returned as a French General in 1812, went to Russia and was mentioned at Danzig where he was captured. Lieutenant-General, Baron, GdOLH and Peer of France in 1839.

Major Grouvel was born at Rouen and became a Squadron Commander of the 10th Chasseurs, then Major of the 17th after Austerlitz. Wounded twice, he was Colonel of the 16th in 1810 and then General in 1813 and Baron in 1814. Inspector of Gendarmes in 1820, Viscount in 1824, he became Lieutenant-General in 1825, GdOLH in 1835. On the non-active list after 1836.

Hullot (called Sabatin), was Adjutant at Friedland, caught at Baylen, he returned from England in 1814 and went into the 8th Lancers. He retired in 1815.

Delaas was Squadron Commander in 1804 then Major in the 22nd in 1806. Retired in 1813, he was recalled as a Major in the 1st Regiment of the Guard of Honour in 1814. He fought against Napoleon during the Hundred Days. He died in 1827.

Also mentioned was Lombard, Adjutant-Major: *"he distinguished himself by leading the 2nd Squadron whose two captains were out of action against a Russian battalion which was overwhelming the regiment with its shooting."*

● The 11th Dragoons

Colonel Bourdon was killed at Hollabrunn was replaced by Bourbier, LH, Squadron commander of the chasseurs of the Guard, Colonel of the regiment on 18 December 1805; he was killed at Eylau.

Also mentioned were Saint-Mard, Adjutant-NCO: *"was the first to enter the enemy ranks, knocking over everything which came his way."*

Verguet, Maréchal des Logis: *"engaged the enemy ranks, had his arm broken by a bullet."*

Major Lefebvre and Squadron Commander Giraud were both killed at Austerlitz; two officers were wounded

— BOUSSART'S THIRD BRIGADE

Boussart was a Cadet in Austria sought refuge in France in 1792, was a veteran of Italy and Egypt. Wounded three times at Mondovi, three times in Egypt, appointed General in 1801 (CtLH), he served at Jena, Prenslow, Lubeck; seriously wounded at Pulutsk, captured at Baylen, returned, Spain wounded again and captured before being freed by Delort; Major-General in 1812, he died from his wounds in 1813.

His aide de camp Bordenave was killed in Spain in 1811 (LH).

● The 13th Dragoons

Colonel De Broc was aide de camp to Louis Bonaparte. Wounded in 1792, Colonel in 1804, he was wounded again at Austerlitz. CtLH, GdCx of Holland; he returned to France, General in 1809, was at Raab and Wagram where he was mentioned. Couronne de Fer. He died of an infection in Milan in 1810.

Goyard took 4 cannon and 800 enemy prisoners in 1800, he was promoted to Lieutenant on the battlefield by Moreau, he was promoted to aide de camp to Roget in 1804. LH. He became a Captain and aide de camp to Milet, he died in Poland in 1807.

Brunon won a Sabre of Honour for the crossing of the Rhine in 1802. Appointed Lieutenant in 1806, he was in Spain then took part in the French Campaign before being retired in 1814.

The regiment lost four officers wounded including the Colonel.

● The 22nd Dragoons

Colonel Carrié de Boissy was born in the Aveyron and became Second-lieutenant in 1782. Colonel in 1800, he obtained the CtLH after Austerlitz? Became General, went to Spain and was made a Baron. He

3rd DRAGOON DIVISION

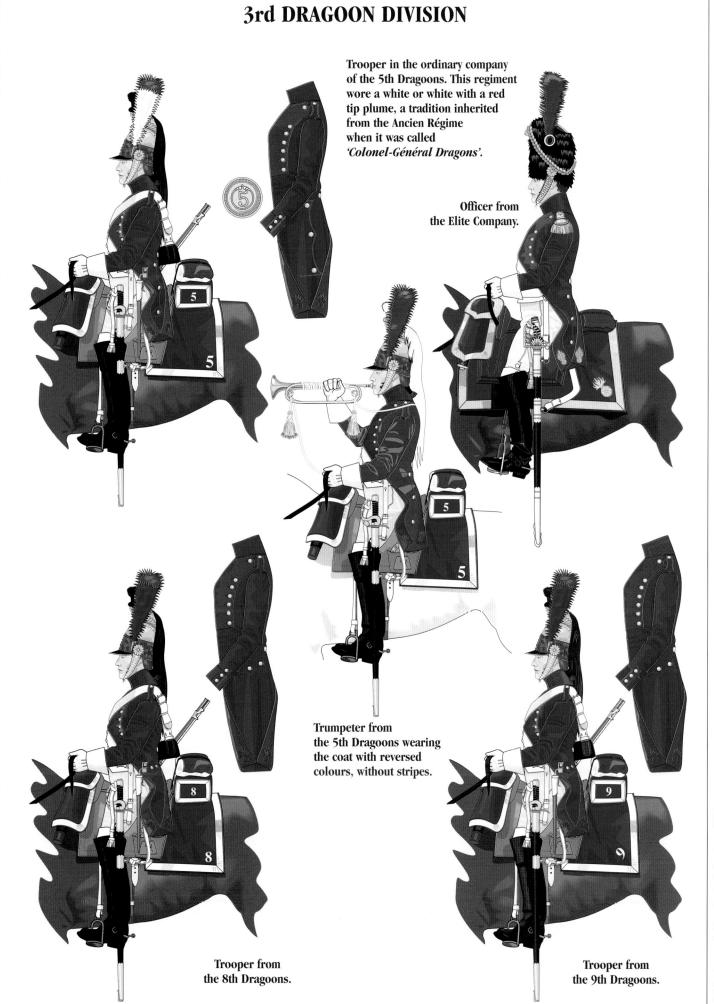

Trooper in the ordinary company of the 5th Dragoons. This regiment wore a white or white with a red tip plume, a tradition inherited from the Ancien Régime when it was called *'Colonel-Général Dragons'*.

Officer from the Elite Company.

Trumpeter from the 5th Dragoons wearing the coat with reversed colours, without stripes.

Trooper from the 8th Dragoons.

Trooper from the 9th Dragoons.

André Jouineau © Histoire & Collections 2003

was wounded twice and captured by the English in 1812. Returned in 1814, he commanded the Aveyron, Deputy for Espalion in 1815, retired in 1843.

Lebarq served on the Danube, LH, was at Eylau and Friedland. He was killed at Logrono in 1810.

Schmidt received a Rifle of Honour in 1802, was promoted to Second-Lieutenant in 1806. He was captured at Baylen, retired in 1814.

The regiment lost one officer killed and two wounded.

BEAUMONT DE LABONNIÈRE'S 3rd DIVISION

Beaumont was first a page to Louis XVI in 1777, dragoon in 1784 and finally General in 1795. He fought at Lodi, Castiglione, Mantua and was wounded at Magnano. Major-General in 1802, he served at Wertingen and Ulm. Ill at Austerlitz he was replaced by Boyé. After Jena he became the First Equerry to Madame Mère (Napoléon's mother). Cr of the Couronne de Fer, Count, Peer of France in 1814; he was in command in Paris in 1815 and voted for Ney's execution. CxLH in 1824; Died in 1830.

The Chief of Staff was Adjudant-Commandant **Devaux**. Dragoon in 1787, he became Squadron Commander in 1796, went to St Domingo then to Italy in 1800. Adjudant-Commandant he returned to St Domingo but returned to France and was appointed to this post; He served in Catalonia in 1808, became General in 1811 and was reformed because of eye trouble. OLH in 1813, he went blind in 1815.

— BOYÉ'S 1st BRIGADE

Boyé was born in Prusse-Rhenane, he served in the 4th Hussars in 1791 and became a General in 1795. His career was interrupted for health reasons in 1797. Taken back in time for Zurich, he served at Hohenlinden (CtLH), Austerlitz then on the staff of the Army of Spain. Baron and retired in 1812, naturalised in 1817. It was he who led the division to Austerlitz. He did not charge keenly enough during the last phase of the battle. Napoleon sent him Gardane to spur him on.

● The 5th Dragoons

Colonel **Guiot de Lacour** was in turn geographer, bridge-layer, Gendarme Squadron Commander before becoming Colonel of the regiment in 1804. He fought at Wertingen and was seriously wounded in his left thigh at Austerlitz. He returned to the Gendarmerie in 1810, retired in December 1815, he was Honorary Maréchal de camp in 1818.

Also mentioned were **Péridiez**, Captain: *"Distinguished himself. He commanded the first squadron and with his first platoon he carried out a charge on a Russian battalion which he managed to break through and where he was wounded by several bayonet thrusts."*

Delaitre, Dragoon: *"Distinguished himself. Had a horse killed under him but mounted one of his dead comrade's horses. On the eve of the battle he was wounded by a lance thrust while standing up to several Cossacks who were bearing down upon him, as he was out in front as a Tirailleur, and he drove them off."*

● The 8th Dragoons

Colonel **Beckler**, appointed in 1800, LH, killed by a cannonball in Poland in 1807.

● The 12th Dragoons

Colonel **Pagés** was born in the Gard, Squadron Commander in 1794, captured a General in 1795 and was wounded at Novi. OLH. General after Austerlitz. Baron, retired in 1810. Died at Lille in 1814.

Duchastel was born at Saumur, Captain of the 12th Hussars in 1797, wounded at Montebello and at Marengo, made Squadron Commander. LH. Served at Ulm, Austerlitz and Jena then became Colonel of the 21st Chasseurs. OLH in 1815, he retired in 1821; Maréchal de camp in 1831 and GdOLH.

Leconte, LH, Captain after Austerlitz, wounded in 1807, wounded again in Spain, he became a Major in 1813 and served during the Hundred Days.

One officer in the regiment was killed and three others wounded.

— SCALFORT'S BRIGADE

Baron Schelfault, called **Scalfort** was born at Douai, became a Dragoon in 1788 and a General in 1803. CtLH. He was wounded on the chin at Austerlitz, left for Italy. Baron, retired in 1809 and joined the Remounts Department in 1812.

● The 9th Dragoons

Colonel **Maupetit** was wounded 15 or 16 times. After Italy he took part in 18 Brumaire and was wounded at Marengo. He was wounded 9 times at Wertingen, he was at Austerlitz (CtLH) at Eylau and Friedland; also in Spain. Made a Baron he was reformed for deafness. He died as a result of his wounds in 1811.

Faget had a horse killed under him and was seriously wounded in 1794. He took a canon, but was wounded seriously in front of Verona in 1799. He received several sabre and bayonet wounds at Austerlitz. He was at Jena, had a horse killed there and was wounded at Eylau. OLH in Russia. Captured in Saxony after having had three horses killed and been wounded twice by lances; he was retired when he returned.

Lebrun was in Italy and in Egypt before becoming Squadron Commander in 1804. OLH after Eylau, he served in Spain. Retired in 1812. Arrested for being a Bonapartist at St Jean d'Angely, he was freed in 1816.

Lefebvre, Squadron commander after Austerlitz, he was wounded at Eylau and retired.

Eight officers were wounded in this regiment among whom Major **Delort** born in Artois. He replaced **Maupetit** who was wounded at Wertingen; he himself was wounded twice by Cossacks at Austerlitz. Colonel of the 2nd Dragoons in 1806, he served in Spain where he was seriously wounded in 1811. Appointed Chevalier and General in 1811, he was wounded at Montereau in 1814. Promoted major-General, he was at Ligny and Waterloo. Wounded and put on the non-active list, he was retired in 1825 then recalled in 1830 and elected as a Deputy. Became aide de camp to the King in 1832, he was re-elected in 1834. GdCxLH in 1837 and Peer of France, he died in 1846.

● The 16th Dragoons

Colonel **Clément de la Roncière** was born at Amiens, Colonel of the regiment in 1799, he was promoted to General in 1806, then Baron. He was wounded twelve times at Eckmuhl and lost his left arm. General in 1809, commanded at Saumur, he replaced Prince Borghese in the Piedmont in 1814. Count in 1815 and retired, he became Inspector-General of the Gendarmerie in 1834. GdOLH in 1835, then retired and died in 1854.

Haugéranville, Berthier's nephew, became his ordnance officer. He served in the 5th then the 12th Hussars and was wounded at Bassano. Captain in the regiment in 1805, he was at Ulm and Austerlitz. He became Squadron Commander of the 2nd Dragoons, Major of the 4th in 1806 then aide de camp to Murat in 1807. He served at Eylau and became the Colonel of the 6th Cuirassiers in 1807. Baron, Major in the Chasseurs à Cheval of the Guard in 1811, he went to Russia. General in 1813, he broke his right leg at Leipzig and was captured and freed. He followed the King to Gand and was appointed to the Lifeguards. He died in 1817.

The regiment had 258 cavalrymen at Austerlitz. Captain Charlet had two 8-pounders and one howitzer. They were behind Caffarelli's Division, and lost 6 NCOs and 19 Dragoons killed; five officers and 25 men were wounded and six died from their wounds. 59 horses were killed.

● The 21st dragoons

Colonel **Mas de Polart** (Comte de) was at this post in 1801. Wounded at Prentzlow and at Eylau, he was promoted to General in the Westphalian Army in 1810, then returned to French service in 1812; general for the French Campaign in 1814, he was Inspector-General, on the reserve List in 1831 and finished as Mayor of la Ferté-Milon.

Faroppa came from the Piedmont Dragoons. LH retired in 1807.

Captain **Gay** was wounded but the regiment was on duty near General Headquarters.

BOURCIER'S 4th DRAGOON DIVISION

Bourcier was already a Dragoon in 1772; He was on Custine's staff in 1793, then as Chief of Staff for the army of the Rhine and General in 1793; He was promoted to Major-General in 1794, GdOLH in 1804. He served at Ulm, Echlingen and Austerlitz then Jena; Count in 1808, Councillor of State in 1810, he supervised the remounts and the depots. He was at Magdeburg in 1814 and was retired in 1815. Elected deputy in 1816 he was re-elected in 1821 and 1824.

His aide de camps were **Lemoyne** who was wounded at Ulm and Austerlitz by a biscayen bullet. Mentioned in the Tyrol in 1809, colonel of the 14th Chasseurs and OLH in 1813. Retired in 1822, he was elected Mayor of Gland in the Aisne. Mentioned by Davout in his report as well as:

Girard, who was born at Lyons, Was Aide de camp to Bourcier in 1797, he was Captain and mentioned by Davout at Austerlitz. Promoted to Squadron Commander in 1806, he became aide de camp to Jerome and a General in Westphalia, then Chamberlain. He returned to France as a General in 1814, he commanded the Departments. OLH, he died in 1818.

The chief of Staff was **Drouhot**; he was a Hussar in 1783, OLH, Chevalier in 1810, he was with Arrighi in 1812, retired in 1813.

— LAPLANCHE'S 1st BRIGADE

Laplanche was born at Montauban and was wounded 22 times at Kaiserslauten in 1793. General in 1803, CtLH he served at Austerlitz and Friedland. Baron, he went to Spain before being retired in 1810. During the Hundred Days, he was captured defending Charleville where he died in 1832.

● The 15th Dragoons

Colonel **Barthélémy** was Squadron commander of Bonaparte's Guides in Italy then in Egypt, OLH he was at Austerlitz. Wounded at Polotsk, he was made a General in 1807.he served in Spain and was dismissed for misappropriation of public funds in 1810. Garrison Commandant, retired in 1815.

Lavie was Squadron Commander in 1803, LH, he was killed at Lugo in 1809.

Laroche was born at Riom. He served in Egypt and joined the 15th Dragoons in 1804. LH He was at Ulm, Austerlitz, Jena and Eylau. Chevalier, he was appointed Under-Inspector of the Reviews for medical reasons.

Louvain de Pescheloche, Major, LH, mentioned at Austerlitz was killed on 3 December 1805.

Fuseau, wounded at Austerlitz, killed in Spain in 1810.

Brunet captured a flag at Arcola, was wounded in Egypt, and won a Sabre of Honour in 1802. He served in Spain, retired in 1810.

Also mentioned were **Imbert**, Maréchal des Logis: *"Distinguished himself. Set out as Tirailleurs with his platoon, with great determination he charged the enemy infantry which he got through and brought back 80 prisoners."*

3rd DRAGOON DIVISION

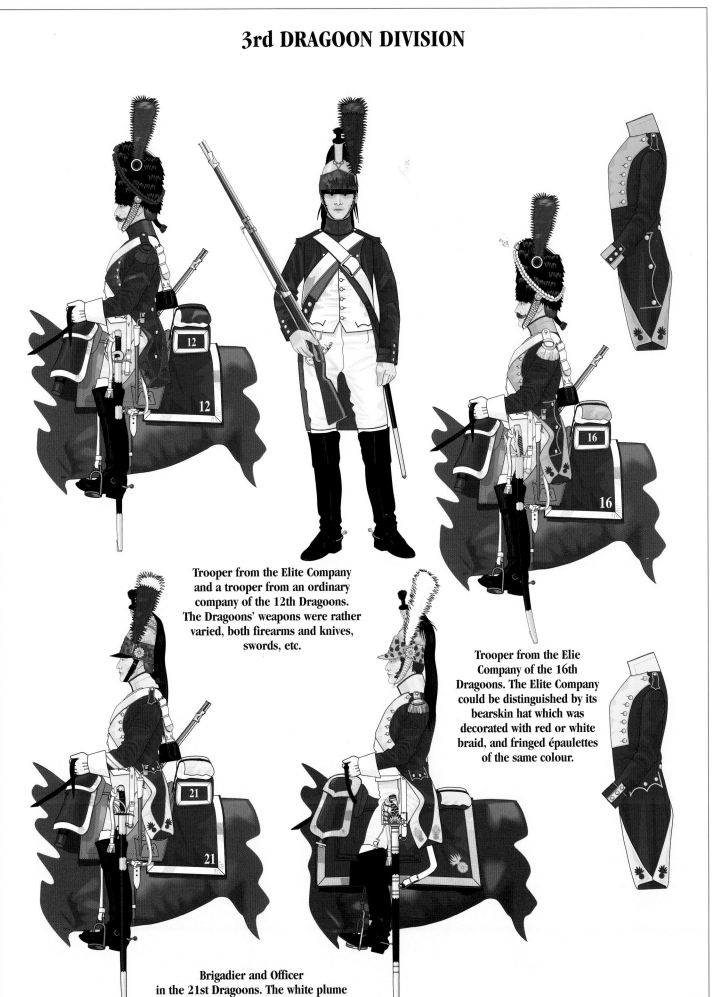

Trooper from the Elite Company
and a trooper from an ordinary
company of the 12th Dragoons.
The Dragoons' weapons were rather
varied, both firearms and knives,
swords, etc.

Trooper from the Elie
Company of the 16th
Dragoons. The Elite Company
could be distinguished by its
bearskin hat which was
decorated with red or white
braid, and fringed épaulettes
of the same colour.

Brigadier and Officer
in the 21st Dragoons. The white plume
shows that the officer belonged
to the Regimental Staff.

André Jouineau © Histoire & Collections 2003

The 18th Dragons of Sahuc's Brigade in Bourcier's Divisions moving up into the Line.
(© J. Girbal, author's collection)

Deschenet, Brigadier: *"Distinguished himself by his bravery: he twice charged the enemy to protect the retreat of two wounded Sergeants; One officer killed and one wounded."*

● **The 17th Dragoons**

Colonel **Saint-Dizier** was killed in a charge at Albeck. In 1806 he was replaced by Beurmann who came from the Chasseurs of the Guard and who was wounded twice at Austerlitz. He defended Metz inn 1814 and committed suicide there in 1815.

Paulus, a child of the regiment, received a Sabre of Honour in 1804. He was wounded twice at Austerlitz, then twice again in 1807. He served during the French Campaign and at Waterloo. Retired as a Captain.

The regiment had three officers wounded.

—SAHUC'S SECOND BRIGADE

Sahuc enrolled in 1772, was a Valmy and with Richepance at Hohenlinden. Appointed General in 1799 (Tribunate, CtLH) he was promoted to Major-General in 1806 and replaced Bourcier. Baron, he served at Lubeck, Raab and was wounded at Wagram. He died of typhus in 1813.

● **The 18th Dragoons**

Colonel **Lefebvre-Desnoettes** was aide de camp to Bonaparte in 1800, he was at Marengo and became a Colonel in 1803. Deputy to the General Headquarters, CtLH for Austerlitz, he was made a general in 1806. Major-Colonel of the Chasseurs à Pied of the Guard in 1808, he was wounded and taken at Benavente. He escaped in 1812. He was in Russia with his Chasseurs of the Guard where he was wounded. GdCx Reunion. In 1815, he tried to take the Arsenal at Cambrai with Lallemand but failed. Peer of France, present at Waterloo he was outlawed and sentenced. He went into exile in the United States and struck off the list of the LH. Drowned in the wreck of the Albion trying to return in 1822.

His aide de camp appointed in 1806 was **Dumas** who had been in Italy and Egypt. LH. He had two horses killed under him at Ulm, was wounded at Austerlitz marching with the 3rd Corps with got him a mention in despatches. Mentioned again at Wagram, OLH, he was wounded four times at Kulm, captured returned in 1814. Retired in 1815 as Lieutenant-Colonel,. Colonel (retired) again in 1832.

Gauthier, called Leclerc was Squadron Commander, fought in Egypt, won a Sabre of Honour and was wounded at Austerlitz. Colonel of the 11th Dragoons in Spain, he served at Waterloo and retired in 1815.

Pistre, Captain, veteran of Egypt, wounded at Austerlitz and then Friedland.

Guiard, captain, LH wounded at Austerlitz, Squadron Commander and OLH in 1809.

Laroche was born at Riom, he was a Guide in Italy and Egypt where he saved Kléber in 1799. Squadron Commander in the regiment in 1802, he joined the 5th Dragons. Colonel of the 13th Dragoons in 1806. He died of illness in Spain 1809.

Also mentioned was **Munier**, Young Recruit: *"Had his left arm blown off, dismounted, passed in front of the regiment and, brandishing his sabre, encouraged his comrades and did not want anyone to take him to the ambulance."*

The regiment numbered 24 officers and 310 troopers in November 1809, it lost 33 Dragoons killed and 44 wounded at Telnitz. Five Officers were wounded and 90 horses lost.

● **The 19th Dragoons**

Comte **Auguste de Caulaincourt** was a Lieutenant in the 1st Carabiniers then with the 1st Dragoons in 1798. OLH. He served at Austerlitz (CtLH) then became aide de camp to Louis Bonaparte and General in Holland then in France. Made a Baron, he captured two flags in Portugal, hero of the Arzobispo Bridge on the Tagus in 1809, he was then promoted to Major-General, Governor of the Pages Count and Gd Cordon Reunion. He commanded General Headquarters in Russia and replaced Montbrun who was killed. He was killed entering the Great Redoubt at the Moskova at the head of the Cuirassiers of the 5th Regiment.

The regiment was mentioned by Davout, who states that it lost 21 men killed, 12 wounded, 22 horses were killed and 15 wounded.

— VERDIÈRE'S 3rd BRIGADE

Verdière joined up in 1767, equerry instructor, General in 1795, Major-general in 1799. CTlh, he died in 1806.

● **The 25th Dragoons stayed at Raygern**

Colonel **Rigau** was born at Agen, Squadron Commander with the 10th Hussars, seriously wounded in 1794, CtLH for Austerlitz. He was present for the French Campaign in 1814. He sheltered Lefebvre-Desnoettes in 1815 after his failure at Cambrai. Outlawed, sentenced to death in 1815, he went into exile at Gand then to the United States to safety in Texas. He received an inheritance from Napoleon.

Degeorges was born at Clermont-Ferrand, LH, served in Spain and in Portugal. Lieutenant in 1809, he was killed at Ciudad-Rodrigo.

Lasne, LH, wounded at Polotsk, was at Salamanca, Leipzig and Montereau. Retired as Captain in 1814.

De Marbeuf was a Lieutenant at Austerlitz, LH In 1807, was Napoleon's Ordnance Officer in 1808. He was an officer in the Chasseurs à Cheval of the Guard in 1810. Baron.

● **The 27th Dragoons**

Colonel **Terreyre** was born at Clermont-Ferrand, joined up in 1776, he took part in the revolt at Nancy. Promoted to Colonel of the 27th in 1803, CtLH after Austerlitz, General after the battle and retired the same day.

Also mentioned were **Bernard**, Adjudant-NCO: *"sent with 8 men to observe the enemy, he went forward to the banks of the lake and having charged several Russian platoons, he made 80 men lay down their arms. General Bourcier met this detachment at the moment he was leading it."*

Tournay, Maréchal des Logis: *"having been put out as Tirailleurs, with great determination he charged a detachment of twenty Russian infantrymen whom he made prisoner."*

Mataillet, Maréchal des Logis *"being set out as Tirailleurs, he vigorously charged a detachment of 65 Russian infantrymen with 6 dragoons which he took prisoner. He also contributed to the capture of an artillery piece."*

Five officers were wounded in this regiment.

— THE LIGHT CAVALRY BRIGADE

Milhaud was born in the Cantal. Second-Lieutenant of a regiment of the Colonies in 1790, was elected Commanding Officer of the Guard at Aurillac, elected to the Convention, voted for the execution of Louis XVI and commanded the 5th Dragoons in 1796. Promoted to general in 1800, he obtained this brigade in October 1805. The Brigade was attached to Walther's division and was mentioned at Wischau.

● **The 16th Chasseurs**

Colonel **Durosnel** was a Scottish Gendarme in 1793, Colonel of the regiment in 179; he was Equerry Cavalcadour to Napoleon on 180. He as Promoted to general On 24 December 1805. He was with Lasalle in 1807. Count in 1808, he was aide de camp to the Emperor in 1809 and Major-General. Captured at Essling, Governor of the Pages, he was in Russia with the Gendarmes d'Elite of the Guard and became Commandant d'Armes at Moscow. He lost a thigh at Leipzig and was captured at Dresden. Aide de camp to Napoleon during the Hundred Days, Peer of France put on the non-active list in 1815, he was retired in 1816. Elected deputy in 1830, GdCxLH in 1832, he became aide de camp to Louis-Philippe. Peer again in 1837, he died in 1849.

Bonnemains was Squadron Commander in the regiment in 1800, major in 1803, served at Lubeck and became Colonel of the 5th Chasseurs in 1806. Baron, he served in Spain and Italy. Lieutenant-General at Waterloo, he became Maréchal de camp in 1815. Inspector-general of the Gendarmerie in 1818, Viscount in 1822, he was promoted Lieutenant-General in Spain in 1823, GdOLH in 1829, Deputy for the Manche in 1830, Inspector-general for the gendarmerie in 1834, he was elected Deputy in 1839, Peer of France in 1845 and retired in 1848.

● **The 22nd Chasseurs.**

Colonel **Latour-Maubourg** was Second-Lieutenant in 1782. Arrested while emigrating with Lafayette, he was released and sent on a mission to Egypt. Aide de camp to Kléber, then to Menou, he became Colonel of the 22nd Chasseurs in 1802. General on 24 December 1805, he was with Lasalle then became Major-General in 18707. He served at Holsberg, was wounded at Friedland, Baron. He fought in Spain and commanded the 4th Cavalry Corps in Russia. Wounded at the Moskova, he was with the 1st Corps in 1813. GdCxReunion, GdCxLH in 1814, Peer of France, he supported the destitution of Napoleon, did not serve during the Hundred days. GdCxSL in 1818, Cr St Esprit in 1820, Governor of the Invalides, he followed the Bourbons into exile.

Gleize had two horses killed under him in the Pyrenees. He served in Egypt, LH. Captain in the 7th

4th DRAGOON DIVISION

Elite Company,
15th Dragoons.

Brigadier,
15th Dragoons

15

15

Trooper from the Elite Company
of the 17th Dragoons.

17

17

Trooper from the 18th
Dragoons.

18

18

André Jouineau © Histoire & Collections 2003

4th DRAGOON DIVISION

Dragoon and trumpeter from 19th Dragoons.

19

19

19

19

Dragoon from 25th Dragoons.

25

25

27

27

Brigadier (Corporal) from 27th Dragoons.

André Jouineau © Histoire & Collections 2003

Chasseurs in 1813, he was at Strasbourg in 1815 and retired the same year. Four officers were wounded at Wischau, 40 troopers were captured or put out of action on the same day.

Kellerman's cavalry . These bussars from the 4th bussars, Van Marisy's Brigade, are charging Russian grenadiers. (© J. Girbal, RR)

THE 5th CORPS' CAVALRY

— FAUCONNET'S BRIGADE

Fauconnet was born in the Meuse, Gendarme in 1766, Captain in 1792, commanding the 6th Dragoons in 1794, he was wounded crossing the Rhine, General in 1796. Accused of contacts with the Emigrés, he served at Hohenlinden, CtLH, here on 21 September 1805, captured Werneck's convoy which had fled from Ulm on 20 October. Appointed to replace Lasalle on 13 December in Klein's Division, Baron, Commandant at Antwerp, half-pay in 1814, served during the Hundred Days at Dunkirk in the National Guard, retired in 1815, and died in 1819.

● **The 13th Chasseurs**

Colonel **Pultière** joined up in 1775, second-lieutenant in 1791, wounded in 1793, Colonel in 1802, OLH in 1804, died in Bavaria in 1806.

● **The 21st Chasseurs**

Colonel **Berruyer** was appointed Colonel in 1803, born in Lyons, wounded twice in Italy, Austerlitz, OLH, Baron congratulated at Jena, retired in 1808.

These two regiments were put in Murat's cavalry reserve in November 1805. They chased Werneck up to Halberstadt. They were sent along the Olmutz to Prague road and behind Vienna. The 13th Chasseurs joined 5th Corps at Brunn on 8 December, so they were not at Austerlitz.

— DE TREILLIARD'S BRIGADE

De Treillard was born in Parma, gentleman cadet in 1780, Lieutenant in 1788, commanding the 11th Chasseurs in 1794, General in 1799, CtLH, Austerlitz, Saalfeld, Jena, Pulutsk; Major-General in 1806. Spain, Portugal with Junot, under Montbrun, Vittoria in 1813, French Campaign, St-Dizier, retired, 1815 then 1832

The Chief of Staff of the Light Brigade of the 5th Corps was **Delage** who was born in Angers; in Vendée with Hoche, mentioned at Marengo, here in September 1805, then Wertingen, Ulm, Hollabrunn and Austerlitz, then Saalfeld and Jena.. Commanded the Treilliard Brigade at Pulutsk, Baron and General at Moscow, CrLH in 1815, retired in 1826.

● **The 9th Hussars**

Colonel **Guyot** was in the regiment in 1801, OLH, charged at Wirschau, wounded several times; Austerlitz, General on 25 December 1805, joined Soult and present at Jena Guttstadt, Eylau, but killed in Prussia on 8 June 1807.

● **The 10th Hussars**

Colonel **Beaumont de Carrière** took part in the Vendée, Italian and Egyptian campaigns, was aide de camp to Murat in 1799. Appointed here in 1805, present at Wertingen, Ulm, Austerlitz, promoted after the battle. Joined Murat as first aide de camp at the end of 1806; then at Eylau, Danzig, Friedland; Baron, CtLH . Went to Spain with Victor, returned to France in 1811 with the 2nd Cavalry Corps in Russia (with Watier de Saint-Alphonse), Major-General in 1812, Leipzig, Hanau; Couronne de Fer, died at Metz in 1813.

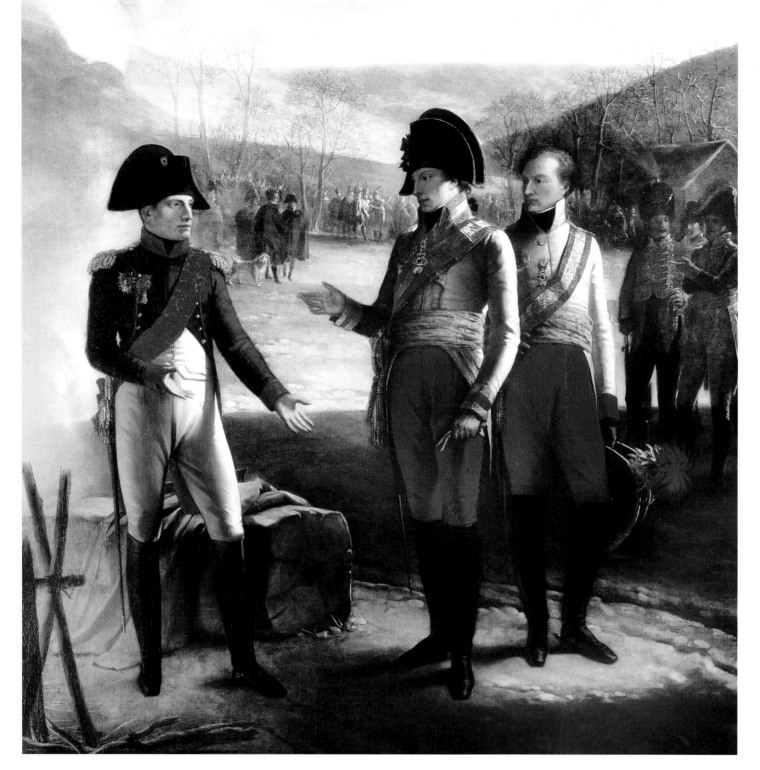

A MODEL BATTLE

This battle was a model in all its different stages.

From a strategic point of view, once again Napoleon surprised his opponents by the speed of his decisions and movements. Surrounding Ulm was marvellous piece of execution which enabled him to get rid of the Austrian Corps, which was the stronger, before the arrival of the Russians.

The Emperor knew how to neglect the sideshows that were Naples and Pomerania. He deemed Archduke Charles to be occupied enough with Masséna's men, and in any case, by capturing Vienna he succeeded in having troops in a fit enough state to deal with any danger coming from Italy.

Strategy and Tactics

The considerable resources which were found in the capital enabled him to restock with arms and ammunition, and supplies of all kinds.

He made the mistake of letting Kutuzov get away – leaving behind him however a large number of feathers, when he sacrificed his many rearguards.

He managed to calm the Prussians down and stop their threatening. He suc-

The two Emperors meet near the Spaleny Windmill to sign the Armistice. Peace had been won.
(© RMN)

ceeded in joining battle too early with his opponents who thought they were far superior. He made believe that he feared them by falling back and letting them take Wischau easily. From the tactical point of view, he thus chose the terrain, which he studied with a lot of care; and he chose the best moment for this decisive battle, sufficiently early so that the enemy had not received its reinforcements which were coming up slowly; whereas he was able, thanks to the exceptional quality of his army, to recover his own, namely Bernadotte and Davout just at the right time, thanks to a forced march made by Friant's Division and Bourcier's Dragoons.

Nevertheless the Allies were able to start their plan. The first two columns did take Telnitz and Sokolnitz and the road to Vienna was almost cut. In theory they had almost won and they only had to wait for their fourth column and break out towards Turas. But Davout, Legrand and Bourcier prevented that breakout thanks to their exceptional courage and that of their men, whose citations can be read in this book. They were a reflection of their quality which made up for the fact that

126

LOSSES DURING THE BATTLE

Danilewski gives an overall estimate and speaks of 21 000 Russians and 6 000 Austrians killed. Colin says that only the number of prisoners is easy to verify since there were 18 convoys of prisoners which entered Brunn with a total of 9 767 Russians and 1 686 Austrians.

For the French, the count is more accurate and gives 1 305 killed and about 6 940 wounded. 573 prisoners were taken and soon freed.

— **Bernadotte** only lost 3 killed and 11 wounded in his 1st Division and 54 killed and 226 wounded for the 2nd — ample testimony to the fact that he did not fight very much that day.

— **Friant** on the other hand lost 325 killed and 1 665 wounded out of 3 500.

— **The Pô Tirailleurs** were almost annihilated losing 29 killed, 154 wounded and 94 prisoners. **Bourcier** gave 11 dead and 25 wounded but **Davout** gave 35 killed and 41 wounded for these Dragoons in his report.

— **In the 10th Light**, St-Hilaire gave 40 killed and 279 out of 1 500 men.

— **Thiébault** gave 52 dead and 592 wounded out of 3 000.

— **Varé** gave 86 dead and 727 wounded.

— With **Vandamme**, Ferey noted 26 killed and 361 wounded.

— **The 28th**: 9 killed and 73 wounded.

— **The 4th**: 18 dead and 193 wounded.

— **The 24th**: 126 dead and 364 wounded

— **Levasseur's Brigade**: 45 killed and 241 wounded.

— For the cavalry, **Beaumont** and **Boyé** lost 48 killed and 95 wounded.

— **The Cavalry of the Guard** had 21 killed and 83 wounded.

— With **Kellermann** there were 29 killed and 123 wounded.

— **Nansouty** had 29 killed and 123 wounded also.

— **Walther**: 20 killed and 63 wounded.

— **D'Hautpoul**: 41 killed and 88 wounded.

The number of dead is very high among the Allies because the French fought without quarter whenever necessary. Two *émigrés* with old names were killed in the Preobrajensky Regiment where they were serving Russia: Broglie-Revel and the Marquis de Villiers.

they were quite obviously out-numbered. It is certain that the assault on the Pratzen Heights relieved the pressure on the French right - Kamenski's return was proof enough, as was the crushing of the fourth column which had become the Allies' centre. It was the stubborn resistance of Davout with Friant and Legrand who blocked the Allied columns, often fighting at one to three or four, which was the determining factor for victory.

Friant lost four horses killed during the fighting and his own losses bear witness to the keenness of the struggle on the French right wing.

Undisputed heroes

If Friant's regiments were the undisputed heroes of the battle, they shared the honours with many others, like Saint-Hilaire, Thiébault, Legrand and Caffarelli, Suchet as well as the cavalry reserve, Troopers, Light Cavalry, Dragoons, Cuirassiers and Cavalry of the Guard alike all contributing to this unique and decisive charge at the end of the battle.

The special case that was Bernadotte started to emerge after Austerlitz. He was jealous and ambitious and here is what Commandant Lachouque thought of him.

"Bernadotte was not in position to prolong Marshal Soult's action, according to the orders received. At 9.00, his divisions were still on the right bank of the Goldbach and around 10.00, only a few had been got over to the other side.

"The Emperor talked with Bernadotte earlier. He talked to him 'with a dry and imperious voice', then he harangued his regiments who acclaimed him. The lethargy if not the lack of goodwill on the Marshal's part is quite clear. The Emperor does not trust him. And through his negligence, a void was beginning to form between Soult's left and Lannes' right." The Marshal made no effort to go beyond Krenowitz and start off an easy chase towards Austerlitz which would have got good results. Indeed, the Marshal was furious with Napoleon for taking Kellermann's vanguard and his cavalry away from him and for not giving him a greater role to play. His passiveness was worrying; it was to

be all the more so at Jena.

This battle was also admirable from the tactical point of view which was based on the mutual trust of the leader in his subordinates, only equalled by the faith of the soldiers in their leader. All the preparations in the Camp at Boulogne had paid off. The Grande Armée at Austerlitz was an exceptional army trained by remarkable, experienced veterans, real professionals with courage tempered by the multitude of fights they had survived, often wounded but still there. A real elite soldier is one who has nearly died so often that he is no longer frightened by death. Those bayonet charges were very impressive; using Tirailleurs (regrouping all the crack shots) was one of the French arm's strengths; but it was charging, without firing which was most effective. At the end of the battle, Napoleon had committed but a small part of his troops, whereas the Allies had given everything.

Nothing but heroes!

At Austerlitz, these fanatical professionals of the Emperor whom they loved and admired made short work of the new recruits in certain regiments which opposed them. Their quality made up for lack of numbers and Napoleon ought not to have forgotten that this tool was needed to obtain victory; the details of the citations are astounding. This exceptional tool was forged in the camp at Boulogne and in the campaigns of the Revolution; there was the risk that it would slowly lose its quality even though the great leader's genius remained intact. This wearing down, losing officers and faithful cadres, aggravated by the Spanish mistake, took place gradually and draft dodgers appeared, then deserters, among the less enthusiastic conscripts, levied in the conquered countries.

But on this 2 December 1805, there were only heroes in the Grande Armée, only veterans shouting very loudly *"Long live the Emperor!"* They deserved Napoleon saying of them:

"Soldiers, I'm pleased with you!"

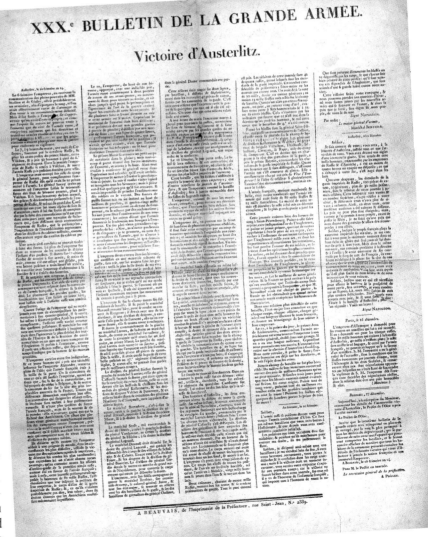

A WORD ON FRENCH MILITARY TERMINOLOGY

In the many biographical notices to be found in this book (especially pp. 55 to 82 and pp. 101 to 111), the following rules have been adopted.

TRANSLATION OF RANKS

In order to avoid confusion, the French officers rank of '*Chef de bataillon*' (foot troops) or '*Chef d'escadron*' (cavalry) has been translated as 'Battalion commander' or 'Squadron commander' respectively. For the Napoleonic period, this rank could not be translated as 'Major' (in English), as there existed also a rank of '*Major*' (in French) immediately above it. When the rank 'Major' is used in this book, it always refers to the original French rank above Battalion commander and below Colonel – cf. plate p. 23).
- '*Général de brigade*' has been translated merely as 'General', or in some cases as 'Brigadier General' (only in the biographical notices).
- '*Général de division*' has been always translated as 'Major General' in the biographical notices.

- '*Lieutenant général*' (in the Royal French Army) has been translated as 'Lieutenant General'. This rank did not exist in the Army of Napoleon.
- '*Maréchal*' has been retained in French or translated in English as 'Marshall'.
- '*Maréchal de camp*' (in the Royal French army) has been retained in French. This rank did not exist in the Army of Napoleon.

ABBREVIATIONS USED FOR ORDERS AND DECORATIONS

LH : Légion d'honneur *(chevalier de la)*.
OLH : officier de la Légion d'honneur.
CtLH : commandant de la Légion d'honneur.
CrLH : commandeur de la Légion d'honneur *(it replaced the* 'commandant' *mentioned above, on the 17th February 1815)*.
GdCxLH : grand-croix de la Légion d'honneur *(it replaced the* 'grand-cordon' *on the 21th June 1814)*.
GdOLH : grand-officier de la Légion d'honneur.
CrSL : croix de Saint-Louis *(chevalier de la)*.
GdCxSL : grand-croix de Saint-Louis.

ACKNOWLEDGEMENTS

The author should like to thank mister Pierre Bréteignier, mister Jacques Garnier and mister Gérard Gorokhoff for their help during the realisation of this book.

SOURCES FOR THE UNIFORM PLATES

— *Planche Le Plumet* n° 78. Drapeau du 4e de Ligne
— *Planche Le Plumet* n° 166. Grenadier d'Oudinot
— *Planche Le Plumet* n° 69. Tirailleurs Corse
— *Planche Le Plumet* n° 248. Tirailleurs du Pô
— *Planche Le Plumet* n° U13. Le 5e hussards
— *Planche Le Plumet* n° U26. Le 10e hussards
— *Planche Le Plumet* n° U25. Le 9e hussards
— *Planche Rousselot* n° 80. Infanterie de ligne
— *Planche Rousselot* n° 81. Eta-major et aides de camp
— *Planche Rousselot* n° 71. Les officiers généraux
— *Planche Rousselot* n° 5 et 33. L'infanterie légère

— *Planche Rousselot* n° 28 et 66. L'artillerie à pied
— *Planche Rousselot* n° 36. L'artillerie à cheval
— *Planche Rousselot* n° 7. Les dragons
— *HS Tradition magazine* n°22. La campagne de 1805
— *Tradition magazine.* Les cuirassiers 1804-1815, Rigo, Pétard, Pigeard, Malvaux
— *Uniformes* n° 20. Le chasseur d'infanterie légère M. Pétard
— *Les équipements militaires,* Tome IV. M. Pétard. Editions de l'auteur
— *L'infanterie.* Comandant Bucquoy, Grancher éditeur
— *Austrian army of Napoleonic War.* P Haythornthwaite & B. Fosten. Osprey n°176 et 181
— *Soldat du temps jadis. Les hussards autrichiens.* R. Forthoffer. Planches n°238, 239
— *L'armée russe du Tsar Alexandre 1er.* M. Gayda & A. Kritjitsky.
Editions de la Sabretache, 1950

Supervision and lay-out : Jean-Marie MONGIN © *Histoire & Collections 203*
Computer drawings : André JOUINEAU.

Un ouvrage édité par
HISTOIRE & COLLECTIONS
SA au capital de 182 938, 82 €

5, avenue de la République
F-75541 Paris Cedex 11
Téléphone 01 40 21 18 20
Fax   01 47 00 51 11

This book has been designed, typed, laid-out and processed by
Studio Graphiqe A&C
entirely on integrated computer equipment.

Printed by KSG-Elkar/KSG-Danona, Spain, European Union.

August 2003